THUNDER PERFECT GNOSIS

THUNDER PERFECT
GNOSIS

INTELLECTUAL
FLOWER OF MIND

OLIVER ST. JOHN

Thunder Perfect Gnosis—Intellectual Flower of Mind
© Oliver St. John 2023

All rights reserved. No part of this publication may be reproduced, distributed, or transmitted in any form or by any means, including photocopying, recording, or other electronic or mechanical methods, without the prior written permission of the publisher, except in the case of brief quotations embodied in critical reviews and certain other noncommercial uses permitted by copyright law.

Cover design and graphics © Oliver St. John 2023

ISBN 978-1-0682715-0-2
Paperback edition (June 2025)
ORDO ASTRI IMPRIMATUR
www.ordoastri.org

Therefore, at all times, constantly remember Me and fight.
With your mind and understanding absorbed in Me,
You will surely come to Me.

Bhagavad Gita

CONTENTS

Concerning Metaphysics	i
Author's Preface	iii

PART ONE: GNOSIS

The Seer and the Warrior	1
Primordial Light	9
Union of the Two Lands	16
The Angel's Egg	21
The Bornless One	27
Enochian Calls	30
Gnosis of the Thirty Aeons	33
Magick	45
Systems of Knowledge	50
Dreaming and Stalking	56
Will and Love	59
House of Bast	63
The Mother MA	69
Thunder Perfect Gnosis	73
Thunder Perfect Mind (translation)	83

PART TWO: YOGA

Yoga	93
The Shankhya Cosmology	100
Yoga of the Mind	105
Love, Devotion and Surrender	116
Vigilance	126
The Way to Samadhi	132
Concentration	138
Attachment and Fascination	149
Patañjali Eight Limbs of Yoga	153
AUM: Reality and Unreality	156

PART THREE: OTHER WORKS & REVIEWS
Uniformity against Unity   165
The Serpent Power   170
The System of Antichrist (review)   185
The Kingdom of Agarttha (review)   192
The Simple Life of René Guénon (review)   197

Illustrations and Figures
Heru-Set   17
Throne of King Senusret   18
Aion Phanes   22
Realm of Sophia   34
Bast   64
René Guénon (portrait)   197

Concerning Metaphysics

Before metaphysics can be explained by discursive means, the terms used must be redefined. Metaphysics is meant here in the etymological sense of the word, which is to say, 'beyond the physical', and so nothing to do with the chemical state of the body or brain, or the psychological domain. Metaphysics refers to the infinite, unlimited universal doctrine that can only be known metaphysically. As it depends from a supra-human source, it can never be a branch of philosophy or some other science. Indeed, philosophy and the other modern theoretical sciences were originally derived from metaphysics and not vice versa.

Symbolism is the only way to convey metaphysical reality without direct knowledge; language itself comprises a set of symbols. Ancient languages, with all their subtlety of etymology, roots of words and phonetics, are nonetheless well equipped to symbolise metaphysics, which is solely concerned with principles that amount to pure knowledge. Such principial knowledge is most adequately set down in the Hindu Vedas and Vedanta. Such knowledge is not in any way derived from an individual author, as is the case with all Western philosophical theories. With the Vedanta, the goal is always that of pure knowledge: untransmissible, infinite and absolute reality. That is what we mean by 'metaphysics'.

This knowledge is not then in any way apprehended by reason or argument as it is derived from a supra-human source. All dialectics of the ancient sciences, including Hermeticism for example—something that in itself has been confused with profane science—form only an outward veil of that which is truly esoteric, which is inevitable. The ordinary meaning of the term 'dialectic', derived from Greek (διαλεκτικη), means 'a discussion', and that word derives from analysis, which is necessarily confined to the domain of reason. The limitation imposed by this is such that the conventional modern dictionary definition, 'enquiry into metaphysical contradictions and their solutions', is confused in its very nature and rests on total misunderstanding of the word's meaning. Such an enquiry removes the enquirer from anything metaphysical, even in the etymological sense. There can be no contradiction in metaphysical or principial reality, which is infinite and contains all possibilities within Itself without any disharmony entering therein. The dictionary will even inform us that metaphysics is concerned with 'abstraction' that has 'no basis in reality'! This owes to the fact that modern science imagines 'concrete existence' to be the only reality.

Some scholars have even attempted to reduce the meaning of metaphysics to the level of the utterly inane, until it becomes no more than 'in addition to' or 'after', as with the appendices of a book![1]

Inevitably, some Sanskrit terms must be used when expressing a metaphysical idea, for there are no words in modern languages to describe Atma or Brahma, for example, let alone the vast array of other technical terms and their different contextual uses. Sanskrit has the vocabulary of a complete science of consciousness itself; this is better understood if the universe is considered as ontological and not material; unfortunately even that completely escapes the grasp of ordinary rational comprehension and is only truly conveyed by direct knowledge. The means of acquiring such knowledge is the subject of the *Yoga-Sutras*, for example, but few are prepared to make the intense and prolonged effort that is needed.

We must then rely on symbolism and language, whatever its shortcomings, if we are to communicate anything at all. That limits our scope to a few that are prepared to work diligently towards an understanding, putting aside any preconceived notions they might hold. It is these few persons that we are addressing, for the rest are as in a deep sleep, lacking the strength or will to awaken. In fact, these sleepers are even the enemies of the knowledge that is our subject and our ultimate goal, which means they will never acquire it. As it is put very succinctly in the alchemical text *Aurora Consurgens*,

> Fools despise this glorious Science of God, and the Doctrine of the Secrets, and the Secret of the Philosophers, and the Medicine of the Physicians, because they do not know what she really is. ... And nor is this kind of wisdom suited to the ignorant because everyone who is ignorant of her is her enemy, and not without cause, as the Observer of All Things says. ... Nor will the spirit of this Wisdom enter into a coarse body, and nor can a fool ever grasp it, due to the poverty of his reasoning, because the wise have not spoken to the foolish, for he who speaks to a fool speaks to someone who is asleep.[2]

---

[1] We refer to S.M. Cohen, 'Aristotle's Metaphysics' [Stanford Encyclopaedia of Philosophy, California].
[2] Book I: 111.

Preface

Sophia is our Guiding Light.

We here follow up points of special interest on Gnostic and other texts, including the truly remarkable *Thunder Perfect Mind*. Our interest is metaphysical; we are not overly concerned with factual references, names, dates and places as are the scholars that write on these subjects. It is the universal meaning of the symbolism that concerns us. The surviving fragments of these ancient texts, as with the *Yoga-Sutras*, have their true origins in times already ancient when the Christian Gospels were composed. The evidence for a yoga practice and science of the mind in those texts will become clear from studying this book. The second part comprises a careful, practical study of the *Yoga-Sutras* attributed to Patañjali and Vyasa. There is no simplification or dilution of the yoga method; yet that method is clearly explained. The goal of yoga remains the same: union with God, immortality and even final liberation for those rare individuals that will renounce the world.

Over thousands of years the teaching on the practices undergoes adaptation. The principles are unchanged by their very nature, as these owe to the supreme principle that does not undergo change or modification by anything. The practices are applications of pure knowledge that has no author as it originates from a supra-human source. There has been a great acceleration in the decline of human civilisation as we near the end of the final phase of the Kali Yuga and that means further and radical adaptation is necessary. There has been a relentless trend over the last century to reduce, simplify and so degrade traditional sciences; there is a need therefore to re-establish the principles that have been lost, forgotten or deliberately abandoned, so spiritual or metaphysical realisation is even possible. In some cases it becomes necessary to rediscover a tradition that is lost, although it is rare when this can be achieved effectively.

Man has been subject to delusion through his senses throughout the Age of Kali Yuga but now we have a 'virtual' field that knows of no intelligence but data and pure quantity, or quantitative evaluation. It is only possible for such a thing to come about because people already trust machines to tell them truth, which is of course an impossibility as even the senses do not do that, let alone discontinuous numbers. Sri Ramakrishna remarked, more than a century ago in Calcutta, that people will not believe anything unless they read it in the newspaper.

But things are as they are, and once our students receive advice from us and then immediately put the key words in a search engine to either verify or refute what has been said, we know the end will not be long in coming. This brings us on to the crucial factor of the teacher and student relationship. All traditional wisdom insists that one cannot follow any initiatic path without a teacher. While this is obvious to anyone that has a sound theoretical basis (at least), legions will deny its truth. Anyone that thinks they can get initiation out of a book, or from 'systematised knowledge', is suffering such delusion that they are disqualified ipso facto from attaining that which they pretend to seek. They inhabit a world of fantasy. The *Yoga-Sutras* call that *viparyaya*, the false knowledge that arises from incorrect cognition (literally 'superimposition').

While on the subject of 'disqualification', it must be said that unless a person is pre-disposed to devotion to God, Ishvara, the Lord of the Universe, Mahadevi Shakti or by whatever name that God is known, then they are not fit for knowledge in any real sense and it is safe to say they will never get that knowledge unless there is some kind of metanoia taking place. The term 'metanoia' is intended here in the etymological not the conventional sense, which only reaches as far as a kind of religious conversion, a purely outward thing. The real meaning of metanoia is a profound 'change of heart'. That means a good deal more than merely changing one's mind about something.

Much of what we wrote previous to *Nu Hermetica* concerned magical practices, and in that, a 'symbolic language' was always used, sometimes without explanation of the terms used or contextual meaning. Owing to the very constrictive conditions of the times in which we now live it has become necessary to be far more exact and discursive. Our use of the term 'magick' was always meant to be inclusive of theurgy and so not limited to the application of Hermetic correspondences to produce effects—although we have never shied away from such natural science; magical practices are only harmful when disconnected from all knowledge of the governing principles. If one will misuse magick then one must suffer the consequences; it is as simple as that.

Theurgy, the 'practice of God' on the other hand, is what might be described as the yoga of other traditions than those of the East, with which the term 'yoga' is most commonly linked. That link owes to the truly vast body of knowledge, inclusive of a complete metaphysics, written in Sanskrit in the Vedas, Puranas and Shastras. Nonetheless, the Chaldean Oracles, Mithraic Rites and all of the so-called 'spells' of the ancient Egyptians indicate a science of the mind and yoga.

Patañjali—a family name that does not necessarily refer to one person—did not invent the *Yoga-Shastra*, so it is wrong to call it a 'philosophy', as is more frequently the case than otherwise, as though it were in any way comparable to the theories of Western thinkers. The knowledge had already existed since times of greater antiquity than the Patañjali Aphorisms, which were the writing down of what was previously an oral tradition. While many will automatically think of yoga as a collection of postures, breathing exercises and so forth, that confuses the means with the goal, which is yoga 'union'.

While a good deal of the present work is concerned with the *Yoga-Sutras* attributed to Patañjali and the commentary of Vyasa, we have devoted the first part of the book to Gnostic and other texts, including the *Thunder Perfect Mind*, from which we took the book's title. As we have said, the ancient texts, some of them written down or copied into other languages around the same time as the Patañjali Aphorisms, have their true origins in times that were already ancient when the Christian Gospels were being composed. The evidence for a yoga and science of the mind in those texts, as well as various oracles of the Goddess, will mean nothing to the academics that profess to specialise in these subjects as it concerns knowledge that they do not and cannot ever possess, owing to their predisposition. That means that so much of what is written on these sacred texts is useful only as 'information', but has no value at all in terms of real knowledge, or as the needful support to effective initiation that was once the sole purpose of such texts, or the oral recitations that preceded them.

Neo-spiritualists have deliberately blurred the distinctions made in the commentaries on sacred texts; for example, confusing the individual practitioner with the Divine Person, Ishvara, and at the same time confusing personal or individual volition or will with the True Will or Sanskrit *Dharma*. This has produced an entire range of counterfeit 'systems of initiation' in popular occultism, where neither the initiated nor the pretended initiator is initiated into anything at all in reality. The consequences of such delusion and the ignorant experimentation that goes with it frequently include deformation of the mentality. In some cases it results in permanent insanity or at least a very serious reduction of the intellectual capacity. But there is worse even than that: diabolism, whether intentional or otherwise, forges links between the foolish practitioner and demonic or sub-infra forces. That can cause ruptures in the subtle framework of our world that would otherwise insulate it against malefic interventions.

The above not only applies to magicians involved in evocation, talismans and so forth but also to those who sincerely imagine they are 'healing' and helping others through various so-called therapies that are in reality remnants of degraded, misappropriated traditional sciences. The practitioners, who often charge fees for their services, fondly imagine they are in contact with 'higher intelligences', when in fact the entities already control their minds from a level much closer to the earth than they imagine. There are also counterfeit versions of some traditions, such as the Native American Indian, that no longer have anything to do with the real tradition but are only another form of the popularised neo-spiritualism that owes more to the nineteenth century Theosophists, with their self-invented 'Great White Lodge' and reincarnationism, than it does to the indigenous peoples of the Americas. The diversity of forms that the counter-initiatic movement takes, in the name of no-matter-what tradition, usually have one thing in common: a theoretical basis, however vague it might be, that is formed from general acceptance of psychological theories with all of the profane, damaging applications formed from them.

It is to make some reparation to this chasm in knowledge, which has come about with the profusion of anti-spiritual teaching and practices that by now abound everywhere, that we have composed the present work.

Sophia be-with-us forever.

Oliver St. John

Land's End Peninsula Sol in ♌ Luna in ♒ 2023

PART ONE: GNOSIS

The Seer and the Warrior

It seems that at some point in very ancient history, perhaps centuries after the onset of the Kali Yuga, which coincides with the beginning of the 'historical period', there was a rebellion of the Kshatriya warrior caste against that of the Aryans, nobles or *brahmins*. The rebellion took place not only in India but also across all civilisations. Similar disequilibrium has taken place throughout recorded history and still goes on in various ways to this day. Legend has it that there were wars on a very large scale as is recorded for example in the *Bhagavad Gita* and on the stone walls of ancient Egypt, as with the battles of Kadesh and elsewhere fought against the 'enemies of Ra'.

In Yugas previous to the present (and final) Dark Age, the priestly or sacerdotal authority was not questioned as it is derived from a supra-human source. The metaphysics in its most perfect form has been preserved in India in the Vedas, the Puranas ('old books') and the Vedanta ('completion of the Vedas'). Nowhere else exists such a complete and perfect knowledge and science, where reality itself, the Real, is the subject and the goal.

Throughout the Age of Kali Yuga the degradation towards final dissolution of the present humanity has inexorably taken its course. In that sense it is quite natural there should be a descent from sacerdotal authority to that of kings and warriors, then at the last stage a further descent where merchants wrest power from the kings. The apparent rule of the people or mob, while merchants control their thoughts, emotions and behaviour through technological means is typified by the present times. We see the ferocious global propagation of Western idealism with an aim to bring about total uniformity and destruction of all real knowledge. Although not of course understood by the advocates of such masked oppression, this is to prepare for the dissolution at the end of time (*mahapralaya*), something that has been in progress for more than half a century. It is a 'sign of the times' among many that the historical rebellion of the warriors against the nobles has been turned upside down by the anti-traditional movement in modern times. While this runs throughout what now passes for 'education', the occult movement took up the cause well over a century ago.

The message insinuated first by the Theosophists and then trumpeted by those who took it as fact because it appealed to their innate prejudice was that all such historical change and 'progress' was wrought because there was a corrupt priesthood. The same explanation, asserted without evidence or real substance, is applied as much to the medieval Christian world as it is to the more ancient Hindu world. In the field of occultism this explanation of a corrupt priesthood that is replaced, as a matter of progress, by a more 'socialistic' kind of order where the 'ordinary man' triumphs with reason, is often in the background of all else. Although the view rests on self-contradiction, it has become instinctive; it is worth bearing in mind that occultists always used the power of hypnotic suggestion, not only on themselves to get 'results', but also on others, to promote their views. Such views involve unquestioned 'scientific' acceptance of evolutionism and progress, where psychological theories are seen as an improvement on anything that went before by the sheer fact of modernity. According to W.E. Butler in his book called *Magic—Its Ritual, Power and Purpose* (1952),

> It is the considered opinion of the present writer that in Jung we have the Darwin of the New Psychology.

Evolutionism and psychologism are here exalted in one stroke.[3] Psychology assimilates all spirituality to a theoretical 'subconscious', which places all power even below the level of reason. The author fills quite a few pages in the same book with the logical end of the inversion of the natural order, finally relegating the spiritual to the domain of mere 'instinct'. The school of thought that was set up by Swami Vivekananda in America to propagate Eastern teaching to the West absorbed much of this evolutionist thought in its efforts to reach those with a modern education. While Swami Nikhilananda and others of that school have done excellent work in translating and commenting on some of the most important Hindu texts, one has to be very wary of what they will sometimes slip in. In his introduction to his translation of Shankara's *Atma-Bodha*, the Swami says, in a section that is otherwise quite sound,

> The brāhmins from time to time abused the power accorded them and received their punishment at the hands of the Kshatriyas.[4]

---

[3] That book and the companion volume, *The Magician—His Training and Work*, is brimful with the pseudo-scientific explanations then in vogue; it would take a volume of equal size to even list them.
[4] *Atma-Bodha*, p. 25 [Ramakrishna-Vivekananda Centre].

The Swami does not supply any evidence to support this claim. While it may not be entirely improbable in the factual sense, that kind of sentiment is one that was very popular with the Theosophists and oft repeated. The latter had both a political and a subversive agenda; they also did quite a lot in the way of fund-raising for the movement. Profane commentators always see history in the light of political, sociological and economic considerations, thus reducing everything to the lowest possible criteria. There are more insidious inferences, put in such a way as to escape the notice of the casual reader:

> As the ancient Āryan-Indians valued spiritual wisdom more than earthly possessions, the brāhmins occupied the highest place in Hindu society.

It is not stated here, as would be the case with Shankaracharya, that the authority of the *brahmins* was based on truth, because the doctrines derive from a supra-human origin. Instead, wisdom is limited to a matter of ordinary human values—something that would please the sociologist, the anthropologist and the psychologist but that automatically reduces the civilised order to the dictates of mere human convenience.

There are many more examples that could be given, but having cleared away some of the misunderstanding that arises with this subject, we can turn now to look at what the way of the Kshatriya, the way of the warrior, should properly be. It is described with great precision in the *Upanishads* that the Kshatriyas can sometimes instruct the *brahmins* in matters that are particular to kings and warriors.[5] This denotes the path, which is that of the Universal Self, and which is at the same time related to *hiranyagarbha*, the world egg from which the heavens and the earth are formed. The Universal Self is called *Vaishvanara*. He is described as the whole of humanity, but this must not be thought of as a kind of collective or group mind; it is more that he is the sum total of all being, not only that of humanity—although some translators place this restriction upon it. The word thus refers to the controller of all phenomenal changes or the Self of all beings.

A story is given where five highly renowned *brahmins* sought to know the answer to the question, 'What is our self and what is Brahma?' And they were directed to a certain son of Aruna. The son of Aruna, however, directed them to another teacher, in case there might be something more, that he did not know. So they followed his advice and they all, along with the son of Aruna, went to visit King Ashvapati.

---

[5] *Chandogya Upanishad* XI–XVIII.

The king first tests them by offering to make sacrifice to give them great wealth. This, they refuse, insisting that he should tell them about the Universal Self. It is significant in this that they approached the king nonetheless with great respect, even though he was a Kshatriya and they *brahmins*, for a teacher must be honoured by his pupils. Also, it is made clear, when the king says they must wait until the morrow for instruction, that the king has no intention of performing any initiatic rites, for a good teacher with capable students has no need of such things.

It then follows that the king first asks each one, 'Whom do you meditate on as the Self?' The first says he meditates only on heaven. He is instructed that this is very good and brings the glory of Brahma to his family, but it is only the head of the Self. Surely, says the king, 'your head would have fallen off if you had not come to see me'. That is to say, he had only a partial idea of Brahma.

The second *brahmin* says that he meditates on the sun only. He is instructed that this is Universal Form, which brings wealth to his family.[6] However, the sun is only the eye of the Self. Surely, says the king, 'you would have become blind if you did not come and see me'.

The third *brahmin* meditates on air only. He is instructed that this is very good, and that many gifts come from it. But that is only the *prana* of the Self, the breath of life. Surely, says the king, 'your *prana* would have left you if you did not come to see me'.

The fourth *brahmin* says he meditates only on *akasha* (spirit). He is instructed that this is very good and brings offspring and pleasant things, but it is only the trunk of the Self; that is to say, the middle part of the body, which also has the meaning of 'pervasive'. Surely, says the king, 'your trunk would have been destroyed if you did not come to see me'.

The fifth *brahmin* says that he meditates only on water. He is instructed that this is very good, wealthy and nourishing, but it is only the bladder of the Self. Surely, says the king, 'your bladder would have burst if you had not come to see me'.

Finally the first teacher, son of Aruna says that he meditates only on the earth. The king instructs him that this is very good, and brings the support of cattle and offspring. However, that is only the feet of the Self. Surely, says the king, 'your feet would have withered if you had not come to see me'.

---

[6] Universal Form is called Vishvarupa in Sanskrit, which is an attribute of the sun as giving forth rays of many colours.

The king then delivers to all of them the instruction concerning the Vaishvanara as the whole Self. He tells them that one that is endowed with limited knowledge only knows the Universal Self as multiplicity. He mistakes the part for the whole, which is none other than the 'one without a second'. But he who worships the measure of the whole span from earth to heaven partakes of sustenance in all worlds, in all beings and all selves. This sustenance is more than physical food alone, which is eaten by the ignorant.

The head is the Beneficent Light; the eye is the Universal Form. The *prana* is all permeating, the trunk is fullness (space), water is wealth, the feet are the earth and the support, the chest is the altar, the hair is as grass on the altar, the heart is the mind that rises from it, the mind is the fire taken from the heart, and the mouth by which speech is made is the offering of this fire made to the *devas*. Here is the relationship of the macrocosm and microcosm, or as it is put in the Hermetic works, 'as above and so it is below'. For this reason, Hermeticism and alchemy, which were a particular development of the Egyptian tradition though not the whole of it, are sometimes described as within the knowledge of warriors or the Kshatriya caste.[7]

It remains to be seen, regarding the Universal Self, that when a person reaches the centre of their individual self, the *jiva*, there is a possibility this may lead to the realisation of the centre called the Universal Self. But that possibility is not in any way a foregone conclusion. Likewise, realisation of the Universal Self may lead to the greater knowledge of the non-dual supreme reality, but that also is not a foregone conclusion.

---

[7] This teaching on the whole Brahma or Universal Self has nothing whatsoever to do with the modern notion of 'holism' or 'holistic therapies', which is in fact a self-contradiction in the sense it is commonly understood. Holism is derived from the Greek *holos*, 'the whole thing', and is taken to mean that nature is more than the sum of its parts. However, because of the total opposition to any metaphysical or supra-human principle involved, this is supposed to be a goal attainable through an ordered grouping or systematisation, which does not in any way take place in nature. In that way, a metaphysical or qualitative truth is reduced to measurable quantity. The selection of criteria and the order of priorities are artificially imposed and wholly dependant on preconceived notions, which vary considerably depending on the individual. What pretends to be a natural or 'alternative' science is governed by the same arbitrary theories as conventional science.

Thus, the *Upanishads* are often thought by some to contain contradictions, but those who think so do not understand that different teaching is given as according to the possibilities within the person, whether this be sage, or warrior or householder, for example.

Turning at last to the ancient Egyptian tradition, from which was developed the Hermetic way of knowledge, Horus is the type of the warrior. All kings were considered to be his embodiment during the course of their reign. Horus has a cosmic and purely transcendental aspect as well, but we are here concerned with the human side, as that relates to initiation and the way of the warrior. Horus is not an individual power; it is the supra-human power, known only by the *boddhi*, or supra-human intellect, which is the 'cause' of the individual self along with all its faculties and senses but is not in any way a part of that individuality. It is the source of the powers of mind and faculties, by which an individual perceives and then mistakes those thoughts based on sensory impressions for the Real.

The eye of Horus symbolises Universal Form. The name *hru* is identical with 'sky' or 'heaven', the cover of earth, which is the support. The hawk's head is covered by the *nemmys* of heaven even as his feet walk upon the earth, the support by which 'lightning', 'rain' or a shower of 'dew' is received as initiatic transmission. This can only happen when the individual realises their centre, as the microcosm of the macrocosm. At the risk of repeating a thing too often, it must be said that it is also not a foregone conclusion that when any person drinks of such a cup, to use a manner of speaking, there will then take place a reciprocal arising or a positive change of state in the being. That which liberates the self may enslave those unprepared for knowledge. For this reason in the Vedanta when a pupil approaches a teacher, the teacher first tests them by asking them a question. According to the answer given, the teacher may then refuse further teaching or otherwise give instruction that is a step beyond that which is known by the pupil.

From the human point of view, which is where all initiation must take its support, action is all-important, and so the way of the warrior is sometimes called *Karma Yoga*. In the Egyptian tradition the hieroglyphs, scarcely understood by those who study them, include 'actions of the eye', 'actions of the ear', 'actions of the mouth' and so forth. The way or path of action then includes the proper and dutiful performance of rites and sacrifices, which include all these, as described by the whole Brahma, from which is derived the relation between the macrocosm and the microcosm.

In the Egyptian tradition Ra is not the visible sun but the sun is used as a symbol of the supreme reality. Particular attributes, such as the eye of Ra or of Horus, convey such things as Universal Form. From the point of view of the seer who knows the supreme Ra or Brahma, all such rites and duties, all partial or separated views of the sole reality, are in the domain of ignorance. But that is not to say that the rites and duties are useless; they are useless for the *sannyasin*, the knower, but they are absolutely necessary for those who dwell upon the earth and who have yet to overcome the sensual desires and passions that control their hearts.

Action and thought are particular to the human being. Horus is a deity or *deva* and so not human at all, though he is able to take on human form. Ritual must always be combined with meditation and therefore the knowledge of the deities; otherwise it can never transcend ignorance. The goal must not be separate from the one goal and purpose, which is knowledge. The way of non-action and not-thinking, or meditation, is the way of the king as according to the Taoist and other Eastern wisdom. It must be made clear that none of that means being passive to the environment. As Universal Self or the integral being, Horus carries the 'potency to act' yet without any involvement in action as such. To compare with Arjuna and Krishna: Arjuna goes into battle while Krishna drives the chariot but the deity does not in any way participate in the battle or actions. All things come about through the mere presence of the Mahadeva, or the Great Neter in the Egyptian tradition, which is the Real.

The ritual called the Cube of Space, which has its equivalent in more than one tradition, is the simplest and most complete symbolic representation of the modality, or modalities (by extension) of any being or individual, including the human. From a cross made by a vertical and horizontal line, a third line at right angles to the first two declares the six directions of space: height, depth, north, south, east and west. The 'seventh ray' is at the centre of all. The Universal Self, sometimes called the Universal Man, is the sum total of all states of being, human and non-human. By the ritual action, the three rays and six radii to the circumference of space are 'illuminated'. This is achieved by the thought, mind, will and imagination and so forth of the ritualist.

It may be seen then that in rites there is a certain kind of imitation of the actions of a God or *deva*. The potency to act of the principle itself and its dynamic effect cannot be invoked, however, as the human is necessarily limited in his will to affect anything outside his own conditions, which are the conditions that define and so limit the human state.[8] Illumination, symbolised by the lightning flash or thunderbolt, carries the possibility of an upward movement through all the states of the being (there must be re-ascent).[9]

This can be realised, as according to the temporal conditions we are bound by, but is never invoked or 'produced' by any man, any more than a man can produce divinity or God. In fact, man can produce nothing from his own side and it is only the delusion of *maya* that leads him to think that he does. The danger in the way of the seer is that of complacency, which leads to inertia and ignorance; the danger in the way of the warrior is enslavement through action, which also leads to ignorance.

---

[8] For example, no individual can affect or change the Cosmic Cycles or even the lesser cycles in the slightest degree.
[9] One may consider Qabalistically the Arabic *Al-barq* (333), which means 'lightning' as well as an initiatic force, and the Hebrew *Zelbarachith* (657), which has exactly the same meaning and is also related to the lion or sphinx.

The Primordial Light

The Vedas and Vedanta, the ancient commentaries on them by sages, hold the keys to the universal primordial tradition. The Vedanta acts as a key because it consists of the most complete metaphysical doctrine. However, Hinduism is one of many forms of the tradition, some of which have been lost or forgotten. All pre-religious traditions derive from the one ancient primordial tradition. Over the course of time, and we are speaking here of vast stretches of time, there has always been adaptation of the tradition according to the requirements of culture, temporal conditions and peoples. The religions that still survive in the modern world, even while some of them are by now in a very degraded form, all carry traces at least of the primordial tradition and its symbolism. The guarding of the way to the Holy Land by the Knights Templar was the outward aspect of a function that was essentially esoteric. The Templars preserved links between exoteric Christianity and its esoteric core, which at that time still existed. As custodians of the primordial tradition, their 'secret' was the universality of this knowledge. They maintained links with other civilisations than that of Christendom, including Hinduism, Islam and the Hebrew and Persian traditions.[10]

A centre of the primordial tradition is likened to a Throne, which can be the seat or foundation of wisdom as well as the crown in any natural order or hierarchy. All initiatic tradition has its source symbolically in this Throne or Seat, and all proper rites serve to establish a reflective 'world centre' or 'seat' on the terrestrial level that is capable of receiving and transmitting that to individuals as a spiritual influence. Such a centre can be regarded as an actual geographic place, an island, continent or world, as well as a symbolic or geometric representation. It can be macrocosmic or microcosmic; it can be 'located' in the celestial sphere or 'heaven' and it can be figured as within the human body, as in the case of spiritual practices such as yoga, which include chakras or centres of force. When temples, shrines or other buildings are properly constructed they can act as centres for the transmission of primordial wisdom.

---

[10] See 'Knights of the Cross', *The Way of Knowledge in the Reign of Antichrist*. From hereafter the book will be referred to as *Way of Knowledge*.

The primordial tradition has a vast array of symbolism, of which the Pole star or circumpolar stars is foremost. The beginning of the Manvantara, a major cosmic cycle, which is to a degree measurable in time through the use of symbolic numbers, is sometimes referred to as the Golden Age.[11] This can only come about at the beginning of a Manvantara, however, and not at the end of one, as is sometimes fondly imagined by those who are ignorant of the cosmic cycles.

At the dawn of our time, humanity inhabited the Arctic region and was so close to the primordial knowledge as to be completely immersed in it.[12] This immersion or total knowledge is symbolised by such things as the 'elixir of life' and the *soma* of the Hindu tradition, which is mentioned as a sacrificial offering in the Vedas. The Holy Grail is a further symbol, and the Tree of Life another and more complex symbol, for it includes a succession of 'cups'.

The earth's climate and even polar alignment was of course very different then from what it now is. Initiation was not then necessary as all lived and moved and breathed in Knowledge. In Sanskrit, the word for this is Ham-Sa, which is also the name of the swan of Brahma. Other white birds, including the ibis, the stork and the heron are symbols of the primordial tradition; the last three happen to be symbols of Christ, although there was a violent disconnection between Christianity and its initiatic core many centuries ago with the destruction of the Knights Templar.[13]

There are various reasons why white is a colour associated with the primordial tradition. It can mean 'purity', in the sense of pure Knowledge undetermined and therefore supra-human, as with the Sanskrit Atma-Brahma supreme principle. White is the colour of the North Star and is also a symbol of the 'seventh ray' or colour. The seventh ray is the centre of the three-dimensional cross, Chi-Rho or Cube of Space—of which the latter term is really descriptive of the 'squaring of the circle' at the end of time, the completion of a cycle of manifestation. We previously described how the Cube of Space or three-dimensional cross relates to the 'warp and weft' of the fabric of the universe:

---

[11] See 'Cosmic Cycles', *Nu Hermetica—Initiation and Metaphysical Reality*. From hereafter the book will be referred to as *Nu Hermetica*.
[12] See *The Arctic Home in the Vedas*, B.G. Tilak (Arktos, first published 1903).
[13] See 'Knights of the Cross', *Way of Knowledge*.

The simplest form of this symbolism is a cross, composed of a vertical and horizontal line, which becomes three-dimensional when another line passes through the centre at right angles to the others. This, the Cube of Space, is identical to the early Christian adoption of the Chi-Rho as the monogram of Christ Jesus. The symbolism can be understood, through the analogy of the weave of warp and weft, as depicting a universal cross that is able to replicate indefinitely, producing numerous worlds or states of being as well as countless individual creatures, which are a microcosmic reflection of the macrocosm.[14]

Each Manvantara is divided unequally into four Yugas, of which the first is longest in terms of terrestrial time and the last, the present Kali Yuga, the shortest and most obscure and dark. There are also lesser cycles within the Yugas. Periodically, a world is destroyed, usually by cataclysm on earth, to make possible a complete renewal or new world. There are also greater and lesser degrees of such cataclysmic events. For example, the last great Ice Age, and the sudden melting of the glaciers that probably accounted for the well known though little understood sinking of Atlantis. Atlantis was a secondary centre, whereas the Hyperborean was the primary. A secondary centre has to be in contact with the primary centre. There are further subsidiary centres, each of which must also be in contact with the higher principle, through the secondary centre. If all conscious connection with a spiritual centre is broken, the spirit of the true doctrine ceases to vivify the symbols that are its outward expression and the tradition is lost.

The Atlantean tradition may not have been exclusively located on the legendary 'island' of Atlantis—a designation that may either be symbolic or literal, or both. Each septenary cycle of Manvantaras, for example, has also seven 'isles' or continents associated with it, and these are really worlds. These islands or worlds are figured in the Hindu tradition as a lotus of seven petals. The centre is Mount Meru, which is a form of the primordial axis. In the Egyptian tradition we find the flower or star of Sesheta or Septet (a name that means 'seven'), and which was also among the royal emblems of the first dynastic kings as 'legislators' identified with sacerdotal authority, an authority that was in itself derived from the primordial wisdom.

---

[14] P. 69 [*ibid*].

While the seven continents can be symbolised as regions of space, that should not be taken as literal fact. It is best to think of them as representing entire terrestrial worlds or states, which in reality are simultaneous but from the human point of view take place in the succession of time. The cycles run concurrently, so that for example the present Manvantara includes the previous six cycles, or to put it another way, is 'backward facing'. The next septenary is forward or future-facing, and contains something of the next six.

When this symbolism is analogously considered as representative of states of being, humanity occupies a central position, or at least should do. There are seven that represent states higher than the human and seven that are lower than the human. One may then consider that these worlds are not entirely separate, and in fact that would be a metaphysical impossibility as all cycles are continuous, not discontinuous as are numbers. And that is one reason why chronological theories can never be exact or reliable, especially when extended over vast aeons of time. What is at least important to know is that there is some 'overlap' between different worlds, and that an individual can descend to lower states of being or ascend to higher states—which is the work of initiation to accomplish.

The Egyptian tradition seems to have continued the Atlantean tradition for long after the disappearance of what must have been presumably its principal centre in the deluge—the same flood that is mentioned in the book of Genesis. The Egyptians referred to a First Time, which equates to the precessional Age of Leo, a whole Great Year before us, which consists of half of a precessional cycle. This would take us back to sometime approximating the ending of the last Ice Age, or perhaps before that. The Atlantean tradition persisted for a period of approximately 12,960 years, the length of the Yuga immediately previous the present Age of Kali or Darkness. The Egyptian tradition to all intents and purposes vanished away itself, along with its language, some two thousand years ago. We may well ask, did the Egyptian tradition withdraw—like the fabled city of Agarttha—or was there a loss of conscious connection with the spiritual or supreme centre?[15] The link was certainly there, for example Neïth is clearly associated with the supreme spiritual centre called Tula in Sanskrit and Thulé in Greek, which is the Hyperborean tradition itself.[16]

---

[15] See Part Three, 'The Kingdom of Agarttha' (review).
[16] See 'Names and Symbolic Representations of Spiritual Centres', *The King of the World*, René Guénon [Sophia Perennis].

In Sanskrit, Tula means 'Scales', specifically the zodiacal sign of Libra, but originally this referred to Ursa Major and Minor, the circumpolar constellations about the Pole or world axis. These two, the Greater and the Lesser Bear, each have seven brightest stars. The bear is a further and more recent symbol of the primordial tradition, as is the stag and wild boar.[17] One may also bring to mind the Celtic tales of King Arthur, son of Uther Pendragon, whose name means 'bear'. Arthur certainly represents the chivalric or warrior caste, the Kshatriyas, and the Scales was transferred to the Bear when a rebellion took place of Kshatriyas against the priesthood, which is recorded in the Vedic tradition.[18] This would have coincided, as we can see by the change of symbolism, with a change from stellar reckoning to that of solar reckoning—the centre was effectively relocated from the Pole star to the Sun as 'zodiacal centre'. Arthur presided over a round table, which symbolises the Zodiac, and the Holy Grail then occupies the centre. The search for the Grail is then a symbol of the search for a 'lost word' or hidden tradition.

A golden ring or crown, with a white jewel or jewels set in it, may symbolise the union of the zodiacal circle with the circumpolar circle—these turn in opposite directions, the former deosil and the latter widdershins, from the terrestrial point of view. According to the Hindu doctrines, in which this knowledge has survived in detail, the Manvantaras are understood to form double septenary cycles turning in opposite directions. These are in reality simultaneous, though from the human point of view we see time as a past that is behind us and a future that is in front of us.[19]

---

[17] The Glastonbury Zodiac, formed from the contours of the landscape across a whole area of Somerset, England, has no equivalent to Libra, but has instead the Swan, which points to the circumpolar stars. The symbol of the Scales was transferred to the Zodiac at a later time.

[18] This most likely occurred at some time approximating the commencement of the present Age of Kali Yuga, where there is increasing separation from the primordial centre until humanity loses sight of it altogether, as at the present time. Cf. *Spiritual Authority and Temporal Power*, René Guénon [Sophia Perennis].

[19] Compare with Janus, the God that looks both ways. The third face that is hidden is the one that is eternally present. It is likewise with Hekate and other gods.

The Scales were integral to the Egyptian tradition, appearing in later dynastic times as the Scales of Ma'at in the Hall of the Judgement of the Soul, presided over by Osiris—a god who was broken into fourteen parts by Set, who is in turn identified with Mentu the 'legislator' or Sanskrit Manu, Lord of the time cycles.[20] Thoth or Tahuti, a Neter of sacerdotal authority, was always the recording angel, writing the names of those who passed judgment in his Book of Life. The crocodile that lurks behind the Scales of Ma'at is part of the symbolism of the Goddess Tawaret, who occupies the very centre position in the Denderah Zodiac—that is, the polar stars.[21] The Egyptians knew Ursa Major as the Thigh constellation, pictured as the foreleg of a Bull. It is a symbolism that occurs very frequently in all hieroglyphic texts, but is scarcely ever recognised for what it really is.

In the Rigveda, the Bull is always 'first'.[22] Now, when the Egyptian tradition was lost, it went out all over the world. Thus it was transferred and adapted for different peoples. It is also true that a subsidiary cosmic cycle began at that time, a precessional passing from the sun entering the fire sign Aries at the vernal equinox to Pisces—a water sign; so there is a strange echo with the 'deluge' in much more ancient times, except this flood signified descent into greater obscurity for mankind. It is important, however, that the centre is never truly lost but is periodically hidden, and that very obscurity is characteristic of the present and last Age of Kali Yuga. So long as there are even a few persons that retain, or reform a link with the spiritual centre, the centre can be established.[23]

Such a link, through direct initiatic transmission, can come about in a most curious and unusual way, in which the law of *apurva* plays a part—for this 'seed' of will-intention is not limited to the corporeal sphere, and neither is it limited by time and space; it can certainly have unexpected or otherwise unknown consequences in a future time.[24]

---

[20] The 72 accomplices of Set are figured by the quinances of the Zodiac.
[21] See 'The Orbicular Tree', *The Enterer of the Threshold*.
[22] The true date of the writing of the Rigveda is far earlier than is supposed by conventional scholarship. It almost certainly coincides with the onset of the Kali Yuga, which places it around the same time as the pre-dynastic and early dynastic kings of Egypt.
[23] See pp. 50–51, *The King of the World*, René Guénon [Sophia Perennis].
[24] See 'The Key to Magick', *Way of Knowledge*.

Apurva is linked to *karma* as 'action', but has nothing to do with any moral attributes, as were attached to the term by the neo-spiritualists in very recent times. What we are alluding to here is very rare, but has been set in operation by certain spiritual masters across even thousands of years, though we know of one case that is much more recent than that. The word 'faith' is sometimes substituted for *apurva* in the Vedanta. As the meaning of this word, as with so many others, has suffered degradation through modern usage, it is necessary to point out that faith has nothing to do whatever with the conventional idea of 'belief'. It is not even generated by human will but in fact is a divine gift that cannot be 'produced' through body or mind or by magical manipulation of some sort. What is important to know is that the tradition will find *you* if you seek it out with a pure heart.

Union of the Two Lands

The story of the fall of man and the subsequent restoration to primordial unity is a universal one that is recounted across traditions. The 'Fall' is a symbol for manifestation, which is necessarily dual, and the consequences of the cyclical law that governs it in time and space.[25] Manifestation, from the metaphysical point of view, is the fullest development of possibilities contained within Pure Being or essential unity. Pure Being is not within manifestation but is the principle of manifestation. Towards the end of a cycle, such as a Manvantara consisting of four Yugas, there is greater distance from the centre of origin. This may be thought of as a spiral moving outward from a central point placed within a sphere, for example. For humanity as a whole, and from the point of view of time and causation, this marks a degradation; spiritual possibilities become obscured and are eventually completely forgotten.

The distancing of man from the primordial consciousness once common to all is marked by disequilibrium. For example, in modern times, disequilibrum is the driving governmental and economic force. This is supported by legislated idealism such as 'equality and diversity'. This objective pretends that stability can be maintained through imposed uniformity; while seeming to exalt the differences between people it only tolerates such differences as will conform to the idealism that ensures universal sameness.[26] Thus, what appears superficially to be tolerant is in reality intolerant, especially towards all tradition; it is even opposed to any real individual expression and development of individual possibilities. Ultimately, the uniformity extends to the whole mentality, the way of thinking and so behaving.

Keeping the masses in a state of permament engrossment with new products, including the technological ones that pretend to be 'personal' while ensuring that all minds are engaged with the same completely simplistic mechanical operations, relies on a continual increase in disequilibrium. This is compensated by the false notion of 'freedom' through majority rule. As this exalts the lowest common denominator, governance is eventually placed in the hands of the most unintelligent individuals.

---

[25] Such consequences include the possible displacement of the earth's pole since the beginning of our Manvantara. See p. 16, 'Atlantis and Hyperborea', *Traditional Forms & Cosmic Cycles*, René Guénon [Sophia Perennis].
[26] See p. 165 'Uniformity against Unity' for more on this.

However, the illusion of democracy is not the first step towards hell; as we have already explained, the first step was taken when the warrior caste rebelled against the priesthood some time after the advent of the Kali Yuga.[27] Further degeneration was then inevitable. Governance passed to the merchants then the utterly profane: thus rulership and governance of both religion and state has effectively passed to the hands of demonic or *sub-infra* forces.

For the individual being, the Fall may symbolise initiation. That is, in terms of consciousness there is descent followed by ascent or a return to the primordial state. In the book of Genesis it is described how Adam is driven out of the Garden of Eden at the very moment that the Tree of Knowledge of Good and Evil appears to him. Eden is the centre, or primordial consciousness to which the Tree of Life corresponds. It is inaccessible to fallen man, whose very mentality makes him impervious to spiritual realisation. To return to the centre by restoration of the primordial state and to reach the Tree of Life is to regain the sense of eternity.[28] There was a legend current in the Middle Ages in which the cross of Christ was made of the Tree of the Knowledge of Good and Evil.[29] The Tree thus becomes the means of both Fall and Redemption. Some depictions of the Tree of Life show an inverse Tree of Knowledge connected to it at the root and hanging below it. This is comparable with the 'upper waters' and the 'lower waters' shown in other cosmic symbols such as the Seal of Solomon, where the exact midpoint between the two runs vertically across an interlaced hexagram. The face of God appears above, as reflected darkly in the waters below.

The sephirotic tree is a ternary symbol that synthesises in itself the nature of the Tree of Life and the Tree of Knowledge. It combines them into a single whole since the ternary can be split into the unity and the duality of which it is the sum. Instead of one single tree, one sometimes finds three trees joined by their roots, the one in the middle being the Tree of Life and the other two corresponding to the duality of the Tree of Knowledge of Good and Evil. The roots are the principle while the branches and leaves form the extension of the manifest possibilities. The sun and moon, mercy and rigour, the elect and the damned and the cross of Christ with the two thieves on either side also figure the duality of the latter.

---

[27] Cf. 'The Seer and the Warrior', p. 1.
[28] It may be noted that the Hebrew word for 'tree' shares a common root with Etz, 'essence'. In the Vedanta, essence or *purusha* is to be understood as no different from Atma Itself, the supreme principle.
[29] See *The Symbolism of the Cross*, René Guénon [Sophia Perennis].

A better-known symbol of the Tree that encompasses the dual aspects has two pillars and a central column of equilibrium. The non-sephira Da'ath or 'Knowledge' is sometimes shown as a dotted circle between the supernal heaven and the lower or inferior waters of the firmament, of which the exact division is called the Abyss.

Ancient symbolism variously shows real unification, which can only take place when all dualities are realised as complementaries, for they depend from the principle that transcends them. The brazen serpent raised by Moses in the desert, as a protection against malefic serpents, was placed upon a rod or staff as being equivalent to the cross and the Tree of Life.[30] Here one serpent corresponds to Christ and therefore the Tree of Life, and the other to Satan and the Tree of Knowledge or Death. This symbolism is also contained within the curious figure of the *amphisbaena*, or two-headed serpent. The staff of Aesculapius has a similar meaning and in the Caduceus of Hermes we see the two serpents in an opposition that is ultimately reconciled.

In the ancient Egyptian tradition there is the two headed Heru-set. Heru-set is a form of the twin gods Heru-Ur and Set as complements such as day and night, or light and darkness. It is only in later times that they were increasingly seen as combatant gods, which is indicative of the current Manvantara cycle moving further away in time from the primordial centre. When there was hostility between the two brothers, it was Tahuti (or Thoth) that prevented the destruction of one god over another in his name of Ap-Rehu, or Ap-Rehui, 'Judge of the two Opponent Gods'.[31] Tahuti, among other things, is the preserver and transmitter of tradition, the embodiment of the Egyptian priesthood. According to René Guénon he is,

> The principle of inspiration from which it held its authority and in whose name it formulated and communicated initiatic knowledge.[32]

In the figure of Heru-set there are two contrary aspects conjoined, one looking back, the other forward. The sense of eternity is beyond both, implied in the union that brings peace and balance. In the Pyramid Texts of Unas it is said,

---

[30] Book of Numbers, 21: 5–9.
[31] See p. 242, *The Gods of the Egyptians Vol. 2*, E.A. Wallis Budge.
[32] See p. 74, 'The Hermetic Tradition', *Traditional Forms & Cosmic Cycles*, René Guénon [Sophia Perennis].

Unas cometh forth upon the Ladder which his father Ra hath made for him, and Horus and Set take the hand of Unas, and they lead him into the Tuat.33

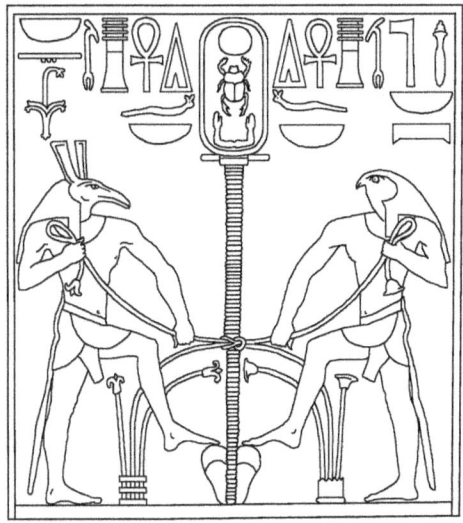

Throne of King Senusret: sma detail

The symbolism of the above illustration of the Egyptian *sma* depicts the ligature of the two lands of ancient Egypt. In its single form, the *sma* hieroglyph comprises the central column (sometimes there are three *smas*). On one side is the bullrush of the South corresponding to the God Set, or sometimes Tahuti—presumably a later dynastic substitution. On the opposite side is the papyrus of the North corresponding to Horus. The stems of the flowers of these two plants make a knot upon the central column and are thus unified in a central principle. The two that carry out this unification, each with both hands grasping the knot of flowers tied around the *sma*, and one foot on the heart that forms the basis, are Set and Horus. This symbol is most often found at the inner most basal corner of the seat of the Iset throne of a God, such as Tahuti, implying primordial beginning and ending.

---

33 Pyramid Texts of Unas, line 493. See p. 242, *Gods of the Egyptians* [ibid]. This is not the only instance of Horus and Set aiding the initiate. For example, on p. 246 Budge translates from the Book of the Dead: 'Tem hath built thy house, Shu and Tefnut have founded thy habitation; lo! drugs [sic] are brought, and Horus purifieth and Set strengtheneth, and Set purifieth and Horus strengtheneth.'

The same symbol is also found on the throne of kings, such as that of King Senusret I shown above.[34] Sma means 'to unite', or 'join oneself to something or someone'. Other meanings of the same word, though the spelling is different, include ideas of slaying. By inverse analogy, the destruction is that which necessarily occurs in the return to the primordial state where peace and order is restored. Sma is also the root of a name sometimes given to Set. According to Budge,

> Smy is Smai, the well known Egyptian name for Set as Arch-fiend. The associates of Set were called Smaiu.[35]

Dual manifestation comes about through non-unified multiplicity, which consists of an indefinite series of disequilibriums.[36] Its return to the principial unity appears as destruction from the viewpoint of manifestation.[37] Viewed from the point of view of the individuality, initiation is similarly understood as involving some kind of sacrifice. In the later dynastic period, Set and Horus are in a state of continual battle until Horus is placed as king of the two lands. In the ligature of the *sma*, the two lands of the South and the North are unified in a central, vertical principle. Set and Horus are thus complements and peacemakers or reconcilers, bound by will to the *sma*. The *sma* is thought to have as its basis the tube of the tracheal artery ending at the heart and lungs. As such, it is a symbol of the divine breath of life, or *prana*, including expiration and inspiration. The latter may also symbolise cosmic manifestation and its withdrawal or dissolution (Sanskrit *pralaya*). A universal truth is thus expressed through the complementary aspects of a single principle, the fundamental quality of manifestation and the means of return to its principle, the unmanifest. The end is with the beginning.

---

[34] Senusret was the second king of the 12th Dynasty (1956–1910 BC). The throne name Ka-Khephra is shown in the cartouche. The original tracing from a relief is by courtesy of Joan Lansberry. It is interesting to note that King Sma, like King Mena, or Aha, is said to be the first, or one of the first kings of ancient Egypt. Net-hotep was the daughter of King Sma and wife of King Mena. See pp. 31 and 453, *The Gods of the Egyptians Vol. 1* [ibid].
[35] P. 247, *The Gods of the Egyptians Vol. 2* [ibid].
[36] One should note that the 'irrational number' Pi is used in calculations of the Cosmic Cycles. Manifest worlds may be symbolised geometrically by circles, but as such a circle of manifestation can never be closed as such, the spiral is the more exact analogy. Manifestation is continuous, not discontinuous as are numbers.
[37] It is difficult not to think there might be an etymological link between the Sanskrit *soma*, the 'elixir of life', and the unification and apparent destruction of the Egyptian *sma*.

The Angel's Egg

The second century depiction of Aion Phanes, the Orphic God of Light (see p. 22), bears striking resemblance to Mithras. It is an apt illustration of a God that is both intermediary and psychopomp, as well as Lord of the Universe. He is sometimes confused with Hermes Trismegistus, but it is easy to see why: the God of light, truth and justice is surrounded by an elliptical or egg-shaped Zodiac and the four holy living creatures. He stands between the two halves of the cosmic egg, which has cracked open to form the heaven and the earth. The flaming Phanes is winged and he holds a thunderbolt in his right hand and a sceptre of sacerdotal and temporal power in his left. A serpent twines about his body, and it is notable that he has cloven hooves, somewhat like the god Pan.

Thus Aion Phanes has attributes that are held in common with many gods, which often leads commentators to assume that he is Greek, or that he is not Greek and really Asian, for example. The fact that the attributes are the same, however, indicates that truth does not change and neither does God, essentially—the Lord is clothed in countless forms, whether male, female or androgyne, according to different cultural and other modifications. It should not be surprising that there is perfect agreement between ancient traditions.

The *Taittiriya Upanishad* places words, prayers and meditations in the context of the discipline necessary for the knowledge of the Atma. The Atma or true Self is subject to conditioning through thought and sensory perceptions. Ignorance comes about through this superimposition upon the Real, the limitation made upon the Self by the faculties of the ego or *ahankara*, which hides or covers the truth and does not reveal it. Only the knowledge of Brahma Nirguna, 'unqualified', can destroy ignorance. Meditation and ritual do not destroy ignorance but they develop discipline that purifies the mind through the *karma* of 'right action'. Ritual assists the aspirant in the development of concentration, self-control and so inner purification. All such actions are performed towards the realisation of Brahma Saguna, 'with qualifications', which is otherwise called the Universal Self. It is the sum total of all beings in the worlds of manifestation, and their 'cause', and this is symbolised variously in all traditions and paths.

AION PHANES (2nd century)

The five traditional elements or *tattvas* ('principles') form a symbol for the contemplation of Saguna Brahma, the 'non-supreme' Brahma with attributes. This is no different from the well-known Hermetic figure of a man within an upright pentagram, as the microcosm of the macrocosm. The figure may equally be that of a woman, or otherwise androgynous, as with the Orphic Phanes—who at the same time bears close resemblance to the solar Persian Mithras, depicted as emerging from the world egg, girded about with a serpent and surrounded by the Zodiac.[38] Mithras was born from a virgin, or otherwise in a cave. It seems that Christianity might have taken quite a lot from the cult of Mithras, including baptism, virgin birth, resurrection and the communion mass. The three magi from the East travelling westward to witness the birth of the Light of the World would have been devotees of Mithras, as the word 'magus' originates from Persia.

According to Swami Nikhilananda, in his modern commentary on the *Taittiriya Upanishad*,

> After the pupil has practiced the recitation of the sounds, rhythms ... he is given instruction as to how to meditate on the combination of words. On account of his long habit of recitation, his mind might have become fixed on the mere letters of the text. Now through meditation he will understand its symbolic significance, which will gradually make his mind pure and one-pointed, enabling him in the end to grasp the subtle meanings of the Vedas.[39]

Once the ritual has been memorised, the subtle meaning of the words and actions is better understood, but then meditation must follow. Such a meditation at the outset involves *nama* and *rupa*, 'name and form'; it is to prepare for the pure meditation (*dhyana*) where there is no distinction between subject and object.

---

[38] Scholars have a strange notion that such symbolism is 'dualistic', and so Phanes has sometimes been described as 'more Asian than Greek'—yet the Asiatic doctrines are not dualistic; there is always a transcendent principle. There is a difference between duality and 'dualism'. The relation between the Roman cult of Mithras and the Indo-Persian doctrines, including that of Zoroaster, is established. It was the Romans that made of it a bull-slaying cult as that suited their disposition; they carried it to the furthest outposts of the Empire; a temple of Mithras was excavated in London. The original cult of Mithras is at least as old as 500 BC and probably much older.

[39] Taittiriya I. iii. i., *The Upanishads Vol. 4* [Advaita Ashrama].

Samadhi, the goal of yoga, has four distinct gradations in its first level, of which the fourth degree is the temporary dissolution of the ego.[40] Knowledge of the Universal Self through yogic union has a correspondence with this fourth degree, the first real *samadhi* ('union with the Lord'). Thus Saguna Brahma is known wholly, without separation into parts or attributes, through the pure heart or higher intellectual intuition (*boddhi*).

> There is this space within the heart; in it lies the Purusha consisting of mind (*manomaya*), immortal and luminous.[41]

That is to say, *purusha* or 'essence' is immortal and luminous. The mind of man is a modality, produced through *purusha* acting upon *prakriti* 'substance'. Atma manifests Itself in the *jivatma* ('creature self'), intelligence and activity having its seat at the heart centre, by virtue of the *jivatma*. It is thus clothed in a series of envelopes representing many phases of manifestation within the individual domain. The sephiroth of the Tree of Life may similarly be regarded as such coverings, the denser of these defined by elemental and planetary attributions. These may also be considered as degrees of knowledge, or otherwise as 'cups' or containers for the Shakti power. Each chakra in the Tantras or sephira in the Qabalah has a colour, which refers to the Sun as the eye of Universal Form. Properly, these may be regarded as determinations of the Shakti herself, forming powers of her *maya* or 'production'. It is worth noting that this subtle art of the Shakti, sometimes called Maya herself, and who is also a form of Universal Self, is often confused with mere illusion and so some have even concluded that the worlds of being are 'nothing at all'. That is a falsehood, because while the productions of Maya are illusionary or nil from the point of view of supreme reality, there are degrees of reality as relative to various states of being.

The central pillar of the Tree of Life corresponds to air and is cognate with the *shushumna* of Kundalini Yoga and the World Axis in various traditions. The trunk of the Tree is 'space' as a container for spirit or *akasha*, the 'middle of the body' of the Universal Self that permeates all. The Universal Self is also the intermediary, occupying the realm between heaven and earth and uniting the three worlds. The aspirant travels the Tree of Life as the Serpent of Wisdom ascending from Malkuth to Kether.

---

[40] See Part Two, 'The Way to Samadhi'.
[41] *Taittiriya Upanishad* I. vi. i.

In Sanskrit the word *vayu* means air, and it also denotes the God of Air or the Cosmic Soul. Vayu is derived from the Sanskrit root *va*, to go, to move; it is the principle of mobility. Consciousness ascends the world tree through various veils or coverings.

> That Shushumna is the path for the realisation of Indra (i.e., the Lord, or Saguna Brahman).[42]

The commentary to the *Taittiriya Upanishad* discusses how Saguna Brahma is identified with the world egg, *hiranyagarbha*, and that the heart is the proper place to contemplate and realise Brahma. In this, it is helpful to recollect that in ancient traditions the heart is identified with the Sun, and the Moon with the mind. The space or 'cave' within the heart is a symbol of Brahma. The *shushumna* or central nerve canal is regarded as the doorway to realisation. The embryonic *hiranyagarbha* envelops Brahma, which is sometimes symbolised by the Sun as the spiritual seed of the macrocosm. There is an important distinction to be made, one that frequently escapes those only able to see a naturalistic explanation for symbolism: the world egg is not a figure of the cosmos but of that from which the cosmos will be effected. The 'starting point' for that development is the centre itself, and that centre is identical with other symbolism referred to such as the heart and the cave, the 'spiritual seed' or the 'golden embryo'. This seed is sometimes an attribute of Christ, who otherwise proclaims himself to be the 'vine', and gold both as a colour and as a metal is associated with fire and the Sun. So it is that the *avatara* is born in a heart or cave. According to René Guénon,

> In fact, these localisations, which are also related to the Hindu doctrine of the chakras, refer to as many conditions of the human being, or phases of his spiritual development: at the base of the spinal column is the state of 'sleep' where the *luz* [seed or kernel] is found in the ordinary man; in the heart it is in the initial phase of its 'germination', which is properly the 'second birth'; in the 'frontal eye' it is the perfection of the human state, that is the reintegration into the 'primordial state'; finally, at the crown of the head, it signifies the passage to supra-individual states.[43]

The 'second birth' is essentially psychic regeneration, a reordering by which real and effective initiation becomes possible. The central channel or *shushumna* continues upwards from Tiphereth to Kether in the Tree of Life schema along the path of union indicated by the letter *gimel*, the desert wanderer or camel that the nomad must tether to the principle in the night.

---

[42] *Taittiriya Upanishad* I. vi. i.
[43] The 'Heart and the World Egg', *Symbols of Sacred Science*.

The cave is only dark relative to the states that are beyond it, and this is why there is a seeming contradiction where the cave is also described as full of light, or a place of illumination—for that is relative to the outer world. The second and third birth are thus the initiations into the lesser and the greater mysteries.

The *boddhi* or higher intellectual intuition (supra-individual) forms the five organs of sense perception: five organs of action, five *vayus* (modifications of *prana*) and the *manas* ('inward sense') within the subtle body of the individual. The subtle body is in its turn formed from five subtle elements: *akasha* or spirit, *vayu*, air, *apas*, water, *agni* or *tejas*, fire and *prithivi*, earth. The five elements are the foundation of the substantial universe. Akasha is associated with Brahma in relation to *maya*. Saguna Brahma (with qualities) is Ishvara, the Lord who creates and transforms through the power of *maya*.

It is curious that while the Hindu doctrines are very clear that Saguna Brahma is the first manifestation and so not the supreme principle, others, especially where there is an almost exclusively theological basis such as the Judeo Christian religions, go no further than the 'personal God'. This at the same time insists on a God that 'creates' the universe, quite often apparently out of 'nothing'. While even Hindu translators and commentators will also refer to Ishvara as a creator God, this does not accurately represent the true doctrine. The anomaly is shown in the first book of Genesis, which appears to begin with Ishvara, which would limit it to a cosmogonic point of view. Cosmic manifestation occurs through the 'presence' of the undetermined, unqualified principle, in the way that shadows appear when a light is shone into darkness. It is also clear, or should be from the New Testament, especially the book of St. John, that Christ as an *avatara* assumes the rôle and function of cosmic intermediary and that he insists always that there is one greater, and that is beyond him. The same might be said for other traditions such as the Hermetic, Mithraic and Orphic.

Hiranyagarbha is the first manifestation of Brahma where all beings live in activity. This first conditioned state of the subtle body is called *kamakala*, the *mula* ('root') of all mantras, words or spoken invocations. Through the various modifications or degrees, Brahma acquires qualities but in reality Brahma is 'one without a second'. The worlds of manifestation are based on contingencies where Atma is the source of *prana* (life) for all the envelopes that cover the Real. Comparison may be made with the light that shines in darkness mentioned in the book of John, 1–5.

The Bornless One

Regarding *hiranyagarbha*, comparison may be made with the Graeco Egyptian (thus Hermetic) spell known as the Bornless One. It is used as an invocation of the Guardian Angel, which is no different in effect from that of *hirangarbha*. One may also easily make comparison with Aeon Phanes and Mithras.[44]

> I am the He the Bornless Spirit, having sight in the feet;
> Strong and the immortal fire.
> I am He the truth.
> I am He who hates that evil should be wrought in the world.
> I am He that lighteneth and thundereth.
> I am He from whom is the shower of the life of earth.
> I am He whose mouth ever flameth.
> I am He, the begetter and manifestor unto the light.
> I am He, the Grace of the World.
> The Heart Girt with a Serpent is my Name.

As we have previously mentioned, the method of Abramelin for obtaining the Knowledge and Conversation of the Guardian Angel has considerable shortcomings and is far too confused to be taken in any way seriously.[45] There is nonetheless a method known as the 'Bornless One' that can be made effective, although it must be said that owing to its popularity countless persons have used it without any real knowledge; in that case they experienced nothing at all or in other cases no more than a spell of delusion owing to the auto-hypnotic methods taught by some 'authorities' on the subject.

It must also be said here that academics, with typical arrogance, have declared the title of the rite to be a 'mistranslation'. Academics will not, save in a covert manner, declare any meaning to the ancient texts they claim to have knowledge of, and so it is an accepted rule of conduct among them to convey only literal translations. The literal translation of ancient languages always results in absurdity; to call this ritual the 'Headless One' is no less such an absurdity. However, such nonsense pleases scholars who wish to show that all ancient knowledge is meaningless; its true significance entirely escapes the reach of their understanding.

---

44 See 'The Angel's Egg'.
45 See *Way of Knowledge*, 'Sacred Magic of Abramelin'.

The 'head' in ancient languages means also 'the chief' and 'the beginning', which has the further meaning of the supreme principle Itself. That which is not born is deathless; it is immortal considered from the point of view of manifest states of being, and eternal from the point of view of Atma-Brahma, or Supreme Identity.

The Bornless Ritual rests on an ancient Coptic spell of exorcism retrieved from a fragment of papyrus. It has very special advantages, not least of these being that, as is most often the case with Egyptian spells, the central Sun of the individuality is never separated from its higher principle called the 'Bornless Spirit'. It seems very likely to be the case that many that have performed this operation, or something like it, whether over six months or even eleven months in some cases, have thought they were performing a ritual only, not realising that the ritual is only a preparation for yoga meditation, as are all rituals when properly understood. This is made absolutely clear in the Hindu *Upanishads*, for example, where ritual without meditation is seen as no different from sheer ignorance.

The most effective adaptation of the ritual is in reality a ritualised form of Kundalini Yoga.[46] In Laya Yoga, the first five chakras of the subtle anatomy correspond to the five elemental *tattvas*. From the foundation, working upwards, these are Earth (*prithivi*), Water (*apas*), Fire (*tejas*), Air (*vayu*) and Spirit (*akasha*). The invocations are thus divided into six sections—the four elements plus spirit 'above' (*purusha*) and spirit 'below' (*prakriti*). The four elements, projected out into the quarters of the circle, are sealed with the pentagram and various deities. The spirit component, above and below, marks the centre of the circle and the vertical axis, and is symbolised by the hexagram, above and below. The twin serpents of Sun and Moon, called Ida and Pingala in the Tantras, are formed by moving widdershins about the circle while simultaneously invoking the elements in the quarters deosil. The natural effect of the contrary motion is to draw the Serpent Power upwards in the central column.

The Spirit *tattva* corresponds to the *vishuddha* chakra and it is in the sixth chakra called *ajna* that even the subtle senses must be withdrawn so that pure knowledge may be apprehended by the higher intellectual intuition (*boddhi*). With the knowledge of the unconditioned Atma the crown or *sahasrara* chakra flowers and a way may be opened beyond even this, through the concentration in its centre, to the supra-human states that are sometimes symbolised as a star posited above the head of the yogin.

---

[46] See *The Phoenix and other Stellar Rites of Initiation*.

At the apotheosis of the ritual the aspirant that has wisdom and integrity passes from the physical and mental activity of the ritual to the silent concentration of yoga in seated *asana*, which is intellectual activity. The physical and even the subtle senses are withdrawn and upwardly assimilated. Thus it is unlikely that a person will have success with this ritual, no matter how many times they perform it, unless they have become accomplished at meditation. They must have achieved sustained *dharana*, which results in *dhyana* or pure meditation. They are then able to approach *samadhi* or 'union', which is the goal of yoga. The ritual, if well understood, acts as a preparation for this. The triumphant song of the Angel continues thus:

> Come thou forth and follow me, and make all spirits subject unto me, so that every spirit of the firmament, and of the aethyr, upon the earth and under the earth, on dry land and in the water, of whirling air and of rushing fire, and every spell and scourge of God, the Vast One, may be made obedient unto me.

The 'gathering' function of both divine intermediary and pharaoh is here invoked, and which was symbolised by the ancient Egyptians as the 'crook', which is really to represent the very exact geometrical curvature of a line about an invisible point, the supreme principle. It is also the form of an ancient needle for stitching or weaving, and so is the gathering of the *sutra* or 'Golden Thread'. All the powers and the principalities of the lower elemental worlds are thus drawn in to the ordered universe of *hiranyagarbha*.

A period of six months, between the equinoxes or solstices of the year, is deemed a reasonable time limit for the operation, which is performed repeatedly on a daily basis, the practice, aspiration and vigilance gradually being intensified over the last two months.

Enochian Calls

It would be very interesting to produce a commentary on the Enochian Calls of the Elizabethan astrologer John Dee, though it is beyond the scope of the present work as there are Eighteen of them plus one to invoke the Thirty Aethyrs. However, to recite the Calls without understanding is to enter into a ritual of superstition. We will here look at the First Call, which is attributed to Spirit (or *akasha*), when this is understood as an elemental principle. The First Call was never meant to be used without the Second Call, which is to invoke the Spirits of the other elements. Why is this? The Calls are obviously all about Ishvara, the Lord of the Universe in various aspects. The First Call is the Justice aspect while the Second Call is Peace. Justice and Peace are complementary.

> I reign over ye, saith the God of Justice, in power exalted above the firmaments of wrath; in Whose hands the Sun is as a sword, and the Moon as a through-thrusting fire; Who measureth your garments in the midst of my vestures, and trussed you together as the palms of my hands; Whose seats I garnished with the fire of gathering; and beautified your garments with admiration.

The Lord is pictured or imaged here as chief of the hierarchical order of things, his governance. He is also the 'King of the World'. He is therefore placed above the firmaments of wrath. What is that? And why is it afflicted with anger, which belongs to the demons (*asuras*)? The explanation is cosmological in nature: The firmament in ancient languages is a dual symbol and represents not sea but sky or heaven, while still being referred to sometimes as 'waters'. What is important to know is that there is an upper firmament and a lower firmament; confusion of these leads to serious misunderstanding. The upper firmament is heaven, or otherwise the celestial, angelic realm. In the Hindu scriptures it is referred to *devas* and *devis*, which are 'gods' but this can include various degrees in the natural order, and is inclusive of human beings that have become *devas* at least for the duration of a cosmic cycle, for example. The lower waters are much closer to the earth, so to speak, and might be thought of as inclusive of a large part of the subtle realm, which neo-spiritualism would have as a 'psychic' domain although it is really much more than that. This marks the really important distinction between Ishvara as Lord of the Universe and the Gnostic Demiurge who is born of the inferior or lower waters.[47]

---

[47] See 'The Sons of Gods', in particular p. 176, *Nu Hermetica*.

It is the inferior or lower waters then that are called 'wrathful', because these lower degrees of manifestation can act as a subtle repository for all the afflictions of men. The *karmasayas*, to use the Sanskrit term, are the retained mental impressions of past deeds, thoughts or actions, whether in the mind of an individual, or a race or any collective entity whatsoever. As the Sanskrit word indicates, these can be latent and yet become active, causing misery. It is for this reason that 'psychism', especially the way in which it is mistaken for something 'spiritual' by neo-spiritualists and others, is in no way condoned in traditional knowledge and spiritual practice.

This makes it very clear that the Lord of the Universe, who has various names in the Enochian or Angelic language, is Ishvara and not the Gnostic Demiurge—although it must be said there are some parts of the Call of the Thirty Aethyrs that blur the difference. It is worth remembering in that respect that there are not two Ishvaras, so the difference is in the point of view. From the ignorant point of view, Ishvara is a 'jealous God', or God made in the image of man. It depends almost entirely on the anthropomorphisation of God that seems to afflict the Judaeo Christian traditions. From the point of view of the sacred science as put forth in Hinduism, it is possible to know God and even that knowledge is not placed as the ultimate limit. God is not an individual being and, as should be obvious, can hardly be human—although that does not presuppose that Krishna or Christ, for example, could not take human form for some special purpose, as is recounted in *Bhagavad Gita* and the Bible.

In his right hand he bears a sword of Justice and in his left hand he bears the Moon, which is as *mal-prji*, 'penetrating fire'. How is this 'peace' then likened to fire in this way? When the mind is made peaceful through prolonged meditation and concentration on a single object, then a certain kind of 'fire' sweeps through, and with devotees this is identified with the deity. It is the fire that purifies the mind of its afflictions and *karmasayas* from previous actions. Over the course of time and with long continued practice the retained mental impressions that give rise to suffering and are also the obstacles or impediments to yoga practice itself, are dissolved.

The symbols held in the right and left hands might be compared with the Egyptian *nekhakha* and *hekat*, often falsely construed as 'crook and flail'. The latter is ordering through discrimination and the former is gathering about the principle—it is also a symbolic needle or hook for weaving a thread. Thus there is a re-ordering that takes place in the individuality with correct practice and intention.

The devotional practice is alluded to in the last line of the quoted verse, where the 'garments' are beautified with admiration. The garments are the clothing or particular form of the God. The form or image of the God is not idolatry when correctly understood. It is to help the meditation. The strange grammatical switching from the first person to the second person serves to help the meditation pass from the *savitarka* 'with words' and inferences to help, to the real engrossment of *nirvitarka*, 'without words'; it breaks up the habitual identifications of subject and object.[48] As the one who 'measureth' the Lord of the Universe is clearly depicted as Mind of Logos, in which all things are named and defined. The seats or thrones are usually an association with ancient cosmologies, for example the twelve zodiacal stations of the sun through the year, which in turn invokes the circle of the heavens with the solar centre as principle.

The 'fire of gathering' is that power of understanding that comes when it is known—through direct experience—that all things are witnessed by the Seer, the supreme principle, yet That (supreme) does not participate in the cognitions directly, and is not changed or in any way moved by them. Thus we are called, through knowledge of the principle upon which the deity acts, to participate in the divinity, which is to achieve true knowledge of the Self.

---

[48] See Part Two for a detailed explanation of *savitarka* and *nirvitarka* and their importance in a spiritual practice; in particular, 'The Way to Samadhi'.

Gnosis of the Thirty Aeons

The Tree of Life model that we are familiar with includes both the Tree of Life and the Tree of Knowledge of Good and Evil—for there was said to be two trees in the Garden of Eden. In fact, the Qabalistic Tree is both a duality and a ternary, consisting of two pillars and a 'middle way' or central path of equilibration. The two pillars of the Gnosis are given various names, usually in Greek or Hebrew. For example, Knowledge and Wisdom. This draws from the Gnostic tradition, which is usually written in Greek, hence *Gnosis* and *Sophia*, Knowledge and Wisdom. Gnosis is the special kind of knowledge, not separate from supreme reality, while Sophia is the world soul or feminine personification of Universal Being. The latter, it should be well noted, has nothing to do with the human collectivity and is descriptive of that which transcends the human individual state entirely—a collection of individual states is no different in this sense than any particular individual being. Gnosis can also be seen as a complement by transposition to another Greek term, *Syneses*, 'Insight', though that is relatively a state of unknowing compared to pure knowledge.

Cosmologies owing to the Hellenic era in which Hermeticism and Gnosticism flourished made frequent use of circular representations for the different worlds or states of being; the Tree of Life of ten emanations or sephiroth that was utilised by the Hebrew Kabbalists is but one of almost countless arrangements that were produced as according to the needs of different schools of thought. Thus, one other frequently occurring schema utilises concentric circles, where the terrestrial realm is placed in the centre as the most material end of manifestation and higher states move outwards and upwards to the furthest edge. With this kind of arrangement, we may find the outermost circle described as the realm of the Father of the Invisible Light, and the next as the realm of the Son of Light.[49] The two are united by *Agape*, the love principle, for they cannot be truly separate in reality. The third circle includes the realm of Sophia, which embraces both the light and darkness in equal measure, as shown in the illustration on the next page.

---

[49] Stephen Edred Flowers produced a synthesis of the complex Gnostic schema in *Hermetic Magic* [Samuel Weiser 1995], which we have made use of here by way of a careful adaptation. We do not in any way agree with his theories or opinions, however, or his inversion of symbolism.

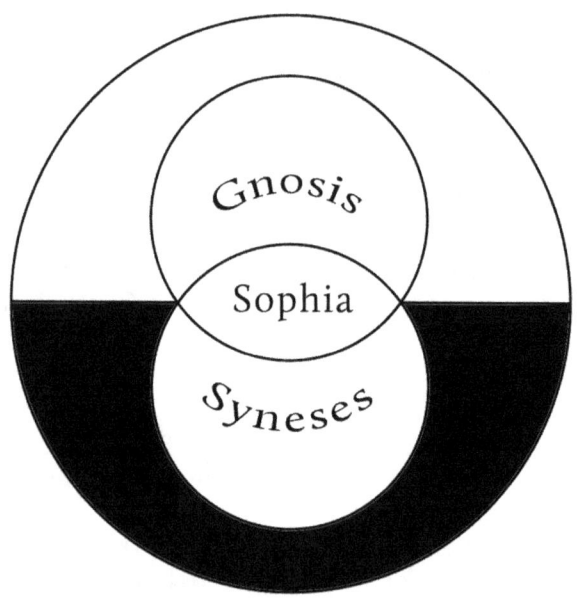

Realm of Sophia within the Gnostic Cosmograph

There is an easy comparison with the Tree of Life, where the only real difference is that the Son and Sophia are placed horizontally as Chokmah and Binah, below Kether the First. Also the names are reversed; in Greek versions the pair are called *Nous*, Mind, and *Sophia*, Wisdom.[50]

The realm of Sophia involves more detail than those of the Father and Son and can be graphically represented by a *vesica piscis* placed within circle. We then have Gnosis as the uppermost of the interlaced circles and Syneses as the lower. The space where the two circles intersect is the special realm of Sophia, as between the light and dark, while the whole of it represents her Nature. If we continue the comparison with the Tree of Life, then this is the 'secret places' of Binah alluded to in the *Sepher Yetzirah* in respect of the Garden of Eden—in which, we should bear in mind, two trees are found.[51]

To recapitulate: the Realm of Sophia as shown above is placed below the first and outermost circle of the Invisible Light and the second of the Son of Light or Logos. One can understand a more or less exact comparison can be made with Binah of the Tree of Life, though the third emanation is here 'Wisdom'. This makes it clear how in the book of Genesis Eve (or Sophia) was supposed to have eaten the apple of the fruit of knowledge, or otherwise to have 'stooped down' towards the Kingdom of Shells, thus precipitating the fateful Fall of Adam. In fact, the true Knowledge or Gnosis is the crown of Sophia; however, if we follow the other circles below Sophia indicative of cosmic manifestation the possibility of 'falling' becomes easier to understand: Immediately below the Realm of Sophia as depicted above is placed the Garden of Eden, in which is the Tree of Life and Tree of Death. The inner abode of the Garden is protected by the flaming sword that turns every way. The sword also has a relation with the four holy creatures called Kerubim, the Lion, the Eagle, the Bull and the Angel. Without the Garden of Eden, or below it in the natural order, are the Zodiac and the constellations. Below this is the great circle of the serpent Ouroboros (Hebraic Leviathan), which is for mankind the outer boundary or threshold.

---

[50] It is sometimes supposed that the Son of Light, as Messiah, is the child of Chokmah and Binah called Da'ath, Knowledge. Da'ath, in its inferior aspect, is the realm of the Demiurge as usurper of any higher principle, however.
[51] See *Thirty-two paths of Wisdom* [Ordo Astri].

There then follow the seven circles of the planetary spheres, commencing with Saturn. Finally the earth is placed in the centre, or the lowest point if regarded as axial hierarchy, encircled by the dragon or beast called Behemoth. Within the earth is also placed the black realm called *Tartaros*, the infernal region. From all this it can be seen how the return to Eden is perilous and beset with difficulty! In fact, it is even more difficult than that, for, according to the ancient Gnostics, divine Sophia, placed below the Invisible Light in the scheme of things, sought to give birth to a son without the aid or intervention of the Light—this is a metaphysical impossibility so long as the 'Father' is placed as superior in the scheme of things, but we will come to that again later.

The illegitimate progeny—really the child of Eve and the Serpent—was the evil Demiurge, Jahweh or Ialdabaoth. This monster usurped the authority of any higher principle, including that of his mother, and with the help of a brood of Archons, created the material (or inferior) universe and with it the race of men. This is what later Christians and Neo-Platonists condemned as unforgivable heresy.[52] While we are not so much troubled in our times by accusations of heresy from the authorities, it is worth noting that neo-spiritualism, psychological occultism, and the entire hybrid concoction of New Age thought and practice is really just as much opposed to the Gnostic point of view, through incomprehension. 'Positivism' regarding the human condition is so central to the postmodern propaganda, now deeply embedded in our civilisation at every level, that it is an article of faith in the same way that evolutionism and 'progress' was to the generations immediately prior to the postmodern era.

The Archons have a certain correspondence with the Asuras, the demons of the Vedic tradition. According to *Isha Upanishad*, V.3:

> Verily, those worlds of the Asura are enveloped in blind darkness; and thereto they all repair after death who are slayers of Ātman.[53]

The 'blind darkness' is the state of ignorance or unknowing. Those who worship the Asuras, who delight in sensory pleasures alone, are the slayers of the Real, for they do not know Atma. According to the comment of Swami Nikhilananda,

---

[52] Plotinus, Enneads II: 9.
[53] Swami Nikhilananda, *Upanishads Vol. 1*, Iśa Upanishad [Advaita Ashrama].

Asuras: Literally, demons, who delight in material enjoyments. Even those who experience in heaven the rewards of their meritorious actions may be called asuras, because they too are devoid of Self-Knowledge. The word 'worlds' in the text [Cf. Aeons] refers to all relative states. Or it may mean 'sunless', that is to say non-luminous.

To continue with our summary of many strands of Gnostic thought, Christ, the Word or Son of Light, was sent into the world, born not of the world but of the Invisible Spirit, to teach humanity the Gnosis and how to escape the prison of the evil demiurge and return to the light. While it seems to be a common notion that Gnosticism, as with the Avestan or Zoroastrian cults, is 'dualistic', we need exercise caution here: the same accusation (which is sometimes used in a slanderous sense) is not usually levelled against the Hindu doctrines, unless by those very ignorant of what they profess to know about. And yet there can be little doubt that Mithraism and Avesta, if not actually spawned in India, were influenced greatly by Hinduism. There is much in common if we allow for the differences in cultural perspective. For example, there is even an invocation to Mithras (or Mitra) in the *Upanishads*.[54]

However, the fragmentary remains of Gnostic texts, as opposed to the complete, unified body of the *Vedas*, appear at least to reach no further than the worlds of being or manifestation. In other words, as with the Greek philosophers, there is no pure metaphysics to provide a principle of supreme reality or Brahma Nirguna, the undetermined Brahma. Modern and postmodern scholastic commentators have no metaphysical comprehension so if the supreme principle is there, they will not see it in any case.

We said earlier that the idea of divine Sophia begetting the demiurge without the aid of the Invisible Spirit is a metaphysical impossibility. This is so if we take the schema 'as read': if the Father of Light principle precedes Sophia, and is supreme in the scheme of things, then Sophia cannot effectively exist or act independently of that principle. This is not to deny that in older times the Goddess bore the divine child without paternal intervention. According to the *Isha Upanishad* 4,

> That non-dual Ātman, though never stirring, is swifter than the mind. The *devas* (the senses) cannot reach It, for It moves ever in front. Though standing still, It overtakes others who are running. Because of Ātman, Vāyu (the World Soul) apportions the activities of all.

---

[54] *Taittirīya Upanishad* I.i.1.

According to the comment of Nikhilananda, Vāyu is,

> The first cosmic manifestation of the Absolute in the relative universe, also known by such epithets as the World Soul, Hiranyagarbha [world egg], and Prāna [breath]. It sustains the whole universe by apportioning to everyone his function. But the World Soul can exercise its lordship because Ātman *is its inner Self.* Without Ātman even the highest cosmic entity becomes powerless and ceases to exist.

And further,

> That fire burns, that the clouds give rain and the sun light, and that the other powers of nature perform their respective functions is due to Ātman. That is why there is no confusion in the universe. The meaning is that all the activities of the universe, following the law of cause and effect, are possible because the eternally conscious Ātman exists as the inmost essence and the ultimate Reality of all.

It is clear then that any confusion in the universe owes not to a truly cosmic state of affairs but to the ignorance of man in the fallen state. The Tantras preserved the exceedingly ancient tradition where the Great Mother of All, Mahamaya, is not only the producer of all worlds of being from her own essence but is also the supreme absolute, equivalent to and not in any way dependent on Brahma Nirguna let alone Brahma Saguna (Brahma *with* determinations, literally 'with gunas'). As *parabrahma* is gender neutral, she is that very *parabrahma*, but can also, through a kind of self-polarisation, be the producer or maker of the worlds of Being and manifestation.

Maya is a name both of the Devi herself and of the 'fabric' or weave of the worlds (*sutratma*). This has led to confusion in Western minds, a confusion compounded by insufficient translations, where Maya is taken to be 'illusion' and therefore non-existent. Nouns and adjectives in Sanskrit and other ancient languages frequently share a common root, and the interpretation depends on the point of view. For example, there is the pure metaphysical view, which is that of the supreme absolute, and there is the strictly relative human and corporeal point of view; between these lies a considerable chasm.

So, there are three possibilities for the apparent Gnostic heresy, or at least one of them—for there are many! The first, most simple, is that the Gnostics were in error, confusing the divine Mother of All with Necessity. That would naturally give rise to the condemnation of the Cosmos as 'evil', a kind of artifice or even virtual world, entirely cut off from any first and true principle. We should also bear in mind that 'good' and 'evil' are in any case moral valuations that belong exclusively to the human corporeal domain.

Secondly, could the notion of the fallen Sophia owe to changes in cyclical time and the deepening darkness of the final phase of the Kali Yuga, where separation and increasing distance between men and women, men and gods, nature and the universe, is inevitable? This much is irrefutable, but when looked at from that perspective, the difference between the Gnostic cosmology and the biblical account of Eve precipitating the Fall might not seem so great.

The truth may include something of all these possibilities, but the third is the one that looks most interesting to us in the light of the present study, and is most worthy of closer examination: the Gnosis requires and is all about initiation, and initiation must have the human state as basis. From the point of view of fallen man at an advanced stage of the Kali Yuga, there is no difference between nature and necessity. When Adam beheld the Tree of Knowledge of Good and Evil (which involves lower states of being) and was instantly chained to a material world by the dragon of time and so made subject to birth and death, he was also separated from Eve or Sophia. Soon he would lose sight of any principle beyond the arbitrary laws and moral prohibitions of his own making. He only knows Eve in her fallen state. If Gnosis is pure knowledge, which must reach the metaphysical, then it cannot be 'dualism', which is solely the product of man's reason. The Invisible Light, placed at the pinnacle of the Gnostic cosmograph, is the 'personal God' Ishvara when considered as the unmanifest state of Pure Being, and certainly not its infernal or inverse reflection in the lower waters as the evil demiurge—something that Gnosticism defines but biblical texts obfuscate, through their need for assertion of the demiurge as the one, sole principle.

Whether the Invisible Light is thought of as 'Father' or 'Mother' is largely irrelevant, other than that the former was acceptable to certain cultures at that particular time. The anthropomorphisation of the supreme deity owes largely to the Judaic tradition and is a consequence of the personification of the demiurge, whose attributes come across as uncannily human and whose demands are frequently very much like those of the king of Persia, who was a considerable political influence at the time.

Pure Being, unmanifest and so not in any way subject to change from an exterior source, contains all possibilities of manifestation, of which the human corporeal state with its male and female modes is one minute fraction. If we look to the Hindu tradition we find that Ishvara may be a form of Mahadevi Shakti, or one of the Trimurti, Brahma, Vishnu and Shiva.

In either case, we must posit that if the Gnostic cosmology begins with Ishvara then it is precisely because it is a cosmology that it does so. It does not presuppose that the Gnostics knew of no person that had attained the Supreme Identity where all is contained within the Brahma Self.[55] Now, it is the Son of Light, placed immediately below the pinnacle, that is the Logos, the Word and ordering principle. The proximity of this Word of God and *Agape*, the love principle, is something made very clear in the first verse of the first chapter of the book of John the Evangelist, and this accords completely with our Gnostic schema.

> In the beginning [*in principio*] was the Word, and the Word was with God, and the Word was God.

The Son and the Spirit are then unified in the love principle. Furthermore, the Son of Light and Sophia are only separate from the perspective of fallen man. In fact, in the Gnostic narratives and even in the Gospels, Sophia, as Mary Magdalene, embodies the love principle in so far as her love of Jesus is absolutely integral to the story of descent and ascent, death and resurrection. In that case, by upward transposition, we have a ternary of Light, Logos and Sophia that is reflected downward towards manifestation through the triadic central function of Sophia as Vāyu or the 'world egg'. This is not 'dualism'. We can look at the diagram above and see Hiranyagarbha, for it is also said that the world egg cracked in two halves; the top half was of gold, and from it the heavens were produced, and the lower half was silver, and from it the earth was produced.[56]

In much earlier traditions, the Son of Light was both the son *and* the consort of the Goddess for, as we have already stated, there was no patriarchal intervention. The restoration of the fallen world and the return of Sophia to her rightful place among the stars, or to be more exact, *beyond* the stars, is presented here from an initiatic point of view, which requires a 'Journey of the Soul' through the ascending states of being, named Aeons ('worlds').

---

[55] See René Guénon, *Man and His Becoming according to the Vedānta*, the closing chapters [Sophia Perennis]. The last utilises Shankaracharya's *Atma Bodha* and is by far the best, most exact commentary on that book.
[56] *Chandogya Upanishad* III.19.2. 'That which was silver became the earth; that which was of gold, heaven. What was of the thick membrane [of the white] became the mountains; the thin membrane [of the yolk], the mist and the clouds. The veins became the rivers, the fluid in the bladder, the ocean.'

As also stated earlier, the Aeons are ruled by Archons, so there must be means to defeat them, or in some way to pass them. This also is not different from the Hindu doctrines, where there are almost countless *devas*, which either bar the way to the unworthy or assist the initiate, providing various magical powers along the way. Essentially, it requires a level of knowledge to get past them; 'unworthiness' is no different from ignorance (*avidya*). In the Tantras, these *devas* and powers are also those of the Mahadevi Shakti, or are sent by her.

It is notable that in the Mithraic rites, the initiate was himself identified with the Lord of Heavenly Light, and that the sense of the followers of Christ becoming Sons of Light in his name is frequently referenced in the Gospels, especially the book of John, of which here are merely two examples:

> Behold, what manner of love the Father hath bestowed upon us, that we should be called the sons of God: therefore the world knoweth us not, because it knew him not.[57]

> Beloved, now are we the sons of God, and it doth not yet appear what we shall be: but we know that, when he shall appear, we shall be like him; for we shall see him as he is.[58]

The first, from 1 John 3: 1, echoes the words of Krishna in the *Bhagavad Gita*, where he tells Arjuna that when he takes on human form, men do not see him, they only see the human form. According to the *Gita*,

> 7: 13 Deluded by these threefold *gunas* constituting Nature, this whole world fails to recognise Me, who am above the *gunas* and immutable.[59]

> 7: 24 Not knowing My supreme Nature, immutable and transcendent, foolish men think that I, the Unmanifest, am endowed with a manifest form.

> 7: 25 Veiled by My *maya* born of the *gunas*, I am not revealed to all. This deluded world knows Me not as the unborn and eternal.

> 8: 20 But beyond this unmanifested [*pralaya* or night of dissolution] there is yet another Unmanifested Eternal Being, who does not perish when all beings perish.

> 8: 22 That Supreme person, in whom all beings abide and by whom the entire universe is pervaded, can be attained, O Pārtha, by whole-souled devotion directed to Him [that is, the supreme, as opposed to worship of the *devas*].

---

[57] I John 3: 1.
[58] I John 3: 2.
[59] Translation by Swami Nikhilananda [Ramakrishna Vedanta Centre].

9: 17 I am the father of this universe, the mother, the sustainer, and the grandsire. I am the knowable, the purifier, and the syllable Om. I am also the Rik, the Saman and the Yajus [that is, the principal Vedas].

It remains now to consider some of the remarkable similarities between the 'Enochian' Thirty Aethyrs of John Dee and the Egypto-Christian-Gnostic Thirty Aeons of Valentinus. Valentinus, often described as an early, possibly even the first, Christian theologian, was an Egyptian man based in Alexandria. Gnosticism undoubtedly influenced his schema of Thirty Aeons.[60] The Thirty Aeons is an initiatic means by which Sophia, in the sense of the soul of fallen man—though also the 'scarlet woman' Magdalene, the consort of Jesus, as was concealed in the Gospel narratives—could be rescued by the Son of Light to effect an escape from the material universe and return to the ineffable source.

Christianity of the 1st or 2nd century AD, it must be added, was not in any way comparable to the Romanised version that emerged later. Neo-Platonism, Hermetic and Gnostic thought, influenced it. It was influenced by traditions as geographically removed from Egypt as Persia and even India—which may have been the source of both Mithraism and Zoroastrianism. One might even say that there are 'two Christianities' in that respect: the original one, involving diverse schools of thought, in which the initiatic element was of primary importance, and the later one, produced through 'repackaging' of the many strands of the Gnosis, in which initiation was excluded and all evidence of the original sources carefully erased.

The Enochian Thirty Aethyrs of John Dee came about through a series of communications with angels during the reign of Elizabeth I of England. Firstly, there are also thirty worlds, called Aires or Aethyrs, to traverse in each phase of the initiatic journey. TEX, the lowest of the Aethyrs (or first on the path of ascent), corresponds to the subtle realm of the terrestrial sphere. As with our Gnostic schema referred to earlier, earth is placed in the middle of concentric circles leading outwards towards the infinite. The letter correspondences of TEX reveal Eve and the Serpent.[61] Both symbols have a dual aspect, superior and inferior. Eve is divine Sophia or Mahamaya Devi. In the lower sense, she is analogous to the soul of the aspirant. She must pass through the perilous Aethyrs before the Kingdom is restored, the Garden of Eden reclaimed.

---

[60] Valentinus is reckoned to have lived from about AD 100 to 180.
[61] By Enochian Geomantic correspondences: T = Draco; E = Virgo; X = Earth.

She is the Graal and the seeker of the Graal. Sophia and the Serpent are one, but terrestrial Eve is bound by the Serpent as Kronos, time, so that she is the bride of the fateful Beast (Behemoth or Leviathan, by which the soul is kept captive). The Aeons of Valentinus provide us with what is otherwise missing. Christ, or as he is sometimes known, Emmanuel (*God be-with-us*) is also identified with the Serpent, and is sometimes also called the Ophite. He is the Nassarene, a name formed from the Hebrew or Aramaic *nachash*, 'serpent'. Indeed, Messiah, another name by which he is known, and *nachash* have the same value by Hebrew number correspondence.[62] The 'anointed one' (Messiah) is one with the Old Serpent, called Satan or Seth in Jewish tradition.[63]

Mary Magdalene, the prostitute or scarlet woman of the Gospel retelling of the initiatic tale, was as stated earlier, the consort of Christ Jesus. This fable of 'Babalon and the Beast' is not as anti-Christian as some would like to think. It is more a veiled allusion to the original Gnostic and Egyptian forms of Christianity, which quite possibly were not even called 'Christian' at that time, and were not unrelated to the Sethian Gnosis. It would take an entire book to examine the symbolism of all the Thirty Aethyrs, so it must suffice here to look at the first and the last only. The First (or highest) is the principle of Pure Being, and is no different from the Invisible Light as it is called in our Gnostic schema, except that here it is called a Virgin, and not the Father.

The First is called LIL. This is both noun and adjective in Hebrew and Sanskrit. The various meanings include 'night', 'virgin', 'child', 'girl' and 'play'—of which the latter is associated with the dance or phenomenal display or productions of Maya, which bewilder and delude men. The Knowledge of LIL requires a return to the Edenic State. Also, a missing key is here that is otherwise omitted or excluded from the Gnostic cosmology: it is stated in the Enochian literature that there is another Aire or Aethyr, beyond the First, not numbered. The metaphysical element is thus restored.

To conclude on a practical note, though this study is by no means exhaustive given the great complexity of the subject: the Thirty Aethyrs symbolise an initiatic Journey of the Soul (or Being), ascending through various states.

---

[62] MShICh counts to 358, as does NChSh.
[63] Curiously, the letter *nachash* was excluded from the Hebrew alphabet at some point in its development, and was replaced with *nun*, 'a fish'—yet both animals are Typhonian and both are a symbol of Christ.

The Aethyrs include the 'three worlds', in common with most if not all traditions.[64] The Operation of the Aethyrs is usually described as 'skrying', but unless the practitioner has at least mastered the yoga of the initial stages of Savikalpa Samadhi, access beyond the first ten or so will not be possible.[65] In fact, without some sure footing in *dharana* (concentration) and *dhyana* (meditation in the true sense), any results from skrying will amount to little of any consequence. From the beginning, with TEX called 'The Realm' (or Kingdom), the practitioner must already have cultivated the 'right mudra' or attitude of the Shakta or Tantrika. Unless some contact is made with the Shakti, Sophia or Babalon (a form of Isis-Hathoor), they may easily achieve no more than a subtle plane projection of their own thoughts and imagining, limited to the psychological domain—which is a non-achievement in initiatic terms.

Although Gnosticism is not a dualistic path in itself—the goal is no different from that of yoga, and *gnosis* is the direct equivalent of Sanskrit *jnana*—the magical working of the Aethyrs is intensely dualistic in so far as the mind is trained on objects of the mind and subtle senses. Rigorous discrimination is needed, as even slight success can overwhelm the inexperienced operator with seductive glamour. They are setting foot on the very ground most liked by Satan, by which we mean in this context the Adversary or opposer to all spiritual knowledge and realisation. If there is no devotional element, no real aspiration beyond the desire to gain the *siddhis* or magical powers, there will be nothing to rescue the soul from the consequences of the indefinite prolongation of ignorance. It is best then to approach the work as theurgic so as not to confuse it with ordinary matters such as divination or 'psychic development'. The very first part of the journey, which must be accomplished before any higher ground is reached, is the domain of Sophia and Christ. One must know something of these, and even a 'mystical' or vague yearning is better than nothing. If we prefer it, we can call TEX the domain of Eve and Adam Kadmon or even Babalon and the Beast, but the name we give it makes little difference to the spiritual realities and the principles, whether greater or lesser, that govern such operations. The basis is love in its highest principle, and those who do not understand this or otherwise misconstrue it deliberately will be amply rewarded by the Asuras.

---

[64] See *The Great Triad*, René Guénon [Sophia Perennis].
[65] See Part Two, 'The Way of Samadhi'.

Magick

Our older works are largely concerned with magick, although our use of the term then included theurgy, which is usually separate and distinct as the 'practice of God'; whereas magick is really concerned with the manipulation of phenomena through the application of the law of correspondences, 'As above and so below'. There is a difference between natural correspondences and syncretic or systematised knowledge, involving tables and lists of more or less arbitrary assignments, though the latter can doubtless achieve some of the effects desired by the practitioner, something that owes more to auto-hypnotic suggestion than anything else. We shall go into this in more detail later.[66]

The limitation, more or less severe, placed on the possibilities for real spiritual realisation by the systematic approach means we had to revise our approach to the subject quite drastically. Since computers became the dominant force in the world for shaping the minds of men, the urge towards classification and tabulation has by now been taken to the extreme where systems analysts produce popular books about magick. Those who produce these—and there are very many of them—usually have university degrees they are proud of but no real knowledge whatsoever. Most of them are even atheists and among these, a degree in psychology is considered a 'qualification', whereas in fact that kind of mentality automatically disqualifies a person from any real initiation or spiritual realisation. These always emphasise a kind of artificial 'psychism', where visualisation techniques are used along with the ubiquitous auto-hypnotism. As a consequence we now have book-learned 'adepts' claiming high degrees of initiation and whose knowledge extends no further than the ordinary man in the street, though that does not it seems prevent them from pretending to teach and even initiate others, sometimes through the convenient means of internet video links and even social media—which is a kind of oxymoron as anything 'social' automatically discounts esotericism.

For all this mania for selling delusion to the masses—who already accept the most fantastic lies from governments, corporations and 'official' science—we now place much greater emphasis on theoretical knowledge, by which is meant traditional cosmology and ontology, and the practice of yoga, than at any time before. According to René Guénon,

---

[66] See the next chapter, 'Systems of Knowledge'.

> Of all preliminary means, theoretical knowledge alone is absolutely indispensible, and that later, when one passes to actual realisation, it is concentration that matters most and that leads to it in the most immediate way, for it is directly bound up with knowledge.[67]

We have always, right from the veriest beginning, insisted that one works from the highest principle. While that is no certain guarantee that heedless fools will not come unstuck, the Hermetic axiom 'As above and so below' has far greater import than is afforded it by today's postmodern 'experts'.[68] Magick, if not torn wholly asunder from its governing principles in the natural and supernatural order, can be very efficacious as a support to the path of true knowledge, and in the times we now live we need all the assistance we can get.

It is seldom realised that many rituals in our older works are fully adaptable to different needs, and that their use can sometimes go much further than the necessarily brief descriptions afforded by such a book.[69] As has by now been frequently pointed out, no one can get initiation 'out of the book' or from merely applying themselves to more or less systematised knowledge. Every tradition insists on the need for a teacher, or nothing of any real worth can be achieved. Such a relation depends a great deal on the student asking the right kind of questions and being prepared to enter into consultation and discussion as well as to follow the advice or direction that is given. There is a *Threefold Obligation* that, while never declared in the way of an oath, insists upon that at the commencement of practical work; it is intended to be a continual observance and should really spring freely from the love, devotion, reverence and enthusiasm of the practitioner.

All of the above requires a certain and very special kind of 'energy' on behalf of the aspirant. Unless they fix their mind wholly on the subject of their devotion, refraining to expend their time and attention in the pursuit of merely personal and ordinary goals in the vain hope of gaining an increase in self-pleasure, that special kind of energy will not be available for the work and no further progress will be made.

---

[67] 'Conclusions', *Introduction to the Study of the Hindu Doctrines*.
[68] Indeed, one of the latter went so far as to reverse the axiom to imply that the higher could be magically forced to change in accordance with the low and very ordinary intentions of the magician. That is a typically 'satanic' inversion of the natural order and while it could certainly effect results in the sphere of the practitioner, such results, owing to the inversion, could only increase ignorance and delusion still further.
[69] For example *Ritual Magick—Initiation of the Star and Snake*.

The 'Ritual for Psychic Self Defence' provides an example of a ritual where the practical operations can go further than as is implied by the titles and brief description given in the textbook.[70] Cases of actual psychic attack, where the antagonist intentionally takes their malice to the Hermetic level, are rare. While there might be many persons in the world today who would indeed use magical means to harm others, given the availability of the rituals and methods in the public domain, few would be prepared to go to the painstaking lengths necessary. It is well indeed that few persons now have the expertise and knowledge necessary, even if that kind of knowledge is relatively ordinary. Anyone that had real knowledge would never consider such a thing. It is more likely that such an attack would be unintentional, arising from anger or some other affliction. It must also be said that to feel disturbance or disequilibrium and then look for external causes in other people is a dangerous road to travel as it might easily result in further derangement. However, it really makes no difference as a psychic attack can only be effective if there is a sympathetic response from the victim, who is more alike the attacker than they care to admit in so far as they have retained harmful mental impressions that lead to what are called *kléshas* in Sanskrit, 'harmful afflictions'.[71]

Thus, in understanding the ritual of Psychic Self Defence, it becomes apparent that whether a cause is seen as external or internal, there is a need to loosen the bonds of attachment to harmful sense impressions that, when retained (through the faculties such as memory), amount to serious obstructions to the goal of yoga. The Ritual of Psychic Self Defence can be taken further than that, as we have indicated, but to explain that we need first to refer to the way the ritual is constructed: it begins as do most rituals with a general opening of the temple that orders the sphere of the practitioner as according to cosmological principles. Every Zelator has a ritually consecrated dagger to symbolise the whole plane of Air, and this is then used to perform a thorough banishing or purification of that element in the name of its various hierarchical names and powers, making the appropriate pentagrams and so forth around the place of work. It should be mentioned that the 'plane of Air' corresponds in this Hermetic schema particularly to Yesod, the ninth sephira called the Foundation in Qabalah.

---

[70] *Ritual Magick* [ibid].
[71] Part Two of this book includes a study of the Vedantic science of the mind. In particular, 'Yoga of the Mind'.

However, the etherial designation is really inclusive of the whole domain of the individual *ruach* or mind-intelligence. The operation of higher principles is always marked in Qabalistic operations; so for example the divine name in Tiphereth (the Sun) is always given first in an invocation of Yesod (the Moon). There then follows a general purification (by holy water) and consecration (by incense perfume) of the person and the place, in all four quarters. The term often used, 'banishing', is a rough and ready one, especially when it is applied to the elemental level. Obviously the element of Air, when symbolising the whole of the mind, cannot really be 'got rid of' unless we are thinking of the 'Arrested' state in yoga, which corresponds to the final stage before ultimate *moksha* liberation; even there, the mind subsists, though it no longer exerts influence over the yogin.

What is really being done here is that the principle corresponding to thought (and what are sometimes called 'thought-forms', implying an accretion), is brought to a state of immobility or stasis; it is returned, temporarily, to its undifferentiated cause. Another way of looking at it is that all objects retained by the mind, and the sense impressions that compose them, are withdrawn. That requires the practitioner to know how to elevate their consciousness beyond the level of gross and subtle elements—the better we are at yoga the better we are at magick and the less chance there is that we are merely acting superstitiously, out of sheer ignorance through the lack of theoretical and direct knowledge.

Following purification, the element is re-invoked and an Egyptian deity is called in to assist in linking the elemental sphere with higher and divine forces, as well as to place a seal upon the sphere of the practitioner to strengthen it against all malefic influences. Having given a sort of 'tour guide' approach to the ritual, we can now make an allusion to some of those further uses mentioned earlier. Even this very brief overview should be enough to show that the ritual is far more than being about 'getting rid of' things, or even of nullifying some external aggression. The deity Anubis is heard to say here,

> I stand between the invisible and the visible.

But more than that, as Guardian of the Threshold he crosses the bridge from the unmanifest to the manifest and so is able to return the way he came:

> My mother is darkness and my father the night: thus do I come forth, bearing the Ineffable Light!

Anyone that has passed through the Neophyte ritual will recollect from this that Anubis guards the temple outside with a sword and also appears within the circle, as the bearer of the Lamp of Light by which the Candidate is conducted around the new world in which they have entered.[72] The effect of the repeated circling about the place from station to station during the ritual—an action that also symbolises the *pranayama* or circulation of breath in yoga—is to weave a way to further knowledge, at the same time strengthening and protecting the aspirant, so he is all the more firmly resolved in his love and devotion to the Great Work. It is not a coincidence that the Sanskrit word *tantra* means literally 'to weave', and that the word *sutra* has a similar meaning, 'stitching together', and is usually applied to a book of knowledge. Such a book should not be thought of only in the literal sense, for the Book of Life is as a book of leaves upon the Tree of Life, and each letter is a tongue of fire that licks up the soul's ardour and transforms it into honeydew.

Such a ritual as has here been described also corresponds to traditional magick lore, involving a 'moving of the air', or 'changing of the winds'. We think that enough has been said here regarding the adaptability of rituals.

---

[72] See *The Phoenix and other Stellar Rites of Initiation*.

Systems of Knowledge

We can now explain in some detail exactly why it is that 'systemised knowledge' fails to act as a support to any real knowledge. Metaphysics is not expressible in words but can be symbolised, and symbolism was always the mode used by the primordial tradition. To a certain extent we cannot dispense entirely with the lists and tabulated classifications that amount to 'systems of knowledge'. For perhaps as long as six thousand years, human beings have lost entirely the knowledge that is called *soma* in Hinduism and ambrosia, or the 'elixir of life' in other traditions, not to mention the Holy Grail itself. Modern commentators love to imagine that these things exist in some gross form, especially drugs or otherwise 'altered states', produced either by auto-hypnotism or some mind-changing substance. This could not be further away from the truth as none of that has any relation at all to real knowledge, which we define as metaphysics, in the etymological sense of the word. And that is to say, 'beyond the physical', and so nothing to do with the chemical state of the body or brain, or the psychological domain.

As *soma* is best described, though there is no word for it, as 'total knowledge', we can only approach the super-sensible from a ground of artifice to a certain extent. The difference between being 'initiated' and the state of unknowing is in some way marked by knowing what is artifice and what is real. As for the super-sensible knowledge, that is only the very beginning of real knowledge.

In *Thirty-two paths of Wisdom* we took some steps towards denouncing the systems of correspondences developed by occultists in relatively modern times. It might seem strange then that more or less complete tables of correspondences were given in the appendices of that same book. We wanted to make a book that shows how the Hebraic Kabbalah can to some extent be viewed metaphysically, not stopping short at cosmology and ontology. At the same time there needed to be some continuity with the Hermetic Qabalah that most of our readers are familiar with. The Hermetic Qabalah, which relies heavily on systems of correspondences, was previously taught to all our students. Some of them learned it so well that they fail to see that the only real use of it is to understand the limitations so as to effect an escape into the unlimited world of metaphysics. That is easier said than done, however, even when the capacity is latent.

For some, learning more or less arbitrary correspondence systems might be as much as they can grasp. In that case, at least they can learn something that does not stop short at a naturalistic explanation for all traditional symbolism, as is the case with the books on the subject by those 'learned' scholars from Oxford—even if that means they can only go as far as a sort of quasi-mystical engrossment. We would hope to do better though; so it seems the time might now be right to explain carefully how it is that closed systems of correspondences do not admit to real knowledge.

There needs to be a clear difference made between such closed systems and the natural correspondences that are integral to alchemy and hermeticism, although the keys to knowledge were already forgotten by the time of the European Renaissance. That is of course quite contrary to the historical propaganda we all learned in school regarding that time, and the so-called Age of Enlightenment that followed. The ancient Egyptian hieroglyphs are largely based on natural correspondences though there is more to them than that. There are subtle linguistic and etymological inferences in even one or two letters of a word in sacred languages. We should also not confuse natural correspondences with 'naturalism', which is a quite modern European invention. If the King of the Mountain should wear a triangular-shaped hat, naturalism will insist the hat is to symbolise a particular mountain location, as if that explains it. It is rather that both the hat and the mountain symbolise something else, and that 'something else' is totally beyond the reach of the average or common intelligence to comprehend.

Similarly, ancient mythology is ignorantly supposed to symbolise such things as constellations as well as weather, topographical features and so on. It is more the case that both the myths and the constellations symbolise something quite other—and that 'other' is the metaphysical knowledge we are interested in. It is said of the *Yoga-Sutras* that the yogin does not seek ordinary knowledge of things; the yogin seeks knowledge of principles.

Systems of correspondences, however, are closed systems. The knowledge produced by the means of any system is limited to the system that produced it. One gains knowledge only of the system and nothing of any other thing. In Sanskrit this is called a *viparyaya*, 'superimposition'. By taking one or two examples, it can be easily shown how the most absurd notions can come about:

According to our tables of correspondences, goats are placed with the twenty-sixth path of the Tree of Life linking Tiphereth the Sun with Hod, the sphere of Mercury. Goats are therefore supposed to have something to do with the *ajna* chakra or 'frontal eye', and that is illustrated in more than one modern deck of the Tarot, for the Devil XV is also corresponded to that same path, which has the Hebrew letter *a'ain*, 'an eye', linked to it. It is a rather strange world we enter in here, for no one has ever seen a goat with three eyes in real life! Goats usually have two eyes, a pair of horns, cloven hooves and a short tail. Given that the *ajna* chakra has the meaning in Sanskrit of 'pure knowledge', and so is nothing to do with seeing things in the ordinary sense, or in the 'psychic' sense, we might also wonder why the goat is then associated with a higher kind of knowledge or 'sense of eternity'? However much we like these quirky, cantankerous creatures, we would not consult with one over the finer points of the *Bhagavad Gita*.

Chapters, indeed entire books and a whole series of books in the case of the occult orientalist Kenneth Grant, have been composed from such fabulous nonsense. To make this perfectly clear, then, lest there be no mistake: the correspondence system referred to here depends in the first case on the allocation of the twenty-two Hebrew letters to the connecting paths of the Tree of Life, of which there are twenty-two in that system. That was adopted by the Golden Dawn (and ourselves) but owes nothing to the Hebraic tradition or the *Sepher Yetzirah*, from which other correspondences were drawn. It came about no earlier than the seventeenth century, and was the invention of one Athanasius Kircher in a book, *Oedipus Aegiptiacus*.

Oddly enough, Kircher's book was a work of early Egyptology but it included a kind of 'Christian' interpretation of Kabbalistic lore. The paths are numbered in a logical order from 11 to 32 and the Hebrew letters are placed accordingly. Although this system is linked with the *Sepher Yetzirah*, it forms no part of that source work, and indeed, while the latter has internal correspondences of elements, zodiacal signs, planets, days of the week and so forth, these differ from modern attributions. In fact, some of these original placements are discredited by 'occult scholars' because they are not systematic enough!

The corresponding of the twenty-two Hebrew letters to the Tarot trumps is a modern invention that seems to go no further than the nineteenth century. It owes more to the fiction of Gustav Meyrink and (perhaps) Eliphas Levi than it does to the Hebrew tradition.

There are various ways of making the Hebrew letters equate to the Tarot trumps but however this is done it can readily be seen how a syncretic correspondence system emerges: the twenty-sixth path of the Tree of Life corresponds to the letter *a'ain*. The letter *a'ain* corresponds to the Devil XV and the zodiacal sign of Capricorn. From there we arrive at our three-eyed mountain goat. We should also know that the sinister relation between the Devil and goats, on which whole swathes of fiction depend, originated with the Greek traveller Herodotus. Herodotus was told by local Egyptian guides that goats were secretly sacrificed to the God of Mendes, which is the Greek corruption of Ba-neb-tattu. In fact, God took the form of a ram at that place, not a goat, and it is highly unlikely, given this, that the Egyptians would have sacrificed rams there, and vastly improbable that they would have sacrificed goats. Nonetheless, Europeans have frequently thought that the Ram god there is the 'Goat of Mendes', especially as this provided much material for entertaining after-dinner story telling. By the twentieth century we then have the appearance of a goat with a third eye on his brow.[73]

The paths are meant to represent the knowledge of the sephiroth or the states of consciousness they represent. The twenty-sixth path connects Tiphereth with Hod. Can a chain of more or less arbitrary symbols stuck on the Tree of Life like the fluttering prayer flags of neo-paganism lead us to true knowledge of Tiphereth, the centre of the individuality, and Hod, the faculty of thought or mentation in the human being? As we have said previously, any system can only give knowledge of that system. One more example, subtler than the previous, might help us further along the way:

To the seventeenth path is corresponded the letter *zain*, 'a sword'; also the astrological sign of Gemini and the Tarot trump the Lovers VI. From there we get the magical powers or *siddhis*, gemstones, symbolic weapons and all the rest. Such a system is easily validated internally. For example, we can say that Gemini and its trump the Lovers shows duality and so might tell us something about human reason, or otherwise how things are manifested in the universe, these last two things not being entirely disconnected in any case.

---

[73] The sagacious goat with the third eye is accompanied on one of the most popular Tarot decks by a phallus penetrating the 'rings of Saturn'. Any association with the Egyptian star goddess Nuit, as was pretended by the author, takes a fantastical stretch of the imagination that is both sordid and perverse; the real meaning, which is sodomitic, was indicated by the said author in a footnote. To add to the testicular nonsense, scientific diagrams of DNA theory are shown in the 'double symbol' below.

Any pair or duality may be seen as contradictory from the exterior point of view, but is complementary from the more advanced perspective. When regarded as a complementary pair no dualism is involved as such, for the unification is effected by the higher principle that transcends both. We can then declare that the number 17 of the path in question shows this. By the sacred geometry of Pythagoras, the seventeenth triangular number is 153 and so this also has a correspondence with the path of Zain.[74]

$$\sum (1-17) = 153$$

The duality of the two-edged sword of the Hebrew letter *zain* is thus transcended by the triangular 'three', and it is the triangle of all symbols that shows most perfectly how two things depend from their higher principle by natural extension.

However, the number 17, the letter *zain*—which happens to add to 717 when spelled in full—the sign of Gemini and the Judgement of Paris are not needed to show that dual symbolism is best understood as complementary. All we needed to do, in fact, was to show an equilateral triangle. And that is how it is usually done in traditional symbolism.

Is there any use at all in systems of correspondences then? Apart from realising the limitation and escaping from that limitation, correspondences of this sort have proved a useful mnemonic. Given that everyone nowadays is subjected to compulsory education, or what passes for that, and is thereby systematically brainwashed from childhood into acceptance of scientific and anti-traditional theories, however absurd they may be, some justification can be made for introducing a system that at least takes the mind outside of the conventional parameters ferociously drummed into it. Nonetheless, at some point we must leave the shallow waters and take our boat to the deeper waters in which to cast our nets. The recounting of the miracle of the fishes from the book of St. John 21: 11 serves as a fine example of both natural correspondences and Pythagorean numbers:

Three would-be disciples, Peter, Thomas and Nathaniel, had been fishing all night and not caught a single fish. The Master tells them to take their boat into the deep waters and cast their nets again.

---

[74] The triangular numbers are called such because in each case the same number of dots, circles or objects can be arranged to fill an equilateral triangle perfectly.

The three fishermen, though reluctant to do this, as they are exhausted from their fruitless activities, do as they are told and are rewarded with a catch of 153 large fish.

The significance of the triangular number 153 has already been explained and we might take special note that, of the three disciples, Peter is the 'rock', which is the foundation stone or capstone on a pyramid. His rôle is to be the keeper of the keys, which symbolises the silver and gold or the lesser and the greater mysteries. While no systematised knowledge, or 'system of thought' as in a philosophy, will lead to any mystery small or great, for some it is at least a way of indicating the two doors—even if it does not supply the means of passing through them, which, however unpopular it may be to declare it, involves considerable time and effort.

Dreaming and Stalking

In *The Way of Knowledge* space was given to some of the more serious aspects of the teachings of don Juan as conveyed in the narratives of Carlos Castaneda. The chapter on the 'Dreaming Attention' particularly interested some of our readers, although it must be said that in spite of all our efforts to be clear, some seem to have read into it the very opposite of what was intended. It will be helpful to give a brief quotation from that here:

> The art of dreaming involves tapping a vital natural resource that is wasted in the normal state of affairs. The chief misunderstanding of this—which has worked its way into becoming a kind of popular myth or folk-lore—is that it involves trying to remain aware while in the dreaming state so that dreams can be controlled. It follows that many people who have tried this failed to fulfil its true purpose, for they have supposed it is only about conjuring dreams and fantasies 'at will', to direct their dreams towards the satisfaction of ordinary desires and goals. It is not so, and the truth of the art of dreaming is almost the complete opposite of that. Any attempt to manipulate the content of dreams can only result in regaining the First Attention. Although the dreaming content can sometimes be manipulated to a certain extent, through various methods, that is a complete waste of energy. The content of dreams is for the most part irrelevant.

Given that the content of dreams is for the most part irrelevant to the art of dreaming, it seems quite extraordinary how anyone could think that we were proposing a method of 'incubating dreams', which is the exact words used by one such person. The word 'incubate' is not used anywhere in that book. Given that an *incubus* has a context in some aspects of demonology, one may well wonder what goes in people's minds when they read a book, so they can ascribe meaning that is totally alien to the author's intentions.

However, in all fairness—whether that is deserved or not—we are conditioned to think about dreams as being about the content. The Dreaming Attention, to use a weaving analogy, is not concerned with the 'picture' formed by the tapestry but with the warp and weft that brings a picture to form. And beyond that, it is about what the warp and weft are 'hung on', which is Brahma in Hinduism and Neïth to the Egyptians. One may also think of *purusha*, 'essence', as the substrata of manifestation that is not involved in manifestation itself.

René Guénon's analogies in *The Multiple States of Being* are in general concord with the teachings of don Juan concerning dreams as subtle modalities.[75] Guénon also had little if any interest in the actual content of dreams. Furthermore, what is meant by 'dreaming' in don Juan's teachings has almost nothing to do with going to sleep and dreaming at night. The modalities of the subtle plane are much closer to the waking state than we generally realise. The fabric of things and events we experience in the waking state include meeting points that amount to a sort of nexus with the countless modalities of the subtle plane. That gives rise to many of the otherwise inexplicable or bizarre phenomena that spice the narratives of Castaneda. It is the very stuff of sorcery in the way that is commonly understood, though of course in our times it is all relegated to a world of pure fantasy or explained away as psychological or symbolic. The word 'symbolic' is itself scarcely understood, as that too is thought to be of the nature of the unreal; whereas in fact true symbolism is expressive of things more real than anything experienced in the sensory world. While the modern magical practitioner tends to immerse their self in fantasy, through the means of auto-suggestion, the yogin is able to see clearly into the nature of all phenomena, and while that is not the focus of his interest, he sees far more of the genuinely strange in things that either would not be noticed at all by the ordinary person or would not in any case be *seen* for what they truly are.

For the most part, dream experiences are contingent modalities of the individual human state, and for that reason they are unworthy of serious attention. Not all dreams are without significance, at least to the dreamer, however. Sometimes, though it is rare, it can even be a matter of individual destiny. In even rarer cases, as in 'prophetic dreams', it might be relevant to a collective *dharma*. This, however, is a dangerus road to travel, and we must exercise caution, for there are countless persons imagining that their dreams, which they think are very special and significant, have even conferred on them some kind of 'awakening', and without even noticing the irony involved!

We did not venture to go far into the subject of Stalking, another aspect particular to the narratives of Castaneda. Before this can even be approached we have to rid ourselves of any notions of that word circulated by the popular press, and used to describe a certain kind of criminal. It has nothing to do with that whatsoever. It is mostly about an aspect of don Juan's teaching to his apprentices on how to gain power, as we shall now explain:

---

[75] 'Analogies Drawn from the Dream State', *The Multiple States of Being*.

Our world is full of what don Juan terms 'petty tyrants', that can enslave others in various ways and make life a misery, even driving them to destruction. According to don Juan, the warrior sees such a petty tyrant as a 'gift', a means to gain power. His story tells that as a young apprentice he fell into the hands of such a petty tyrant with a gang of armed guards who enslaved Indians and stole their money. Don Juan worked his art by pretending to be totally subservient to them, putting up no resistance no matter how cruel they were. He suffered the torture for years, always watching and waiting with warrior *intention*. One day the opportunity came, which had to be seized in the moment, and don Juan took the action that led to the tyrant's horrible downfall. This tale can be understood in relation to 'action through non-action' where the moment to act comes only once. The reason the stalking aspect was not gone into in *Way of Knowledge* was because in today's world it is rarely possible, at least as according to the kind of examples given. Everything is automated; there are plenty of the petty tyrants, perhaps more than ever, but they are now protected by law or are part of the faceless corporations and institutions that serve the System of Antichrist.[76]

There is another aspect to the Stalking method where the seer himself uses it on those he has chosen to be his apprentices. Not to destroy them, obviously, only to destroy the many obstructions they will put in the way of initiation, owing to their mentality. He plays Castaneda's fears against him, for example, and sometimes it takes many, many years for Castaneda to work out what was really going on all the while. That is also quite natural to the path; it is not something that is necessarily contrived by a seer or sorcerer, so it can all be a matter of point of view. It is said in the *Upanishads* that Agni had to live with his teacher for one hundred years before he obtained full spiritual realisation. Whether that is a symbolic number or not, the point is that it takes time and considerable dedication.

There are countless other applications to this theory of Stalking; these are not necessarily about dealing with enemies and neither are they about doing harm to others. However, we will not go into any of that in detail. Those that are able to understand how to do this from what has been put down here will also understand the level of their responsibility that is involved; they will need no further help from us in working out the practicalities of the operation.

---

[76] The System of Antichrist is explained in *Way of Knowledge* throughout the book. The theme was introduced in the previous book, *Nu Hermetica*, written between 2020 and 2021.

Will and Love

According to the Vedanta, any person that could actually put into practice or action (or non-action) perfect True Will would be no less than a Jivanmukti, one that has achieved *moksha* or complete Deliverance while still living in the mortal flesh.[77] Given that such Deliverance, as is asserted exhaustively in the Vedanta, requires total world renunciation, it is easy to know then why the meaning of a spiritual will, in anything but the most ordinary sense, escapes those conditioned by a modern education. Divine will is also divine ordinance. The will, as having something to do with a spiritual practice, appears at first to be the lesser path, because 'to do' implies action (*karma*). No action can result in liberation from action, which is ignorance (*avidya*). Action limits all to the individual state, though that does not necessarily limit it to the corporeal modality. According to Shankaracharya's commentary on the *Isha Upanishad*,

> Action has been prescribed in the scriptures to suit the understanding of worldly people, who associate with Ātman such characteristics as multiplicity, agency, enjoyment, impurity, sinfulness, and so on.[78]

Divine will belongs to the formless state, where it is *potency to act* without involvement in action itself. A True Will is then only known through complete union with the very essence of Being, Ishvara, the Lord of the Universe, or Shakti. The formless state is suprahuman as the human state, by definition, involves form, whether corporeal or subtle (as pre-condition). It seems needless to add that love and devotion cannot be separated from will, understood in this sense.

One that has attained permanent liberation from the individual states acts only through non-action. The latter term is commonly misunderstood; it does not in any way imply passivity. In so far as action can transcend the corporeal state, we need to understand something of the Hindu law of *apurva*, a word that does not translate into any modern language. We have previously described the law of *apurva* as the 'Key of Magick'.[79] It may easily have escaped the attention of some that the use of the term 'magick' there declares its limitation, even when it is considered as a traditional science.

---

[77] For a description of what a Jivanmukti is, see *Way of Knowledge*, p. 149. For the complete explanation, see René Guénon, *Man and His becoming according to the Vedānta*, chapters 21–24 in particular.
[78] *The Upanishads Vol. 2*, as translated by Swami Nikhilananda, p. 198 [Advaita Ashrama].
[79] *Way of Knowledge*.

This becomes evident in the light of what follows here: *apurva*, as 'seed' or 'germ' implicit in any cause and effect, which is the relationship between the two, is only known through union with the divine essence, pure Being. It therefore requires a more or less complete and perfect knowledge. The divine essence is the domain of the Shakti—the name itself means 'power' and also 'divine presence' in Sanskrit, Hebrew (the Shekinah) and ancient Egyptian (Sekhet). For this reason, of the limitation implicit, the practice of magick is usually restricted to the fulfilment of quite ordinary desires; a full or complete understanding of the laws that govern its operations means that all such desires vanish away to nothing, are transcended. It is likewise with the so-called magical powers (*siddhis*), for as soon as they are known for what they truly are they are automatically renounced. The Shakti may grant any wish, as according to her divine grace, but the fulfilment of any particular desire other than the desire for pure knowledge means that the person stays in ignorance. This is put very clearly by Shankaracharya in his love poem to the Goddess:

> Others worship with reverence the plant with leaves and particular qualities,
> But I know that Aparnā [without qualities] alone in this world should be worshipped.
> Then the old Shiva garlanded with space
> Surely grants to Thy worshipper the fruit of full liberation [*moksha*].
> O Ishani, as the old Lotus-Born [Brahma] and others have said,
> The rule is that if others than Thyself art worshipped,
> Only the particular fruit desired is gained;
> But Thou giveth more even than is asked for.
> Make me, then, ever attached to Thee by day and night.[80]

Of all magical spells, there is one supreme and superior to all else. This is the spell of invisibility, if that is understood metaphysically, which excludes most persons from ever making use of it.[81] To become invisible in the true sense is to enter the formless state we have already mentioned. Neither True Will nor the law of *apurva* can be understood in any other state, including all that is defined as human. While this may cause astonishment and might even provoke hostility among those habitually accustomed to limiting all things in the universe to the individual human state, it is nonetheless a true and unalterable fact.

---

[80] Sir John Woodroffe, *Hymns to the Goddess*, 'Waves of Bliss', vs 7 and 13.
[81] P. 70, *Way of Knowledge*.

Love or devotion (*bhakti*) is the lesser path, relative to that of pure knowledge. At the same time the lesser mystery or 'second birth' is more easily attainable in the time we have now entered, right at the end of the Kali Yuga and Manvantara cycle. And as Ramakrishna pointed out one time, while there are greater and lesser paths, all paths, so long as they are legitimate, may lead to the same goal finally. In the *Bhagavad Gita* the question is asked by Arjuna, 'Supposing a person does yoga but they still don't know Brahma?' The reply is along the lines that all they need do is keep doing the yoga, and so long as they do that they can get there in the end. In all these things, the yoga, combined with the rites, is the one absolutely indispensable thing. Shankaracharya's commentary on verse ten of the *Isha Upanishad* insists on the harmonisation of ritual (action) with meditation (knowledge), but condemns the practice of either one without the other:

> In order to emphasise this harmonisation, work (or ritualistic action) and meditation on a deity (without appropriate ritual action) pursued separately have been condemned in verse nine.[82]

With regard to what results are expected by those who harmonise ritual action with meditation on the deities and those who do not—neither of which is regarded as equivalent to Self-Knowledge from the Advaitan point of view, Swami Nikhilananda has added:

> It seems, according to verse ten, that those who contemplate a deity (without harmonising their contemplation with action) go, after death, to Devaloka [realm of the Gods] and dwell there till the result of their good action is exhausted, and those who perform ritualistic actions [alone] go to Pitriloka [realm of the 'ancestors'] to enjoy the fruits of their actions. According to verse eleven, it appears that those who harmonise both attain, in the end, the status of a deity and dwell in the heavenly world as long as the cycle [i.e. the Manvantara] lasts, enjoying, as gods, what is called relative immortality.

Of supreme Self-Knowledge, verse sixteen exalts Brahma Nirguna, or Brahma 'without determinations', which is eternity, not limited by time or space or anything at all:

> O Nourisher, lone Traveller of the sky! Controller! O Sun, Offspring of Prajāpati! Gather your rays; withdraw Your light. I would see, through Your grace, that form of yours which is the fairest. I am indeed He, that Purusha, who dwells there.

---

[82] *The Upanishads Vol. 1*, Iśa Upanishad [*ibid*].

With the path of Love, the devotion (*bhakti*) or worship given to the Shakti, in whatever name or form, is implicit—without this it has no meaning and cannot be considered a path as such. The devotion suggests a certain duality, but when the goal is union, no less than yoga, then this may lead to the highest possible states, full, complete and permanent knowledge and transcendence. The disadvantage of the path of Love or devotion, though it is more easily attainable than that of pure knowledge (*jnana*), is that in our times it is rare to find any person to have even the smallest grain of real devotion in them. Even their idea of what that might be is no more than a deformed caricature, based on sentimental ideas of love and morality. It must be said that unless devotion to deity is a real and at least latent possibility in an individual, there is no chance of it being realised—nothing can come into existence that does not already exist.

However, though such souls are by now rare, there may be those who have this in them and do not yet know it. And for these, the latency can be awakened to full and effective realisation by following out the necessary rites and yoga practices, for this acts as a support to knowledge. For this reason it is said at Mass, 'So cometh ye all'. That is, may all those who are able to, partake of this knowledge and achieve liberation in due course. That is the idea; and it is no vain hope. By the immutable laws that govern these things, it will come to pass even if we can never be certain of when that will be or what conditions will by then prevail, and by which such things are subject to modification.[83]

---

[83] It is revealed and at the same time concealed in the works of René Guénon, through scattered allusions and footnotes, that he used the law of *apurva* to reach us, across time; the few of us that have a serious interest in such things in the West are without an unbroken esoteric tradition. Guénon worked to repair this breach, across time and space.

House of Bast

There is very little written or known about Bast. We can always find more about her sister Sekhmet, which owes to the accounts of her legends as filtered down to us from Greek travellers. And yet what is known even of Sekhmet amounts to very little; ignorance however does not prevent Egyptologists from inventing what they do not know; they superimpose their modern prejudice and particular interests, always of a very limited nature, upon the subject they pretend to know of.[84]

We must not think that the ancient Egyptians, any more than the Hindus or any other ancient civilisation, were in any way concerned with 'pantheism'. The seeming plurality of what we term as 'Gods' comes about through the different attributes of the one Universal Being. The Gods, called Neteru in Egyptian, Devas in Hindu, are not separate individual beings like humans. The error of so thinking is derived from the anthropomorphisation of God in human form, which is something particular to some religions of a relatively modern era. Ancient civilisations had no word in their language for 'religion', and yet orientalists and now scholars almost universally insist on describing their doctrines as a 'set of beliefs', when it has nothing to do with that. Likewise they talk of 'religion' where none existed.[85] The countless variety of Gods, really Neteru, 'principles', which is the most exact term, is there to assist with meditation on what is really formless. The God or Neter is not the form and if we think so, we fall into a mistaken idolatry, mistaking the symbol for that which it represents.

According to an article we wrote previously, the feline Bast and lioness goddess Sekhet were representative of the regions of Lower and Upper Egypt respectively.[86] The centres where Bast figured prominently were therefore situated in the swampier Delta regions, a strange country of rivers and islands, where one did one's travelling by means of a boat. By way of contrast, the regions of Upper Egypt, populated with countless statues of Sekhmet, are generally hot and fiery and prone to being blasted by the heat coming up from the Sahara desert: fire and water; heat and coolness; the light and the dark; the dry and the moist.

---

[84] In that way, although Egyptologists are contemptous of occultists, there is not so much difference between these as Egyptologists like to imagine.
[85] A religion requires three things: dogma, ritual and moral teaching.
[86] 'The Way to Bubastis', *Babalon Unveiled! Thelemic Monographs.*

Figure of Bast

While the above description conveys some obvious comparisons, associating Bast with the sublunary worlds or dreaming state, the island temple of Bast that is described in the article was raised up in height, probably to an extent easily comparable to say, Glastonbury Tor in Somerset, England. As with the Tor, the temple of Bast looked from the ground like a tower with a lantern placed at the summit. However, it is clear from the description given by Herodotus that the tower on the island of Bast was far more impressive than the little stone turret of Glastonbury, which can seat about four persons at the most.

We should bear in mind here that when Herodotus says 'house of Hermes' he is using the name of the Greek God; it is actually the temple of Tahuti, the God of Knowledge and writing:

> Round about the tower is a wall, engraved with hieroglyphics and depictions of various beasts. The inner temple is enclosed by a high grove of cultivated trees, and in it is set up an image. The length of the temple is 220 yards each way. From the entrance of the temple Eastward, there is a fairly large causeway leading to the house of Hermes, 660 yards long and four acres broad, all of good stone. It is bordered on each side with tall trees.

The Delta region may remind us of the lower parts of the human anatomy, where we may imagine that amphibious creatures, snakes and other reptiles lurk, whether seductively or to menace us; it is where the womb is situated, by analogy that dark place where we all begin the fleeting journey of life lived out in a body of flesh. And yet in such dark, moist regions, the supreme principle is everywhere present. Even the creatures of the night, like the shadows on the wall of Plato's cave, appear by the light of the self-luminous Witness.

At the pinnacle or summit of a tower it is brightest but in the depth it is no less present but cloaked in the darkness and obscurity of our perceptions. Likewise the cat, even as a very little creature that frequents the night when she is not curled up asleep, or that is friendly enough to be given the freedom of our homes, is nonetheless as a principle 'like unto Ra, the Sun'. In fact Mau, one of the names given to Bast, as well as being onomatopoeic, carries the meaning of 'alike' or 'in the likeness of'.

The Egyptians identified the cat goddess Bast with the cobra goddess at *per Wadjet*, which the Greeks called Buto.[87] It seems that the ancient oracles produced by the temple virgins of the Egyptian Delta region, to whom Bast was sacred, preceded the famous Greek Delphic oracle. Ancient Egyptian symbolism involving the royal solar serpent as cognate with the Eye of Ra, or of Hathoor or Sekhet, bears comparison with Kundalini Shakti of the Hindu Tantras. However, the yoga practices that are integral to the Tantras are not aimed at producing an oracle. Oracles are generally associated with divination, and that is a branch of quite ordinary natural magick. The snake in a basket is commonly identified with illusionists, tricksters, Hindu fakirs, travelling magicians or jugglers, but is also frequently found among ancient Egyptian hieroglyphs, sometimes used in conjunction with the names of goddesses, especially those particular to the Delta region. It is possible then that magical tricks involving the power of suggestion or otherwise the means of producing phenomena were a later corruption of a function of the priestess or yogini, or of the Goddess herself, that has now become very obscure.

Certainly, as the power of fascination or the 'evil eye' is always associated with Typhon in snake-form, the slaying of the serpent of evil, sometimes at the foot of the Tree of Life, was associated with the cat, or Ra in the form of a cat. That may account for why depictions of Bast were often adorned with the scarab Khephra, the form taken by Ra when he rises in the morning. There are many depictions of Ra in the form of a cat, or Bast, slaying a serpent, removing its head from its body by means of a knife. The snake is especially the principle of motion, the particular nature of that owing to the fact that the snake can go forth without the need of legs, which normally symbolise action or mobility. Motion belongs to Ra, the supreme principle, and thus when the faculty of action is realised in its higher principle, the poisons or afflictions owing from past and future actions are dissolved. In Sanskrit the mental impressions left by past actions that can recur and cause new actions leading to further misery and suffering are called *karmasayas*. That is literally, 'actions that continue to go forth', which comes about through the retention of the mental impressions.[88]

---

[87] Per Wadjet—House of the Cobra: the cobra was identified with the Eye of Ra or Eye of Horus, also called Wadjet.
[88] See Part Two, especially 'Yoga of the Mind'.

According to Budge, the cat was the incarnation of the goddess Bast, in the same way that the cobra snake is a form of Isis.[89] However, listing places, names, facts and histories after the manner of scholars, or compiling all the references to cats in sacred texts, such as the Metternich Stele (which includes the Book of the Cat), will not much further our understanding of Bast, or why the cat and the snake are associated with oracles, and why the cat in particular, as sacred to Ra and the Goddess, was seen as a protection against the evil forces summed up in the name of Typhon.

The cat is typified by its long, subtle spine and tail and its distinctive purr, as well as its agility and prowess. The spinal cord, associated with the Kundalini force in the Tantras, which includes three primary principles of fire, sun and moon, is likened to the snake or 'Serpent Power'. Sometimes, depictions of Bast include a snake extending along the whole length of her spine as well as the emblem of Khephra worn upon her breast. The *Upanishads* tell of the same cosmological principles of fire, sun and moon as involved in the manifestation of the universe, to which is added lightning as a fourth.[90] Lightning also is associated with the serpent force, as a reciprocal or downward-striking influence and it is that which unites heaven and earth in simultaneity. Thus in the Qabalah we have the 'Sword and Serpent'. While the serpent with its undulatory motion frequently symbolises time and space, which is a limiting condition pertaining strictly to the human state, the lightning flash symbolises an illumination of the present 'moment', which, as simultaneous, is inclusive of past, present and future. It is the root of the traditional science called 'oracular', where the oracle is particularly associated with word, speech or language. Likewise, the sword as either the antithesis or complement of the snake is sometimes shown as issuing from the mouth of God, as the Word that brings forth the worlds.

In the Tantras, the arising of the Serpent Kundalini is to affect a return to the supreme principle, which is the meaning of *yoga*. And this is brought about by a reversal of the cosmological hierarchy or natural order. In Shankhya yoga the difference is only in the detail not the principle. The elemental *tattvas* are followed back through the power of concentration to their higher or subtler source until only the knower or cogniser remains.

---

[89] Budge, *The Gods of the Egyptians*.
[90] *Chandogya* Chapter VII, 'Instruction of the Swan'.

The purr of the cat is more or less unique to that creature and resembles the continuous sounding of AUM, which in the yoga of Patañjali is often placed in the heart lotus, 'cave' or 'cavity', wherein it is said resides Brahma, or sometimes *purusha*, the 'essence' of Brahma. At other times this is described as the heart or shrine of Brahma. The near equivalent in ancient Egyptian is the hieroglyphic AUR, which has the 'heart' vessel as determinative, and is identified with 'light', in the sense of intelligence or consciousness itself, the pure I-sense. MAU is a name of Bast, or Ra in the form of a cat, and it is notable that the letters are a rearrangement of the word AUM, the continuous cosmic or universal vibration.

We only need recollect that Ra is never the visible sun and is more the equivalent of Brahma, both 'with attributes' (as Ishvara) and 'without attributes' as supreme all-transcendent principle, to appreciate that ancient symbolisms are all reflective of one very exact and complete science depending from the highest metaphysical principles.

Bast is the protector of Ra, the slayer of evil and the driver out of poisons: As supreme principle, Ra hardly needs protecting for he is the 'unmoved mover', infinite, eternal and changeless, not affected by any other thing. However, the knowledge of the principles and true meaning of the sacred sciences becomes increasingly obscure to humanity towards the end of a cosmic cycle. For many thousands of years it was not necessary for any knowledge to be written down, and when it was first written down, in sacred languages, the writing itself was the 'sacrifice' as recounted in the *Vedas*, else the knowledge be lost completely. It is notable that Fire (*Agni*) is the first kind of sacrifice mentioned in the Vedas and the first word of the first book. The fiery solar principle Ra, the divine Word, is sometimes called 'the Cat', in which case it is clear that the principle is its own protection. But for humanity, the knowledge must be preserved, and in diverse ways. Bast, as in the case of her sister lion Sekhmet, is then both the principle Itself and the protector and upholder of that principle, and guardian of the sacred ways.

The Mother MA

MA is the Great Mother in almost all languages, both ancient and modern. The Sun enters her astrological sign at the solstice when he attains his height; so it is said that he enters the house of his mother. Modern astrologers and others interpret the sign of Cancer weakly; some will see in the glyph female breasts, in which they find the confirmation of their psychological theories, which always reduce ancient symbolism to mere human instinct. They will prattle on about 'nurturing', as they see in this a 'positive' quality that will be of benefit to their clients. However, divine attributes figured by cosmological symbolism, such as the 'All Provider', are properly used in devotional practices and are never applied to oneself—as is now commonplace in societies regulated by profane governance, in turn controlled by commercial interests, as indeed are todays professional therapists. All psychological teaching, if it can be called that, is 'satanic' in so far as it rests upon atheism and so total rejection of the Holy Spirit; it encourages its disciples to practice self-worship, which is believed to promote 'wellbeing' and betterment for the soul and society in general.

Occultists, on the other hand, wishing to find darker and more glamorous ground for stupefaction, will see in this sign the 'devouring' aspect of the Great Mother, which they will then gleefully point to as an indicator of vampirism or some other insatiable and uncontrolled appetites of the flesh. Most occultists today also accept the psychological counterfeit initiation instigated by CG Jung and his followers, and so these will even encourage the use, by simplistic means, of forces that have a domain in the infernal regions. There are others, whose knowledge of Eastern traditions does not surpass erudition, that will even argue that the destruction of the souls of such persons is part of their initiation!

The confusions regarding the Eastern traditions that abound in neo-spiritualism have certainly reached a diabolical level; perhaps it was always the case but never so blatant as now. While none of the aforementioned notions regarding the Supernal Great Mother are completely wrong, it is their misuse and the monotonous emphasis on what are only minor and specialised aspects of the symbol that is injurious to those that would 'take the bait' and then see nothing beyond.

The glyph of Cancer has more in common with the Chinese *yin-yang* symbol than it does with any part of the human anatomy. Here then is a complete symbol for the union of Heaven and Earth through the seed principle that transcends all dualities. We do not mean that the astrological glyph for Cancer is the same symbol, which owes to a different tradition. Earlier forms of the glyph looked more like two lines ending in circles than modern depictions, similar though not identical to the sign of the Fishes. It is more that the meaning of the symbol can be no different in effect from that of *yin-yang*. This is not in any way to deny the special place of the Great Mother in the fourth house of astrology, that when looked at one way is the producer of all forms, as Maya, and when looked at another way is indeed the 'devourer', or the way of exit from the manifest worlds either to the undifferentiated state (*prakriti*), unmanifest, or to the realm of Pure Being (*purusha*), unmanifest.

In the Qabalah the special domain of the Great Mother is Binah, the third path and sephira that is the summation of the supernal trinity. The aspect of the Supernal Mother that is associated with the Holy Grail is well known but would require a separate study even to provide an overview of the subject. Let it suffice to say here that the 'waters' of Binah that reside within the Heart of the Mother drop down like *mezla* or 'starry dew' to fill the cups below. However, the transmission of spiritual influence, should that even come about, will affect the recipients each as according to their own nature. What may be a blessing for one is a curse for another. It is a great error to apply modern ideals to the Great Work, imagining that 'all are equal' and so all entitled to all knowledge, regardless of their state of readiness, their habitual disposition or innate qualifications. The secrecy of some of the traditional organisations (excluding modern ones) was to protect foolish persons from injury and not, as is often supposed, to protect the preceptors.

The third path and sephira is variously called Understanding or Wisdom (Sophia) as according to different interpretations. The Hebrew names of the Supernal Mother include AMA and AIMA, and herein is a curious cosmology capable of upward transposition to the metaphysical level. Ama refers to Binah as the Divine Mother of All, without production or cause; when considered as the producer of worlds or forms, she is Aima, enclosing the principial *yod* (the letter 'I' in transliteration). It is probably more than a mere coincidence that Aima is identical to Maia (Maya) but for the arrangement of the letters.

Ama is called the 'sterile mother' of Binah, which is sometimes given negative connotations—negative in the sense of 'inferior'. However, that is an inversion, for while Aima is the Mother of the Gods (Aima Elohim) and also the mother of language or words—the *yod* being the seed principle of all of the letters—Ama is in fact the Gate of the Gods, by which the seed or *yod* principle is devoured, or apparently so. One may compare this with the Egyptian Amma and also Tawret, placed at the centre of the stellar wheel and so identified with polar North. The devouring gods, sometimes taking the form of the bear, crocodile or hippo, for example, are symbolic of the gateway that leads *beyond* manifestation, not into manifest existence. Ama is the principle resting within Itself, not manifested, not manifesting or productive of anything.

We can see then where Ama gets her fearsome reputation. Yet Ama is really superior in the order of production to Aima, not inferior. While Aima carries the seed (*yod* or *bindi*) of all the letters or words that form the worlds and creatures of manifestation, and so is the Gate of Men at the summer solstice (the door by which they enter the path of initiation), Ama is the Gate of the Gods or winter solstice, by which one passes beyond manifest existence altogether, which is *moksha* liberation and the ultimate goal of yoga.

The horror of Ama, manifested in gross terms by simple cultural aversion to widows or women without husbands or children, is in truth the fear of the ego or individual self that owes to its sense of separation from all else. Ama is neither the cause of anything, nor is it caused by anything. In the Age of the Kali Yuga, the final phase of manifestation of a humanity, the supreme principle was transferred to the heavenly Father, whereas in previous ages it rested with the Mother of All. This seems implicit in the remnants of the primordial tradition that have survived. While Hindu sages, for example, abstain from marriage, children and family life so that they can devote themselves to God, in times of great antiquity it would not have been unusual for women, even though they are the child-bearers, to renounce all family and worldly ties and duties, including the not inconsiderable task of producing progeny. We can see this surviving in some of the ancient traditions that supported temple virgins, such as that of Egypt. It also survived to some extent even in modern times where women can still leave the world and enter a convent or some other form of monastic life.

The root word MA forms many words in ancient Egyptian, of which the most well known is Ma'at, Goddess of Truth and Justice, and the complement or holder of Peace. The 'perfect balance' that she represents is yet another example of an irrefutable link between yoga practice and teaching, and the Supernal Mother as cosmic or inner guru. Other words include the name for a truth-speaker or justified priest, *ma'a-kheru*, and *ma'a*, the word for 'seeing' or 'beholding', a word that has the hieroglyphic determinative of an owl. That much is self-explanatory as the owl is noted for its very large eyes and the ability to see in the dark; however, the Mother of Wisdom, also associated with the owl in many traditions, is the Witness and the Seer, verb and noun, and no less than Atma Itself.

Furthermore, the fluting cry of the owl is heard most frequently at the two ends of the year—the end of summer and the end of winter. As the ghostly call is also heard at dusk, this bird of prey, which can sometimes attain a very large size, is most apt to symbolise the supreme principle that partakes of both the manifest and the unmanifest, yet is neither of these.

Thunder Perfect Gnosis

In an earlier work, we presented the Gnostic text *Thunder Perfect Mind*, but without a commentary.[91] We have sought to rectify the omission here to some extent. The sacred text is laden with metaphysical symbolism and yogic instruction in its form and content. It would take at least a small book to fully explore it; we will give merely a few pointers that we hope will provide a basis for further study and contemplation. Following the advice of René Guénon, we will use the Vedanta to assist us.

Thunder Perfect Mind is written in Coptic and is thought to date approximately to a period before 350 AD. It is among the Gnostic manuscripts in the Nag Hammadi library said to be discovered in 1945 by a local farmer boy who had dug them up from a burial site in the desert, near the tombs of the Sixth Dynasty of Egypt. Scholars have suggested the text was originally composed in Greek due to its meter and phrasing, although no earlier version exists. Although we will not discuss it fully here as that would be be far too much of a digression, there are good reasons to refute this suggestion. Western prejudice cannot be ruled out, since scholars tend to think of all civilisation and learning as derived from the Greek and Roman model, upon which our own is based.

The Gnostic oracle was not composed in the 'literary' sense. This corresponds with what is termed *shruti* in the Hindu traditions, for directly received as opposed to secondary or reflected knowledge (*smriti*). It is purely metaphysical in nature, and so in perfect agreement with the primordial doctrines in common with ancient cultures. It is not comparable with Greek philosophy, or any other philosophy or religion. The language of the oracle is universal, and as direct transmission such an oracle has no individual author. It is natural to assume the identity of the first person as Isis, though she is beyond name and form, as we shall explain:

> I am the one whose Image is great in Egypt,
> And the one who has no Image among the barbarians.
> I am the one who has been hated everywhere,
> And the one who has been loved everywhere.
> I am the one whom they call Life,
> And that you have called Death.

---

[91] *Babalon Unveiled! Thelemic Monographs.*

The one whose Image was great in Egypt, at the time this text was supposed to have been written down, could be no other than Isis.[92] The colossal statue of Hathoor, whose name means House of Horus, that once stood at the gates of Aunnu (Heliopolis) was by that time known as Isis, also the mother of Horus. The barbarians were already busy with the work of tearing down ancient statues and defacing the images of the Gods in ancient temples. We are fortunate that any of it remains to this day. Principial truth is beyond form. The ancient Egyptian civilisation died out, its language no longer spoken, but some of her doctrines spread all over the world to be assimilated by other traditions. This is perfectly natural, for when cosmic time cycles change, civilisations disappear and the primordial doctrine clothes itself in new forms adapting to the times and peoples so as to express and communicate itself anew. As Isis says in many places, she is the principle or tradition that is the truth of all diverse peoples. Life and death are two phases of being where death marks the ending of one state and birth the beginning of another.

It is a feminine voice who speaks here in the first person; the source is from within the ancient Egyptian tradition where the feminine deity was afforded the place of supreme principle, for example Hathoor and Neïth. According to the Hindu doctrines, the Shakti is the will, omnipotence and power of the supreme principle's actionless activity. However, as Isis is also the intermediary between Heaven and Earth, some of the text concerns initiatic transmission. Traditional doctrine has no human author; it is knowledge from a supra-human source, transmitted to the higher intellectual plane of the mind. As the Great Power, sent forth from beyond the known, she is here the activity of heaven passing to the plane of reflection. As 'thunder', a word that is synonymous with both lightning and rain in ancient languages, her power takes the form of spiritual transmission from heaven to earth. The individual mind is but a clouded reflection of the Perfect Mind, perfect intellect or *boddhi*. If the individual mind believes only in itself, which is a superimposition upon the real, it is ignorant of the Perfect Mind and consequently truth. If it reflects only the Perfect Mind, then through initiation the being may achieve realisation of the primordial unity, and pass beyond even that, to liberation.

---

[92] However, this does place a certain limit on one that also calls herself the 'Great Power' and at the end of the third verse says that she is 'the Oracle whose utterance is my name'. In other words, she is known as Isis but in reality she is beyond name and form (Sanskrit *nama* and *rupa*).

Isis speaks in a series of complements and apparent opposites. Complementaries are, for example, the active and the passive, a duality that has no meaning except in relationship. At different levels either term may take on an active or passive rôle according to what is being placed in correlation with it. In Hinduism the active principle is always *purusha*, 'essence' and the passive that of *prakriti*, the substantial. Prakriti should not be thought of as 'matter' as such, for that is a purely modern notion. Prakriti is not truly separate from *purusha*, and neither are within manifestation.

The union of complements constitutes the primordial androgyne also described in traditional doctrines as Universal Man, or Adam and Eve. In the totality of integral being all complements are in perfect equilibrium. In a series of dualities that cover almost every conceivable relationship, where she is variously in the active or passive mode but always equally balanced, Isis is the primordial androgyne, unmanifest yet with all possibilities inherent as she is outside of time and space. Manifestation must take place through a series of disequilibriums, the sum of which constitutes the total equilibrium of all things. By listing all disequilibriums equally, she establishes the total equilibrium with herself as the principle. Opposite pairs only appear as such when seen outwardly. They become complementary when they are reconciled in primordial unity, which is the higher understanding.[93] Isis gives both points of view, which she is only able to do because of her superior state. For example,

I am the one whom they call Law,
And that you have called Lawlessness.

She is the Law, or ordinance, and as such is beyond the Law herself, for the principle Itself cannot be contained by anything or known by anything that is not Itself. In the Edenic State, there is no outside or inside, no difference. The return to that state appears as destruction only from the side of manifestation. From the Edenic viewpoint, however, the sum of all disorders constitutes total order. When things are no longer seen as isolated and distinctive but in the light of their essential unity then order and harmony is restored, a viewpoint that is above multiplicity. When all things are known from within the divine abode, multiplicity is transformed: unity is in multiplicity and multiplicity is in unity.

I am war and I am peace.

---

[93] The manifest and unmanifest are not dualities, however, for the latter is the principle of the former.

War is descriptive of the oppositions within man who does not yet know the Real. In the primordial state, there is Shekinah who has two aspects: one is the inward glory and the other the outward peace. Unity is a meeting point of concentration and expansion, but there is that which is beyond. She is the principle of both. As reconciler and supreme principle she leads to *turiya*, the fourth state mentioned in the *Upanishads*, completely unconditioned and non-dual.

> Come forward to me, you who know me
> And you who know my members,
> Then you will establish the great ones
> Among the smallest of creatures.

Expansion and contraction are a complementary duality. When considered simultaneously, they are differing aspects of principial immutability. This is the state equivalent to what is called *prajna* in the Hindu doctrines. There is nothing outside of the principle, either manifested or non-manifested, for It is infinite and nothing that is infinite can leave anything outside of Itself. It cannot be determined or limited in any way. The whole of universal manifestation is only distinguishable from It in an illusory way; manifestation is but a reflection of the Real, and whilst the universe only exists because of the supreme principle, the principle is not in the universe because It cannot be contained in any way. According to the Hindu doctrines, there is no reciprocity between the world and Brahma as absolute. Brahma is everything for Brahma is the whole, the infinite; but everything is not Brahma since all else is relative and conditioned. Anything that is 'this', or 'that' is not Brahma.[94] In the presence of Brahma, knowing and being are one essence, or non-dual. Brahma is more than the sum of Its parts. It is superior to what is known, and in fact cannot be known in the same way—it is said in the *Upanishads* that fire can burn other things, but cannot burn itself.

> I am the First and the Last.
> I am the rod of his power in his youth,
> And he is the staff of my old age.

She is the origin and the end of things. The First and the Last is the Alpha and Omega, the Beginning and the Ending of all things as variously described in all traditions.

---

[94] 'That' is nonetheless a name given to Brahma: Om Tat Sat. 'That', as noun, does not indicate a particular, limited thing or plurality. To know Brahma one must *be* Brahma.

In Christianity, Alpha and Omega is a name of the Cosmic Christ as given in the book of John, 22: 13.[95] This may also be understood as *purusha* and *prakriti*, the first and last of the *tattva* principles of Shankhya, but which have a higher analogue with the holy spirit. The series of seemingly impossible relationships are beyond time and space, and are therefore in the eternal realm of principial unity. The rod and the staff are symbols of rigour and mercy, and also symbols of ordinance and right action, which are the supports to knowledge. Youth and old age have a double meaning: youth is manifest whereas old age is akin to the unmanifest; youth is the return to the beginning whereas old age is the end of the cycle; youth is ignorance whereas old age is wisdom. Thus Isis links both states with the staff of power or of ordinance, the vertical axis of the cross that reconciles all oppositions.

> I am forever within.
> I am always of the qualities.
> I am forever the principalities and the spirits.
> I am control and that which is uncontrollable,
> I am unity and dissolution.
> I am the one that is below,
> And yet they have come up to me.
> I am judgement and acquittal.
> For what is within you is what is outside of you,
> And the one who fashions you on the outside
> Is the one who shaped the inside of you.
> And what you see outside of you, you will see inside of you.
> It is visible, and it is your garment.

Isis is forever within the centre of all. The qualities, including all elements and conditions of manifestation, belong to her for they are made from her own essence. As the principle of control, she is uncontrollable. She is unity and dissolution; for in unity the self is dissolved. She is below, as *prakriti* or unmanifested sub-strata, yet above, as *purusha* 'essence'. As judgement and acquittal she is the twin pillars of rigour and mercy, or Justice and Peace, which are the powers of Shekinah, or Shekinah and Metatron.[96]

---

[95] 'I am Alpha and Omega, the beginning and the end, the first and the last.'
[96] Cf. René Guénon, *The King of the World*.

One may find comparison here with the transcendent seamless garment of Christ Jesus as related in the Gnostic *Pistis Sophia*.[97] All things appear, become knowable, by virtue of the supreme Knower. Much of the text, while metaphysical, consists of yoga instruction of a very practical nature:

> You who deny me, confess me,
> And you who confess me, deny me.
> You who tell the truth about me, lie about me,
> And you who have lied about me, tell the truth about me.
> You who know me, do not know me,
> And those who have not known me, let them know me.

To help explain this, it is worth quoting a passage from the *Keña Upanishad*. The commentary in parantheses is from Guénon.[98]

> If you think that you know [Brahma] well, what you know of Its nature is in reality but little; for this reason Brahma should be still more attentively considered by you. [The reply is as follows]: I do not think that I know It; by that I mean to say that I do not know It well [distinctively, as I should know an object capable of being described or defined]; nevertheless, I know It [according to the instruction I have received concerning Its nature]. Whoever among us understands the following words [in their true meaning]: 'I do not know It, and yet I know It,' verily that man knows It. He who thinks that Brahma is not comprehended [for by the knowledge of Brahma he has become really and effectively identical with Brahma Itself]; but he who thinks that Brahma is comprehended [by some sensible or mental faculty] knows It not. Brahma [in Itself, in Its incommunicable essence] is unknown to those who know It [after the manner of some object of knowledge, be it a particular being or Universal Being] and It is known to those who do not know It at all [as 'this', or 'that'].

> I was sent forth from Mystery,
> And I will come to them that reflect upon me,
> For those that seek me, shall find me.
> Behold me, ye who reflect upon me,
> And listen to me, ye that have ears to hear.

---

[97] See 'The Ass of God', *Nu Hermetica*. The seamless robe is mentioned in *Pistis Sophia*, Chapter 10.
[98] *Man and His Becoming according to the Vedānta*, p. 107.

To be sent forth from Mystery means to appear or be manifested from the unknown, the unmanifested. To 'reflect' is to practice yoga meditation or contemplation, in which recollection is an important part of the discipline. It is also a very precise term to use as we are but the reflected light of Atma. 'Listen to me' is a directive on the practice of meditation; concentration implies returning to the centre of the heart or being, the abode of elemental *akasha*, for example, corresponding to the faculty of hearing.

> Ye who have waited for me, take me to yourselves,
> And do not banish me from your sight.
> Do not say hateful things of me, do not hear them spoken.
> Do not be ignorant of me anywhere or at any time.
> Be vigilant! Do not forget me.

The practice of discrimination requires continuous vigilance for the elimination of profane or harmful thoughts, and recollection of that which is helpful to the path. Abstinence from ignorant or profane speech or thoughts is vital to the practice of yoga; ignorance is the absence of all knowledge derived from the Perfect Mind or intellect.

> I am the Silence beyond knowing,
> And the Idea of continuous recollection.

There is that which is beyond the ego self, thought, sensation and feeling. As 'beyond knowing' she is beyond time and space, infinite and simultaneous. There is no subject and object in unity; she is saying she is beyond what you know and yet she is everything. As the Idea she is the cosmic Logos, which can be apprehended, and of which the knowledge is supported by the practice of recollection.

> I am the one you have hidden from,
> And thus do you appear to me!
> And wherever you hide yourselves,
> I myself will appear.
> And whenever you appear,
> I myself will hide from you.

To make oneself 'as small a mustard seed' is to know the Real, which is beyond the self. Thus she appears when the self withdraws into the centre of all and disappears when the self reappears.

> You that would know me
> Will yet darken my understanding,
> And embrace my wisdom with sorrow.
> You embrace me in places that are ugly and ruined,
> And steal from those which are true, even in your falsehood.

This has a ring of prophecy where the anti-initiatic force of our times has taken from tradition and subverted it so as to destroy and wipe out all memory of it.[99]

> Do not separate me from those who once knew you.
> And do not cast anyone out, nor turn anyone away.

There is no 'separate' in the Edenic State.

> Hear me, o ye that have ears to hear,
> And learn of my words, ye who know me!

Hearing in this sense is the higher faculty, which corresponds to *akasha* or spirit. Hearing is transposed to pure vibration, or sound that is not heard by the ears but within the 'space' or cavity of the heart. This is a form of direct cognition of deity. Those who 'know me' in this context are those who know Brahma, for example, only through scriptural study; theoretical knowledge is indispensible as a support to direct knowledge but the latter also requires meditation and concentration of the mind. This fluctuation of the meaning in different kinds of sound or hearing is continued:

> I am the sound that is attainable by all;
> I am the voice beyond reason.

This affirms the previous two lines. There is ordinary knowledge or sound, that is nonetheless necessary, and there is direct knowledge; and that direct knowledge is beyond reason as is the *manas* or the 'inward sense', which in turn is an intermediary between thought and the essential principles depending from the I-sense or knower.

> I am the name of the sound,
> And the sound of the name.
> I am the signature of the letter
> And the seal of the division.
> And I am the darkness and the light.

---

[99] This part of the text, and some other parts, have remarkable similarity to the 'Oracle of Babalon'—see *Babalon Unveiled*. *Thunder Perfect Mind* was not discovered until centuries after the time of John Dee, however.

Nama and Rupa are 'Name and Form', which is integral to the individual and so also the means of knowing Isis when still in the individual state. The 'signature' is an exact description of what the Nama is, as defining the essence of any individual creature. Through such definition and so determination, division comes about. Isis is also both the unmanifest, unknowable, and the manifest, knowable. She is known by Name and Form but she is beyond that too.

> And I am the voice of my listeners,
> And the one who listens to you.
> For I am the Great Power
> And he that sends forth to me will hear my name.
> And he that delivers me shall be as one who created me.
> And I will speak forth his name.

As the voice of both the listeners and the one that speaks, Isis is the cogniser of the self, and the pure I-sense, for she is the supreme Knower, beyond all duality of subject and object, of the knower and the thing that is known. As such she is the Great Power. The devotee of Isis will be rewarded with knowledge of her true name, through the super-sensible faculties. 'He that delivers' refers to the *moksha* or final liberation; for in that, Isis is the soul. If Isis should speak forth the name of the devotee, then that name is said to be written in the Book of Tahuti, or Book of Life, which is the gift of immortality.

In the final verse Isis once again says that she is the principle of everything that can exist. The verse is metaphysical and has nothing to do with any moral sense that might be construed outwardly:

> Take heed then, ye that hear me.
> And ye Angels also, and those who have been sent,
> And ye spirits who have arisen from the dead.
> For I am the one who alone exists,
> And I have no-one who will judge me.

Isis here speaks of other states or modalities of being, in both formal and formless worlds. According to the Hindu doctrines, men that have achieved knowledge but not yet the final *moksha* liberation can become as gods or angels, *devas* and *devis*, for the duration of a cosmic cycle. This may include avatars and prophets, that 'have been sent'. Yet all are reminded never to forget her, in the Supreme Identity, for she is 'the one who alone exists'. As such, she may not be judged for she is not affected in any way by external or contingent things such as the human state, for example.

> Many are the pleasant forms that exist in
> Numerous sins, and poisons,
> Even in disgraceful passions, and fleeting pleasures,
> Which men embrace weakly.

There are 'weak pleasures' that arise from ignorance, for these are limited to the corporeal state and all such pleasure is measured by pain and affliction, bringing further suffering.

> When they seek, and attain clarity,
> And go up to their place of peace
> Then at last shall they find me.
> And they shall have life,
> And they will not die again.

We are instructed to turn aside from such weak pleasures and to seek Isis in all things, or in other words, to become practitioners. The 'clarity' is that of pure knowledge, beyond reason, and that is only attained through meditation and concentration. Tranquility or peace is the necessary condition for knowledge, and signifies freedom from all afflictions that are the consequence of desiring the sensual and temporary pleasures. At the same time this can allude to death, and the possibility of attaining either immortality or liberation then. In final deliverance, the being will not return to manifestation. This is the promise of Isis, her true words spoken to the seekers of truth.

Thunder Perfect Mind

I was sent forth from Mystery,
And I will come to them that reflect upon me,
For those that seek me, shall find me.
Behold me, ye who reflect upon me,
And listen to me, ye that have ears to hear!
Ye who have waited for me, take me to yourselves,
And do not banish me from your sight.
Do not say hateful things of me, do not hear them spoken.
Do not be ignorant of me anywhere or at any time.
Be vigilant! Do not forget me.

I am the First and the Last.
I am the blessed one and the forsaken one.
I am the whore and the holy one.
I am the wife and the virgin.
I am the mother and the daughter.
I am the members of my mother.
I am the barren one—and yet many are her sons.
I am she whose wedding is of great nobility,
And I have not taken a husband.
I am the midwife and she who does not bear,
And I am the solace of my labour pains.
I am the bride and the bridegroom,
And it is my husband who begot me.
I am the mother of my father,
And the sister of my husband,
And yet he is my offspring.

I am the slave of him who prepared me,
And I am the governor of my offspring.
Yet he is the one who begot me,
Before the time of my coming.
And he is my offspring in due course,
And from him I take my power.
I am the rod of his power in his youth,
And he is the staff of my old age.
Whatever he wills shall come about.
I am the Silence beyond knowing,
And the Idea of continuous recollection.
I am the Voice whose tongues are legion,
And the Word whose forms are many.
I am the Oracle, whose utterance is my name.

Why, you who hate me, do you love me
And hate those who love me?
You who deny me, confess me,
And you who confess me, deny me.
You who tell the truth about me, lie about me,
And you who have lied about me, tell the truth about me.
You who know me, do not know me,
And those who have not known me, let them know me.
For I am knowledge and ignorance.
I am shame and pride.
I am shameless and I am ashamed.
I am strength and I am fear.
I am war and I am peace.
Take heed of me! For I am the one who is disgraced,
And the one who is exalted greatly.

Take heed of my poverty and my wealth.
Do not be arrogant to me when I am cast out upon the earth,
And then you will find me in those that are to come.
Do not look down upon me on the dung-heap,
Nor go and leave me cast out,
And then you will find me in all the kingdoms.
Do not look upon me when I am cast out among those who
Are disgraced, and in the meanest places,
Nor ever laugh at me!
Do not cast me out among those who are slain in violence.
I, I am compassionate as I am cruel.
Therefore be on your guard!
Do not hate me when I am obedient,
And do not love my powerful self-control.
Do not forsake me in my weakness,
And do not fear my power.

For why do you despise my fear
And curse my pride?
I am she who exists in all fears,
And there is strength in trembling.
I am she who is weak,
And I am strong in the place of comfort.
I am senseless and I am also wise.
Why have you hated me in your councils?
For I shall be silent among those who are silent,
And yet I shall appear and speak unto you.
Why have you hated me, you Greeks?
Do you think I am a barbarian among the barbarians?
I am the wisdom of the Greeks,
And the knowledge of the barbarians!

I am the judgement of the Greeks and of the barbarians.
I am the one whose Image is great in Egypt,
And the one who has no Image among the barbarians.
I am the one who has been hated everywhere,
And who has been loved everywhere.
I am the one whom they call Life,
And that you have called Death.
I am the one whom they call Law,
And that you have called Lawlessness.
I am the one whom you have pursued,
And I am the one whom you have seized.
I am the one whom you have scattered,
Even while ye have gathered me together.
I am the one before whom you were ashamed,
And you have been shameless unto me.

I am she who does not keep the festival,
And I am she whose festivals are many.
I, I am godless, and I am the one whose God is great.
I am the one whom you have reflected upon,
And yet you have forsaken me.
I am unlearned, and yet they learn from me.
I am the one whom you have despised,
And yet you reflect upon me.
I am the one you have hidden from,
And thus do you appear to me!
And wherever you hide yourselves,
I myself will appear.
And whenever you appear,
I myself will hide from you.

Those who have my knowledge
Will cleave to my ignorance.
You that would understand me
Will yet darken my understanding,
And embrace my wisdom with sorrow.

You embrace me in places that are ugly and ruined,
And steal from those which are true, even in your falsehood.
Out of shame, take me to yourselves shamelessly.
And when you find fault in my members,
Look for that fault in yourselves.
Come forward to me, you who know me
And you who know my members,
Then you will establish the great ones
Among the smallest of creatures.
Come forward to childhood,
And do not despise it because it is small and it is little.
Do not turn away greatness in some parts from the
Smallness in others,
For the small is known from the great.

Why do you curse me and pretend to honour me?
When you were wounded, I gave you mercy.
Do not separate me from those who once knew you.
And do not cast anyone out, nor turn anyone away.
For then I shall turn you away and I shall know him not.
For I know who is mine.
I know the first ones,
And those who came after them shall know me.

I am the Mind of Thunderous Perfection.
I am the answer to my own question,
And the knowledge of those who seek after me,
And the will of those who ask of me.
I am the power of the powers in my knowledge
Of the angels, who have been sent at my word,
And of gods in their seasons by my counsel,
And of the spirits of every man who dwells with me,
And of the women who dwell within me.
I am the one who is blessed, and who is praised,
And yet who is scornfully despised.
I am peace, and war has come because of me.
And I am an alien and a citizen.
I am the substance and the one who has no substance.

There are those who cannot know me from their ignorance,
And those who know me, that are of my very substance.
Yet those who are close to me have yet been ignorant of me,
And those who are far away from me have yet known me a little.
On the day when I am close to you,
You are far away from me,
And on the day when I am far away from you,
I am closer to you than I can ever be.

I am forever within.
I am always of the qualities.
I am forever of the principalities and the spirits.
I am always that which the soul seeks.
I am control and that which is uncontrollable.
I am unity and dissolution.
I am the one that is below,
And yet they come up to me.
I am judgement and acquittal.

I am sinless, and the root of sin derives from me.
I am the weak lust in the appearance of things,
And the strong will to the eternal is within me.
I am the sound that may be heard by everyone,
And the voice that is beyond reason.
I am a mute who does not speak forth,
And yet great is the multitude of my words.

Hear me in peace and learn of me in unrest.
I am she who cries out,
And I am cast forth upon the face of the earth.
I prepare the bread and my Mind is within it.
I am the knowledge of my own name.
I am the one who cries out, and who hears.
I appear and yet I walk in the shadow of invisibility.
I am the attacked and the defended.
I am the one who is called Truth,
And who is known to be iniquitous.

You honour me loudly, and you whisper against me.
You who are vanquished, judge them who vanquish you
Before they give judgement against you,
For the impartial and the partial exist in you.
If you are condemned by this one, who will acquit you?
Or if you are acquitted by him, who then will detain you?
For what is within you is what is outside of you,
And the one who fashions you on the outside
Is the one who shaped the inside of you.
And what you see outside of you, you will see inside of you.
It is visible, and it is your garment.

Hear me, o ye that have ears to hear,
And learn of my words, ye who know me!
I am the sound that is attainable by all;
I am the voice beyond reason.
I am the name of the sound,
And the sound of the name.
I am the signature of the letter,
And the seal of the division.
And I am the darkness and the light.
And I am the voice of my listeners,
And the one who listens to you.
For I am the Great Power.
And he that sends forth to me will hear my name.
And he that delivers me shall be as one who created me.
And I will speak forth his name.
Look then at his words, and all the writings complete.
Take heed then, ye that hear me,
And ye angels also, and those who have been sent,
And ye spirits who have arisen from the dead.
For I am the one who alone exists,
And I have no one who will judge me.

Many are the pleasant forms that exist in
Numerous sins, and poisons,
Even in disgraceful passions, and fleeting pleasures,
Which men embrace weakly.
When they seek, and attain clarity,
And go up to their place of peace,
Then at last shall they find me.
And they shall have life,
And they will not die again.

PART TWO: YOGA

Yoga

Everyone imagines they know what yoga is, but the notion commonly rests on the misconception that yoga is all about postures and breathing exercises. In fact, the development of postures and breathing came at a relatively late time and only forms a branch of Hatha Yoga—a branch that is not in any way a sum of even that specialised knowledge. Yoga, which is linked etymologically to 'yoke', includes both the goal and the means. The 'union' that is implicit is also mistaken for a uniting that takes place between two distinctly separate things, whereas it is really more of a return to one principle that has no second, so is more in the way of a fullness of realisation or total knowledge that involves the destruction of all ignorance concerning the true state of affairs.

The origin of yoga is far more ancient than is usually supposed. There are two *darshanas* or points of view within the Hindu doctrines that are closely linked, these being the principial cosmology of Shankhya, and the *Yoga-Sutras* attributed to Patañjali. Modern scholarship always insists on attributing traditional knowledge to an individual author, whereas names like 'Shankhya' are not the names of a personage but descriptive more of a specialised knowledge or science not in any way comparable to conventional scientific theories. *Shankhya* literally has the meaning of 'category', which is meant in the sense of synthetic knowledge of true principles (*tattvas*). Patañjali, who wrote down the aphorisms (*sutras*) of the yoga theory and practice, based on the Shankhya cosmology, does not refer to one person; it is a family name, indicative of a school of thought as a collective entity.

Furthermore, the great antiquity of yoga is made clear in the Sanskrit source texts and the commentaries on them by the ancient sages. Yoga practice is inseparable from the Shankhya teaching and that is attributed to Kapila, who is identified with Hiranyagarbha, the Lord of the Universe in the present cycle or Manvantara. It is written that Kapila had acquired the sum total of all knowledge of the Manvantara previous to this present one, of which according to Hindu cosmology we are now at the end of the final phase called Kali Yuga.[100] Owing to the degradation that takes place at the end of a cosmic cycle it thus became necessary to write down the theory and practice of yoga about two thousand years ago—before that it was not necessary as knowledge was passed down through oral tradition.

---

[100] See 'Cosmic Cycles', *Nu Hermetica*.

When the knowledge was in danger of being forgotten and lost forever, Patañjali wrote it down in a concise form, which is known as the aphorisms or *Yoga-Sutras*. The nature of the ancient Sanskrit language is such that it requires commentaries to determine the meaning. The true meaning can only be construed by those who have direct knowledge of what is being written about, as opposed to the study of scriptures alone. For this reason much gets lost in translation into modern languages; this is all the more so when the translators lack the knowledge, as is the case with scholarly or academic commentators. The important thing is that knowledge in the way it is meant here cannot be learned without a valid teacher.

To repeat what was said earlier, the Shankhya *darshana* is a synthetic cosmology or a 'natural science' that was drawn from what already existed in the *Vedas*, and even thousands of years earlier, before anything was written down. It rests on 'true principles' (*tattvas*). It is not in any way a material science, in so far especially as 'matter' has no direct equivalent word in any ancient language. Matter itself is a modern theoretical notion based on a strictly limited view of causality, which shall here be briefly explained: Conventional scientific theories are insistent that all things perceptible by the senses, or perceptible by the senses supported by special machines or instruments, have a causal relation with other things of a similar 'material' class, and that also rests on an assumption that matter is in itself inert, requiring something else to move it. A material cause is not only sought for material things but is also sought for in things that are obviously subtler than gross matter. For example, it is becoming increasingly accepted, especially by the public, whose access to conventional science is limited to generalised presentations of what are in fact extremely specialised theories, that the mind, or what composes the mind, is caused by the brain, the physical organ. That owes to neuroscience, which as with all conventional sciences, seeks to restrict reality to what its own specialised and so extremely limited field can imagine. All such theories are, by their very nature as 'invented knowledge', constantly changed when new theories are produced; so there is always a kind of 'falling behind' where public acceptance of the 'new facts' amounts to acceptance of an 'old fact'.

Such a way of theorising about nature and reality is the complete reverse of all ancient and traditional knowledge, which while prone to adaptation over time, never changes in its essential principles. Traditional doctrines assert that all things have a causal basis in a higher or subtler principle and are known thereby.

It should be added, lest there be any mistake here, that by 'subtler' is not in any way implied 'smaller' or 'greater' in terms of space and the objects that fill space. It is by the higher or subtler principles that any thing can be truly known; all other kinds of knowledge about a thing are secondary and so already a further step removed from what that thing is in reality. The senses defined as hearing, touch, sight, taste and smell enable the mind, a subtler principle, to perceive all things in nature of the same class as those senses, which are the instruments of the mind. The mind creates objects and things from such cognitions that are based on sensory perceptions. According to the teaching, our ignorance mistakes these self-created cognitions for reality and through identification we mistake them for the self.

The mind (*manas*) is treated as a sixth sense when considered apart from sensorial objects. The qualification needs to be added here that by 'sixth sense' is not meant the popular idea of what that means, which has nothing to do with the inward sense referred to in the *Yoga-Sutras*. The mind, however, only has a seeming existence through its higher principle, which is the I-sense or pure self-awareness. When pure awareness rests in itself and its own higher principle, called *boddhi*, devoid of all self-created objects, then the mind and its objects effectively disappear. This is experienced so that it becomes self-evident only through concentration of the mind as instructed by the *Yoga-Sutras* and commentaries, knowledge which is in turn supported by the body of the *Upanishads* and *Vedanta*.

Such knowledge cannot be proved by any physical or material means, such as weighing and measuring—for such means are a contrivance as they are external to the thing that one wishes to know about. All classification, systematisation and placing things in arbitrary categories for comparison, similarly produce a kind of artificial or virtual knowledge that is strictly limited to the very system that produces it. It must be added that in spite of what even Indian translators sometimes produce in modern commentaries, where they will sometimes refer to the teaching of Shankhya and Patañjali as 'systems' and even 'philosophical systems', there is no relation between any of this and systems of knowledge such as are produced by the theories of Western philosophy or psychology, or other sciences. They will also refer to 'religion' where no such thing exists. At the same time, yoga and all other forms of traditional knowledge can never correctly be called 'atheist', which presupposes the religious point of view and is only a negation of that.

From the point of view of the individual human being—and that which is defined as such has its own necessary limitations—things are known through experience; the conventional sciences rest on theories produced 'experientially', though this is then subsequently mistaken for 'fact', admitting no higher or subtler principle. While self awareness, devoid of mental impressions resting on sensorial phenomena, can be experienced—though only with continued effort of concentration of the mind—the principles that transcend the ego or I-sense awareness are only known by those same transcendent principles. That is what is called 'direct knowledge', which is metaphysical and can only be understood 'metaphysically' and by no other means. The yogin therefore does not seek ordinary knowledge of things; the yogin seeks knowledge of the principles.

It has been said that through identification with the self-created objects, there is a mistaken idea of the self that arises, which owes to ignorance of the higher principles. While we have mostly been concerned here with the yoga *darshana* of Patañjali, there is no fundamental disagreement between that and the non-dualism of Shankaracharya, whose commentaries are the essence of absolute Advaita Vedanta. The 'non-dual conclusion of all knowledge' is the purest form of the doctrines, so it will be necessary to define more closely what is meant by the 'ego'. It must also be pointed out that while some, even from inside the tradition, assert that the *Yoga-Sutras* are dualistic and therefore in some way opposed to Advaita, that is not at all the case. Dualism only comes about when no higher or transcendent principle is known or admitted, and that is not the case with the *Yoga-Sutras*. The mind creates sensory objects from impressions received through the senses but is not self-caused, and as with everything else is dependant from the immediately higher principle, which in this case is called *ahankara* (loosely 'ego'), of which the central principle is called *jivatma*, the 'creature self' as individuality. The conventional idea of ego, which is the only word we have for *ahankara*, falls short of the mark because it is generally used to indicate only the mental impressions, sphere of actions and so forth, as though these were defining characteristics; whereas in fact they are but limiting determinations leading us further and further away from what the ego or self really is. And that is how we can arrive at an idea of the self that is erroneous—and which is 'conventional knowledge'; for psychological sciences, and all derived or related disciplines in agreement with it, support the error, called simply 'ignorance' in the teachings.

What we call 'ego' here is something that can only be understood exactly through ancient sciences including metaphysics, cosmology and ontology: the individual mind of the creature self or human being is in fact dependant from the ego, when that is correctly understood; it is not the other way round. What defines a difference between beings then is much more than the mind and what the mind creates through its sense impressions, including its false idea of self composed from merely outward appearances of behaviours, actions, temperament and so forth. The supreme principle that is called Atma cannot in any way be specified for that would imply limitation through determination, and the Atma is not determined, moved, changed, qualified or affected by any other thing; in Itself, it contains all 'other things' but neither does it 'create' them. So individualities owe their differences to contingencies, determinations, placed as a superimposition upon the Reality or Atma, considered as Self.

The ego or *ahankara*, including *jivatma* and the five *tanmatras* or subtle elemental principles, is already a modification or mode of being of what is called the higher intellect or spiritual intuition called *boddhi*, and that is itself a ray from the Atma principle, analogously comparable to a ray of the sun, which is not the sun itself. That ray causes a reflection as of the sun upon water, for example. So the highest and transcendent principle of the ego that is not actually within the individuality is already one step removed from Atma, and the individuality is three steps removed from Atma. The 'ego' as it is meant here will only ever be known or realised by a very few persons that have practiced concentration and meditation over a long time. It cannot be realised any other way, because the instruments, to use an analogy, only perceive the instruments; the faculty of action makes it possible for us to know that a person or a thing travels, has motion. If we did not have the faculty of action, we could not know action.

It is for this reason that we must exercise caution, for example, over 'experience' and what is sometimes called 'experiential'. It is needed for crossing the street, buying food from a shop, for talking to people and writing a book; but in yoga it only gets in the way of reaching further than an ordinary kind of knowledge. The mind then is an impediment in so far as the knowledge of higher principles is concerned; it has to be got out of the way, and there are various means. The mind is needed for ordinary things; but to know any supra-sensible things, something more is required.

The above may often lead to a discussion of 'higher forms' but a qualification is then needed: all forms, whether 'higher' or 'lower', express the formal order, inclusive of what has been described above. But even the *boddhi* ray, that reflects Atma to the waters of the self, is in the formless realm. In that way even 'higher forms' limits us to what is human or comparable to the human, and may possibly include other creatures and things that are in a way co-dependant with the human, as either part of the terrestrial or cosmological domain.

This leads to the consideration of the environmental influence, which, while part of that which normally defines individuality, is something that must ultimately be overcome, as such conditions are imposed upon the Self (i.e., Atma). These are necessary conditions so long as we are within the human state, as it is what defines the human as individuality. But such conditions prevent access to what are really 'higher states', which is not about form as such. And in fact, there is far more to the individual being than is realised by any conventional science as we have here indicated. Social conditioning, to give but one example of a set of contingent determinations, is a minute portion of the total conditions that make up the individuality, not in any way producing a sum of even the most exterior part of the latter.

The mind is shaped by the objects of its own cognition, and this is what is meant by a mistaken identification. Why is it impossible then for most human beings to ever free themselves from ignorance concerning the true state of affairs or reality? Human beings are not in any way equal or the same in reality; they have different possibilities for knowledge. Furthermore, modern education, which comes with an inherent anti-traditional prejudice, deforms the mentality to such an extent that it becomes impossible for many persons to realise their spiritual possibilities to even the slightest degree, assuming they should have these possibilities latent within them. Spiritual realisation is not possible for every person even from birth, as we are born with certain defining characteristics and possibilities. We cannot be 'another person' in that sense, even when what seems to be a radical change has taken place; we become what we know, since knowledge and identity are simultaneous but such knowledge is latent in the being and does not truly come from a place 'outside' the being. Nonetheless, true spiritual realisation can and does effect a permanent change in the being, and this comes about because knowledge and identification are simultaneous. There is what can be called 'total being', which amounts to the sum total of all the possibilities of the being, and these are not limited to the human.

In the present context, however, there are some that are fitted to become shopkeepers or heads of government for example—it makes little odds really as such things are wholly exterior—and it will never occur to them to doubt that what they do, their actions, and what they think, their thoughts, are real and worthwhile. To the person that has achieved even a small measure of spiritual realisation, that possibility being already latent within their being, they will find at some point that they are surrounded by sleepers, in a sort of trance. Nothing can be done about that and in fact it is harmful (an affliction) to the path to worry about it or become overly concerned. When a person has latency of knowledge within them they will then seek that knowledge—the principle seeks Itself in what It is. When God is even admitted as a possibility then it is sometimes said that it is by grace, or due to compassion or benevolence. And that is equally true.

The mind then is a reflection of a reflection if we consider that the mind 'comes about' through the constituents of the individuality. What is pertinent to the present context is that the mind can, in spite of its limitations, receive spiritual influence; that is what the meaning of initiation is, or at least it is that which makes it possible—spiritual realisation always being the goal. The mind itself can only receive or know such influence through determinations, so it is then explained as a reflection but seen through a cloudy mirror. The knowledge of the mind is necessarily imperfect for it rests upon the objects of its perception based on the same senses, conveying an impression of reality that is only phenomenal.

While there is a difference between exterior objects such as a tree, cat or pot, and interior objects such as a dream of a tree, cat or a pot, or some other imagining, from the point of view of this science there is not really much difference and in many ways waking and dreaming can be regarded in the same light. It seems that exterior objects are seen by the light of the sun or moon and interior or dream objects are seen by our own light, or mind, but in fact all are objects created by the mind; the mind is not the source of that luminosity in reality but some steps removed from it. Atma is self-luminous; It does not shine by any other light than what It is in Itself. This is further explained by the Sanskrit sacred syllable Om, which really has three visible parts: AUM. These symbolise the whole universe and relate to the three states of waking, dreaming and dreamless sleep. This is a complete science and so there is one 'point' in the Sanskrit word Om, called *turiya*, that transcends all three and is at the same time the causal sub-strata. All of this will now be gone into in further detail.

The Shankhya Cosmology

The Sanskrit name for that which is called the Self, but which has nothing to do with the ego and mind, is Atma (sometimes *atman*). When the word 'Self' is capitalised then we do not mean the self of the mind, memory, actions, senses or even the *ahankara* 'ego' but at least the pure I-sense, and even that is but a reflection of Atma—though it is much more than ordinary knowledge. There is no single word by which Atma can be accurately translated into a modern language; unfortunately there are no words in modern languages to symbolise metaphysical realities. One way to define the meaning of Atma would be to put it thus:

> *It* is the smallest and the greatest and yet *It* is truly neither small nor great for *It* does not occupy space and time; Atma is without birth and death and has no cause other than what *It* is, always has been and always will be. Atma is eternal, infinite, immutable and untransmissible.

Yet Atma can be known as the Self. This takes a long time and is not possible without rigorous self-control and the concentration of the mind. That is the concern of the *Yoga-Sutras*. The practice of yoga is first aimed at analysing thought, which involves the precise method of discrimination that will be described later. This is supported at the same time through *dharana*, which is the controlling of thought through concentration on a single object. The attainment of *dhyana* or true meditation involves the suppression of thought altogether. The *dhyana* of having 'no thoughts' is not at all the same thing as nescience, which is called an impediment to the practice in the *Yoga-Sutras* and is no different from ignorance (*avidya*). Even *dhyana* is a means to an end, and that end is usually called *samadhi*, 'union with God', though there are gradations or different levels of *samadhi*. For the present purpose we only need to know that while *dhyana* meditation is achieved with effort, real *samadhi* is without effort. And yet the effort must be put in by the *sadhaka* (practitioner).

With the practice of discrimination we must, in a manner of speaking, step outside of our mind to look back in at what the mind is doing. Some have this already in them as an innate quality and it only needs to be more fully realised before going on further. Others do not have it and so for them a very great effort is needed if they are to stop believing that their own thoughts are somehow 'real', instead of the self-created impressions they really are. This yoga practice is not without its hazards; there are some that will not take kindly to being told that they are chasing phantoms, and that is because it is beyond their reach to think it could be so. Others already know this is true and only need to have it pointed out to them. It is as if they recollect it. There is nothing that can exist that did not already exist.

The famous 'Know Thyself' maxim attributed to the Greeks but often given a completely superficial (e.g. 'psychological') explanation is an exact science in the *Yoga-Sutras*. All images, thoughts, things heard or felt, seen, tasted or smelled, support the mind in forming an impression of these things or objects, mistaking them for the real. Similarly, because the objects of the mind and senses are really what constitute 'mind'—consisting of impressions resting on sense objects combined with recollection of previous impressions—we also mistake that for our Self. What follows is an overview of the cosmology of the Shankhya *darshana*, which even in its entirety is but a small part of the vast body of the *Yoga-Shastra*.

Let us suppose then the object meditated on for the purpose of achieving *dhyana* is the Sun, which is alike to fire and light and heat (as consequence). This will be better understood if we make a brief list of the five elements. These have nothing to do with the material elements as understood in conventional science, they are subtle, yet they come before the gross level in the natural order, and without them, gross objects could not exist as such. Each element (*bhuta*) is associated with one of the five senses as traditionally understood. We here place them in the order of their production from *prakriti* 'non-material substance' (undifferentiated), from the subtle to the gross:

Akasha or ether	sound, hearing
Vayu or air	movement, touch
Tejas or fire	light, vision (seeing)
Apas or water	prehensile, tasting
Prithivi or earth	solidity, sense of smell

One should know the symbols of the five *bhuta-tattvas*. When we contemplate these, the ideas that emerge are different from modern conventional notions that have grown up around them. We give them here in the order of their production from *prakriti* (undifferentiated substantial ground):

Akasha (ether or spirit)	violet or indigo oval (or egg) shape
Vayu (air)	sky-blue circle
Tejas (fire)	red equilateral triangle
Apas (water)	silver crescent with points upward
Prithivi (earth)	yellow square

Akasha is all-permeating. It has no beginning or end. All other elements are derived from it, through determinations.

Vayu is movement and extension or reach (as is the sky, when a symbol). It is also 'breath' or *prana*, and yet *prana* (the vital) is everything.

Tejas is light and vision, as we cannot see things without luminosity. The same applies whether the objects are external or internal, as in a dream. The luminosity is in fact that of the knower, not the object itself. The cogniser imagines it is their own light but that light is derived through a ray of the Sun that is Atma, the supreme Self.

Apas is prehensile and mobile; it is also transparent.

Prithivi holds together and is solidifying.

Although we can reduce things to a single element for convenience, such a thing does not occur in nature and so these are understood as combining in different ways. For example, fire can partake of earth in so far as it has 'body'. It partakes of water in that it can be fluidic. It partakes of air in that it has movement (and so does the sun, or apparently so). Now the sound or 'voice' of fire is subtler still. The nature of *akasha* or ether in this doctrine is that it fills space. Space, in contradiction to what is often supposed, is not empty or full of 'nothing'. Space must be a container for something, otherwise it does not exist at all; that something is *akasha* or ether, all permeating.

There is a fragment of an oracle or instruction attributed to the Persian sage Zoroaster, where it is said, 'Hear thou the voice of fire'. Such a 'voice' is not heard and can best be described as soundless vibration. It is the sound that is not sound. And yet it can be known through meditation *dhyana*.

At this stage we are moving up the natural order of things, away from the gross towards the subtle, although we are still really in the domain of what is called 'subtle form', because form does not necessarily have a body that is seen or touched, etc. The *bhutas* are subtler than the gross elements that happen to share the same names in nature. Between the elements that form the basis of sense perceptions and the mind that creates objects from these are five *vayus*. These are at the *prana* level of sensation and action that governs all functions of the corporeal body. Prana has no exact translation but can loosely be thought of as 'breath', though not the physical breath, and also 'vital force', so long as it is remembered that *prana* does not depend on anything physical as, like the five elements, it precedes all gross objects.[101]

In meditation practice we speak of circulating the (physical) breath in a rhythmic way at the same time associating this with *prana*, a subtler force even than the elements. This is important to understand, because *prana* is the vital link between the domain of sensation and actions and the mind itself, called *manas* (inward sense), which creates objects. The mind creates all these objects from memory, imagination, senses and recollection.

Yet what then is the 'mind' if it is more than the thoughts or objects it creates? We must as always look to the higher principle. Above the realm of the mind (*manas*) are five *tanmatras*, the essential roots of the elements. The *tanmatras* cannot be perceived by the mind and senses and so are called imperceptible; yet they can be known truly through *dhyana* meditation upon an object. It is worth repeating something that has been said previously, which is that the *jivatma*, which is the centre of the individual self and its five *tanmatras*, can be likened to the Egyptian star, sometimes called 'Hand of Orion'.[102] The star has five radials and in the centre is a point within a circle. The *ahankara* or 'ego' (which is rather imprecise and is a very general term) is composed of the *jivatma* and the five *tanmatras*, which all together constitute what is called the I-sense. In the ordinary case this I-sense, which is but a reflection of the Atma, is much clouded and darkened by the mind and its sense perceptions, which are mistaken for the Self. When the sense impressions have been stilled by yoga, so these no longer modify the mind, then what remains is called the pure I-sense.

---

[101] The five *vayus*—not to be confused with the air element of the same name—are the principle of the vital functions of aspiration, inspiration, expiration, circulating blood and digesting food.
[102] See 'The Star of Man', p. 178 *Way of Knowledge*.

There is an instruction in our previous works to 'worship the star' so that the light of Nuit (the Egyptian equivalent of Mahadevi Shakti) is poured down upon us. This is not of course a prescription for 'self worship'. Above the *jivatma* and I-sense in the natural order of things is the supra-human, non-individual *boddhi* that reflects the ray of pure knowledge into the mirror of the unclouded individual consciousness. The ray does not stop there in reality but below the I-sense it is modified by the mind and senses and is dark as the night compared to what is above and beyond. That is why all productions of the mind, including the reason, are ignorance when seen as relative even to the pure I-sense, let alone the immutable Atma Self, the source that is pure Knowledge by its very nature.

The *boddhi*, sometimes called the higher intellect or spiritual intuition—though that must not be mistaken for reasoning mind or the conventional notion of intuition as depending from the senses—is cognate with all ideals of the Shakti Devi in ancient traditions.[103] Gods and angels are all called *devas* (or *devis*) in Hinduism, while in Egypt all such were called Neteru, 'principles', which is the most exact and metaphysical term of all.

However inadequate may be the terms we use for the symbols of ancient civilisations that were far superior in intellect to our very degraded one, no one can attain spiritual knowledge and realisation if they insist on limiting their self by imagining they are an atheist or an agnostic. Certainly there are very many that would disagree with that, whether with a good measure of anger and ferocity or with contemptuous silence, but it happens to be true.

Unreserved devotion to God or to Shakti is an indispensible requirement of the path of knowledge and yoga, and it must also be said, as there is so much falsehood around this, that the path of knowledge as defined in Sanskrit (*jnana*) is not in any way opposed to that of *bhakti* or devotion. Likewise, rites and rituals (*karma* yoga) are a support to devotion and knowledge, unless they should be done without theoretical knowledge and meditation, in which case they amount to ignorance.

---

[103] We would not be wrong to use the term 'Goddess', although that tends to place an anthropomorphic notion of God in the minds of those with a modern mentality. It also has certain New Age connotations that we wish to avoid; for these reasons the word is used sparingly in the present book.

Yoga of the Mind

To understand the following it is necessary to know something of the ancient science of the mind. In particular, with regard to how the mind forms objects of attachment that are a major obstruction to yoga even taking place in the real sense of the word. The *boddhi* or higher intellect has its proper or natural abode entirely outside of and beyond the human individuality and ego self. It is as a ray of light from the Sun that is reflected downward into the waters of the mind. The mind, with its faculties such as thought (cognition), memory and feelings produced by the elemental composition of the universe it imagines existing as separate from itself, creates or re-creates a world based on sensory impressions. This is essentially an illusion. However, it is a very compelling illusion not least because all these faculties of the mind and its supporting senses—sound, touch, light, taste and smell—awaken desire and a will to take action based upon such desire. The strength of such desire and will can be so great that it amounts to a kind of false concentration, for we must remember in this that the concentration of the mind is essential to yoga, though it is the means, and not the yoga itself. As we shall see later, the false kind of concentration, that does not involve any control of thought, is nothing but a perpetuation of the state of delusion common to most men.

It is needful to elaborate further on these objects created by the mind that are mistaken for the real, for in that the self that perceives such objects is also mistaken for the real Self (Atma). When we see a tree or a cat, we think we know what it is. But that knowledge is based on the faculty of memory or recollection, the impressions gained from past experience. We perceive a tree or a cat but in fact we only perceive an illusion created by the mind and senses. Now a sceptic, that has never known *samadhi*, might then say: 'What you are telling me is false. I see a cat over there. I can call the cat and it will come to me and sit on my lap and purr. I know this cat is perfectly as real as you or I, but you are telling me that the cat is an illusion. What sort of fool do you take me for?' The reply is as follows: Firstly, we did not say that the cat is an illusion! What we said was that your idea of knowing the cat from your mind and senses is an illusion. Nothing that exists can be said not to exist. And anything that does not exist truly does not exist, never did and never will. 'What is here is there also (within Atma, the Real), and what is not here is not there either.' The whole world also is not an illusion; only the way we perceive it forms an illusion, a superimposition upon the Real.

Wisdom teaches us that through concentration of the mind upon an object and entering into the meditative state (*dhyana*) it is possible to gain the true and total knowledge of that thing. It is the *boddhi*, mentioned earlier, that is able to discriminate between what is real and what is not real. But that which is produced by the mind and senses is a modification of the *boddhi*, and in relation to the Real (Atma) it is of the nature of illusion. This science can be explained and understood perfectly through ordinary rational means—there is nothing 'mystical' about any of it—but to know it for real one has to practice yoga through control of mind and concentration.

We can now move on to discuss some of the things that make it hard or even impossible for some people to enter into true yoga states and gain real and lasting knowledge. Pursuing the objects of desire, as already described, creates habits of the mind, through the mental impressions. In Sanskrit these are called *samskaras*. These pile up like hills and mounds, so we are not able to see beyond them. They are also like clouds that hide the sun. The sun is still there but we cannot see it when clouds hide it. We might even see the hill that is in front of us and mistake it for the horizon. We might even see the clouds and mistake them for the sun. This is in fact the usual condition of the human mind, and which the sages call delusion.

Because of this habitual tendency, which Shankara often describes as being like seeing a rope that is in half darkness and mistakenly believing it to be a snake instead of a rope, even some of those who take up a practice of yoga will never reach the goal of realisation. It was said in fact, many centuries ago now, that even those men that will worship the gods (*devas*), and which is considered to be a lesser path than that of true knowledge of the Self, are one in a thousand. Most will worship gross objects and unworthy things, things that pass and are merely temporary and illusionary, such as wealth and property. Even the pursuit of happiness itself leads to delusion and misery, so long as happiness is sought for in such worthless objects. So a person that becomes a practitioner of yoga, and that still hankers after all those things that most men will covet, will not attain spiritual realisation and in all probability will not even attain the knowledge of gods, *devas* or angels, because those things they desire belong to the domain of devils or *asuras* and are controlled by them.

Having said this, we would wish to place some distance between ourselves and those who profess to teach about this subject and that would have it that real knowledge is an impossibility. If a person has no direct experience of what they are teaching then they are not in any way qualified to teach it. It is as 'the blind leading the blind'. It is also worth repeating that one thing that totally disqualifies a person from this knowledge is when the person declares they are either an atheist or an agnostic. In that case, it is a simple matter of self-exclusion.

Such practices involving concentration of the mind are aimed at the eventual restraint of the mind to a single object and no other, which is called 'one-pointed' concentration. At first this might be done for a short time but gradually the duration is increased so that more strength is gained. The beginner and even the person that has done a practice for some time will suffer breaks in concentration, some more serious than others. The worst kind of break comes from an object of mind that has nothing at all to do with the meditation subject, and that is some ordinary worry or anxiety or fear, or a recollection of something done earlier in the day, or of a conversation one was having and so forth. When a break in concentration or a lapse into ordinary thought is related to the subject in some clear way it is not so bad, and that is why there is a legitimate practice for beginners that involves a kind of 'thinking around the subject', so that related thoughts are allowed and all else disallowed.[104] With real meditation (*dhyana*) however, the thought and sense perceptions are restrained, and that includes even the subtle sense perceptions—for the physical senses have their subtle or non-material counterpart. The subtle senses are yet still products of the mind and its inward sense (*manas*). When there is no longer a subject and an object, a knower and a thing known, then one of the degrees of *samadhi* has been entered, at least temporarily.[105]

With the meditation on an object, whether gross or subtle (*savitarka* or *savichara*), silencing of the habitual mental chatter must still be observed for some length of time before any real knowledge of the object can be gained. The real knowledge of a thing comes about when the *boddhi* (higher intellect) has made it luminous. However, this must not be mistaken for the modifications created by the mind, inward sense and the other faculties including the gross and the subtle senses.

---

[104] In our textbooks this practice is called the *Logos* method.
[105] See 'The Way to Samadhi'.

Mental distractions in the yoga practice itself should lessen with persistence and regularity. However, these only come about at all because the habitual state of mind is dominant at all times, throughout the waking and dreaming states. This means that while it might be possible to concentrate the mind for a short period of time, the habitual mode of thought is in the background and distracting or anti-yogic objects of thought will quickly come to the surface as soon as an opportunity arises, or the concentration is relaxed. Not being able to concentrate at all means we are not practicing indifference to the ordinary things that go on and are continually engrossed in worthless objects. Discrimination has to be done constantly, to remember the real and never forget the world is not the Self (Atma), let alone the virtual constructs of the empty thoughts and desires of other people, or such purely modern inventions as films, television and the like. The body is not the Self, the mind is not the Self, the thoughts and emotions are not the Self. When everything is stripped away only the Self remains.

> The winds of the world are like waves and surges of water. The trick is to keep still and let the waves pass. They will still do exactly what they do without us needing to do anything at all.

It is needful to understand the five states of mind. The practice goes nowhere and is not yoga as such unless it is supported by discrimination the whole of the rest of the time, not just in one hour in the day. This is very hard to do for most people. Each must do the practice as according to their ability. As one practices discrimination the latent impressions retained by the mind that lead the soul away from union are gradually dissolved. The gates of knowledge are opened. One begins to realise that nothing has been lost of any worth but a lot of imbecilic nonsense, and indeed, something of real and lasting value is being gained.

There are different kinds of concentration and some of these are anti-yogic (as in the case of the pursuit of worthless objects). There are five mental states, of which two are yogic and three are non-yogic. For the sake of clarity we will list them here from the highest to the lowest states.

1. Arrested: Through long practice the thought processes have been arrested. All thoughts are shut out of the mind for a long time. Liberation (*moksha*) can come about through this, the final or last state of mind. In that case, this is permanent; it is not here today and gone tomorrow.

2. One-pointed: The concentration on an object (such as devotion to God) has become a habit of the mind so that the idea continues even in dream. This concentration leads towards real Samadhi. While the yogin may still experience some evil thought coming into the mind, whether because it is irresistible or has come about in some way unconsciously, or unwilled, the yogin is not in any way overpowered by the thought. He remains indifferent.

3. Distracted: While the lowest two states typify a person that is totally unable to gain knowledge of any subtle or super-sensorial things, the state called Distraction is very common with those who are spiritually-minded enough to do a practice and study the right materials for a long time. The distracted person is able to concentrate sometimes and so gain temporary knowledge, but it is soon emptied away in the never-ending sea of things that cause the distracted state of mind. The knowledge melts away, there is no firm hold gained. This can go on and on, fluctuating from Distraction sometimes to Stupefaction (see below) and back again.

4. Stupefied: This is the habitual or ordinary mode for most persons. It is allied to infatuation. The person has no control of mind or will and follows one object after another. Each fixation is temporary and is soon replaced by another, equally delusionary. The reason it is such a common state for many persons is that it can manifest in what might seem as worthy objects, for example concern over family, property, wealth, job of work and so forth. While this is not as bad as the next and lowest, it can easily slip down into that and precisely because of the concentration on objects of delusion—a sort of false concentration or anti-yoga—it is difficult to rise up from this.

5. Restless: Of the last three non-yogic states, this one is the worst. It is more than that word implies because there is a concentration on wholly negative things belonging to the demonic realms, such as greed, envy, pride, malice, anger, impatience, harmful thoughts and so forth.

Through self-enquiry we must identify which of these states is our 'normal' or habitual mode. Unless one is a master of yoga then it will be one of the last three. The habitual state of mind determines whether real and effective yoga and knowledge is possible. All of these states involve a mixture of the Gunas. The lowest two correspond to *tamas* and *rajas*, mostly *tamas*, which induces torpor or inertia. The Distracted state owes mostly to *rajas*, which impels to action.

None of these last three states are conducive to yoga or *samadhi*, which is the aim of yoga and that requires one-pointed concentration for long duration of time. The *sattvic* state with the real yogin is a permanent condition that owes to long practice of discipline and exertion of will, fixed and unalterable.

It should be added that we are nearing the end of the final phase of the Kali Yuga or Age of Darkness. At this time, and until the end, the general condition of humanity corresponds to the lowest states of mind, dominated by *rajas* and *tamas*. So long as we have to deal with the worldly in any way, through work or family life, as in the case of a householder for example, then we are susceptible to all three of the non-yogic states to some extent. That is why in the Age of Kali Yuga traditional wisdom has it that the tantras are very efficacious. The word 'tantra' has the literal meaning of 'weaving' and is sometimes taken to indicate rituals and devotional practices. Ritual and even magick, if that is understood to be not different from theurgy in its aim, can act as a support to yoga and to real and effective initiation. We need all the help we can get if we inhabit a world that is covertly or even openly opposed to the 'practice of God'. The more we inhabit that world, the more we need the assistance of ritual and devotion when away from the public eye. Having said that, it is too easy to play a game of discrimination where other people are concerned. None of that is any use at all in furthering yoga. To use discrimination with serious intent—and there is no other way to gain real and lasting knowledge—we have to apply it to ourselves, rigorously and at all times. When very distracted it is helpful to repeat the mantram that was given by the teacher. When concentration on a single super-sensible idea-object is even followed through in the dreaming state, then some measure of success is being gained.

It can help the householder a great deal to take a few days or a week off from work and mundane duties every so often so as to carry out a full practice, because a person with such responsibilities cannot otherwise do a full practice and must use what time they have to read, study, contemplate and do the rituals and the meditation. Ramakrishna gave some very pertinent advice on meditation to a devotee in response to questions on how to know God and how to live in the world at the same time, as for most of us it is the case:

> If you apply your mind to meditation on the Lord in solitude and silence, you will acquire dispassion, knowledge and devotion to the Lord. But if you give your mind to worldly thoughts, it becomes degraded. In the world, the only thoughts are of lust and greed. The world may be likened to water and the mind to milk. If you pour milk into water, they mingle, and the pure milk can no longer be found. But if you first curdle the milk and churn the curd into butter, you can put it into water and it will float. So you must first practise spiritual disciplines and obtain the butter of knowledge and devotion. This cannot be contaminated by the water of the world. It will float, as it were.[106]

Ramakrishna repeatedly advised that those who have to live in the world must practice as stated above and also go into solitude now and again. When the time is right, one may be released from worldly duties. Also, that we should refrain from worrying about this.

The practice involves a subject and an object. The subject is the knower. The object is what is being meditated on. As yoga practice (not yoga as such) begins with the meditation on an object, it will be useful to mention what kind of objects or symbols are most suitable for this. The best is a form of God or the Shakti. Even the Sanskrit Aum (or Om) is a name of God, and so a mantram or sound can also be used. While mantra yoga is a practice in itself, it can effectively be used in combination with other forms of worship—'worship' here is taken to mean the use of any form, image or symbol of deity. Whatever the object of meditation, it is best if it is one that arouses a sense of bliss or happiness in the practitioner, for this helps the practice, which is very difficult at the outset. In a previous work a Hermetic symbol was given as an example, that of the Cross and Triangle of the Golden Dawn, as one familiar with our students.[107] Through the faculty of recollection such a symbol has many associations. The red cross of sacrifice bringing down the white triangle of spiritual light amidst the darkness of the world will for some evoke a sense of nobility, beauty, awe and reverence. One is reminded of the ascent and descent of the *avatara*.

For others, however, such a symbol may not evoke such majestic feelings. It might seem like a work of austerity concentrating the mind on what to them is no more than any comparable geometric symbolism such as was learned in school textbooks. That is certainly a difficulty that besets many aspirants today, for the education we have all received is anti-metaphysical in its very nature:

---

[106] *Ramakrishna and his Disciples*, Christopher Isherwood.
[107] 'Considerations on Yoga Practice', *Way of Knowledge*.

We learn from an early age that gods, angels and such-like are no more than figments of the imagination. At best, we might learn that such things only have a 'psychological' value, and may be called 'archetypes', for example, that have an abode in the 'subconscious' or some sort of collective psychic realm. Psychology reaches no further than the level of the human psyche, no matter what else some of its advocates claim. Some persons are more resilient than others when it comes to resisting the influence of false, anti-initiatic propaganda. Most succumb to it absolutely.[108]

It may be expedient then to choose an object for the meditation that does inspire at least an ordinary bliss or rapture. If Egyptian, alchemical or Hermetic symbolism fails to move the practitioner in the right direction, and the form of a God or Devi still seems an abstraction of mind, or something that seems unnatural, then we may wonder why the person is doing such a practice at all!

Some further remarks will be helpful regarding the five mental states. Quite often those that have passed through neo-spiritualist or occult training will over-estimate the reach of their development when it comes to yoga. We could count many instances of persons that have contacted us and that have reached quite stupendously 'high grades' in organisations that claim to be initiatic. It is clear enough to us when these possess no real knowledge of anything whatsoever, even if that is not clear to the individuals in question, who truly believe they have advanced far beyond the level of any ordinary human. Unfortunately, we live in times when almost all occult organisations can only offer a pseudo-initiation, or even worse, the persons that manage the organisations are anti-initiatic in their whole disposition.

---

[108] The coronation of the British monarchs involves very ancient primordial symbolism, of which foremost is the crown, the sceptre and the orb. These symbolise the unity of the sacerdotal authority and the temporal power, so that traditional knowledge is renewed, upheld and maintained. The king or the queen is privately anointed with holy (consecrated) oil, such as is described in the book of Exodus, an ancient Egyptian formula. Even in very recent times, the king and the bishops still know what they are doing, but to most persons outside of that narrow circle both the sacraments and the symbolism mean absolutely nothing. If they pay any attention to it at all, they will only wonder at the monetary value in the gold and jewels and that may well provoke in them *tamasic* thoughts of envy, resentment, malice and so forth. And that is because, unlike any true king, they ignobly covet such treasures for their price alone and see no further.

While we must be encouraging and positive to our students regarding the practice, we must also be realistic. It is harmful for a person to have ideas of their 'attainment' that are blown out of all proportion and helped, perhaps, by years spent in practices that amount to a form of self-hypnosis. Very often, and as has been proved by those many cases of persons with 'high grades' contacting us, the individuals will never pass beyond the limitations of their personal delusion.

The Arrested state is permanent and final. It is more or less the end of the road from our point of view. A person that knows the Arrested state is of the order of a great sage like Sri Ramakrishna or Shankaracharya himself. It involves total world renunciation. Possibly, such a person might not even be in a human body. They might be a *bodhisattva* or of a supra-human order. If they held a degree in a Hermetic Order it would be that of Ipsissimus 10=1. No one could teach them anything at all as they would already have passed beyond the realm of Total Universal Knowledge.

It is doubtful if there is anyone in the world today that is in the permanent Arrested state, and if there is then we can only suppose they might be hidden in a cave in the Himalayas or in some part of a desert not yet frequented by helicopters and hang-glider adventurers. Such a master will not be giving talks in a room upstairs of a shop that sells *saris* in Delhi. An adept of that order was rare even at the time when Patañjali wrote down the Aphorisms, estimated to have been some two thousand years ago. A century ago or more at the time of Ramakrishna hardly anyone in India had even seen a *sadhu* in the deep Samadhi that Ramakrishna habitually entered. People travelled hundred of miles on foot, by boat or horse and carriage simply to see him.

The One-pointed state, in the present context, is permanent and one would need to be a master of yoga such as must be rare in our world today. It does not involve thought at all, or thinking about things. The mentality is left behind with the pure I-sense. How much more so then with the states beyond that? With these first two, which are to be considered as states of being and not merely meditation results, the yogin is entirely unmoved by phenomena.

Although the five states are called 'mental' states, in reality the first two have nothing to do with the human mentality, which comes somewhat below the I-sense in the scheme of things to the extent there might as well be a sort of abyss between them. An analogy could be made where the mentality is like a ladder by which real yoga *samadhi* can be reached but the ladder disappears once the yoga state is entered truly. In the case of Arrested, it disappears forever.

Most of us occupy the Distracted state for a lot of the time in waking and dreaming and we can slip down into the lower hell worlds sometimes unless we practice constant vigilance. We can pass upwards and get glimpses of the one-pointed concentration in yoga practice and we can even prolong that, or otherwise prolongation can take place in some rare and exceptional way. But we cannot be in that state all of the time and manage the kind of things we have to manage if we have anything to do with the world or the worldly at all. There are Three Parts of Practice:

Ritual	sacrifice (in the Vedic sense)
Meditation	concentration of mind
Discrimination	intellective process

Ritual involves sacrifice to the Gods. It is indispensible to devotion (*bhakti*). 'Sacrifice' here is meant in the etymological (and original) sense of the word. It has nothing to do with killing things as such. The Vedic sense of sacrifice is anything that is 'sent up', as it were, to heaven. For example, the flames of a fire or a candle go upward, as does the smoke of incense. The writing of the Vedas was considered to be a form of sacrifice in itself. When a thing is revealed it is also concealed or 're-veiled', covered. Thus to put a truth that is really indescribable in language or symbolism is to sacrifice or give up the direct knowledge that preceded it, once common to all. Yet it was necessary, owing to the onset of the Age of Kali Yuga, to write the knowledge down otherwise it would have been forgotten forever.

The practice of meditation, involving concentration of mind, is not separate from discrimination as without discrimination the mind is clouded, impure. We must identify each thought as it arises before it drags us along with it like a wild horse, as we shall see later in the section on yoga concentration. This must be done not only during a meditation practice for one hour in the day but also as a constant vigilance, or as frequently as we can afford given the limits of our conditions.

Each thought will be identified as owing to one of the five *vrittis* or types of cognition. They are often a combination but can be traced to one *vritti* that predominates. One must think, is it a true cognition or a false cognition? Is it recollection? And if so, is the recollection based on what was once a true cognition or was it false or imaginary to start with? That way the *samskaras* or retained mental impressions, and the harmful *kléshas* or 'afflictions' can gradually be eliminated. It takes much patience and continuous, uninterrupted practice. According to the *Mandukya Upanishad*,

> When the wise man exerts himself in this way, his soul reaches the abode of Brahma.

Love, Devotion and Surrender

The work requires strong mental, moral and physical discipline. The practice must include devotion, which is more than an imagined dedication to some vague ideal. Devotion, if we are really serious about this, requires reverence, faith, discipline, self-control and austerity. If these qualities are missing then the student can learn nothing. If a practice is started half-heartedly, the *sadhaka* is soon overwhelmed by the afflictions (*kleshas*) and the mental fluctuations that form part of 'ordinary life' of any person. But worse than that, he imagines that these ordinary obstacles to the path are something more than what they are. A teacher must select his students carefully, which, if he is qualified in the inner sense of what that means, he is able to do. In the same way, once he is satisfied that the *chela* is ready to go from theory to practice, he is able to determine through the powers invested in him exactly what is suitable for that person—there is no 'one size fits all' when it comes to yoga.

When the practice is continued for a long time without a break, with all the aforementioned qualities present in the practitioner, then it is said that the 'foundation is made firm'. That is to say, the mind is no longer disturbed by its own fluctuations, caused by the latent impressions (*samskaras*).

The controlled state of the *boddhi* in the yoga state of Nirvikalpa Samadhi, 'true knowledge free from falsehood', is attained when there is indifference to all objects of desire; not only such common things as what Sri Ramakrishna liked to term 'woman and gold' but also the desire to attain immortality or the realm of gods and angels, and so forth. Through the special knowledge that is only gained by discrimination one is eventually freed from the influence of such things. They continue to exist but one is no longer moved by them. We may then pass beyond good and evil, being perfectly indifferent to these.[109] According to the *Katha Upanishad*,

---

[109] The Western distortions of this doctrine include some very strange notions, formed to suit the perverse dispositions of some so-called authorities. The passing beyond good and evil, for example, is sometimes used as an excuse to do evil! That arises from impure attachment to objects and only brings yet more suffering into the world—suffering that even continues beyond the human scale, and that carries the afflicted person to lower states of being than the human.

The wise, knowing of the eternal bliss, do not look for the immutable in ephemeral things.

The practice of discrimination teaches us that willingly engaging with the objects of the mind leads only to suffering. However, the way to such total non-attachment as has been described here is a gradual process. When the practices are properly and methodically done, even the *savitarka samadhi* on a gross object already implies a partial spirit of renunciation, and if the practice is continued then eventually there is no longer any desire for sense objects at all. Once such control is no longer needed, the *sadhaka* becomes a real yogin, an adept.[110] Not only worldly things but also super-mundane things do not move him in any way. He is indifferent to the things of the world. At the further reaches, a yogin with the knowledge of *purusha* (or Atma), the supreme principle, is thus indifferent to manifest and unmanifest states of the three Gunas. When the Arrested state is unbroken, liberation (*moksha*) ensues. Vyasa has marked a subtle distinction between those who rid themselves of worldly attachments but who meditate on the 'void' or unmanifest as the highest principle, such as Buddhists. Unknowing of the difference between the *boddhi* and *purusha*, these have incomplete knowledge and are merged in the undifferentiated *prakriti*. From this rather subtle *avidya*, these suffer rebirth, which, as we have explained elsewhere has nothing to do with 'reincarnationism'.[111] When there is complete separation from the three Gunas and their mutations or modifications, the highest knowledge is possible, and liberation (*kaivalya*), with total cessation of mind, is possible.

Various practices act as a support to yoga. One should remember at all times that the goal is to become one-pointed, which means escaping from the three non-yogic states of Distracted, Stupefied and Restless. The one-pointed state alone leads towards constant and permanent awareness of the I-Self (as Atma), the goal of *jnana* yoga. Subsidiary practices may include mantras, yantras and worship or devotion (*bhakti*). In all these one must practice discrimination, an attribute of the *boddhi* and therefore of the Shakti, to identify the distractions and realise their falsity. From here we begin to discriminate the whole time and not only in the hour or so that we are doing a yoga practice. Discrimination is born of the love of truth, which is also the attribute of the Shakti.

---

[110] Neo-spiritualist organisations use the word 'adept' when that is only descriptive of ordinary and sometimes even quite inferior states of mind.
[111] See 'Karma and Sin', p. 142, *Way of Knowledge*.

Mantras usually consist of a single word or a short phrase, which is repeated in meditation or at any time when feeling distracted. The best mantra is that given by the teacher, who will give instructions on how to pronounce it. The mantra is usually taken from a sacred text; there are many of them in the *Upanishads* for example. It is not a word that is merely made up or invented. The mantra may be sounded aloud but it is best done silently. Sometimes it is vibrated on the in-breath and out-breath rhythmically for a short time until there is no need and one enters into silent meditation. When the mantra is repeated for a long time, it can quite easily fade into the background so that it is possible to have other thoughts or be talking to someone and the mantra is still sounding. While this can be helpful if in a very distracted state of mind or ill, it is not yoga to do it like that. The yogic use of the mantra involves concentration on the mantra and nothing else; one must first meditate on the meaning of each word. After a time, the mind is shaped into the sound and meaning until there is no difference between the I-sense awareness and the object of meditation. That is the beginning of success with the mantra.

The three-fold word *sat-chit-ananda* is one example of a phrase that can be used for such a mantra. This needs to be properly understood. The word *chit* is sometimes used in the lower sense (*chitta*), which is restricted to that of the individual mentality and thought, which is part of the formal level of manifestation. One must know that in the universal sense, *chit* is the total consciousness of the I-Self (Atma) and its own object, *ananda* or beatitude, usually translated as 'bliss', though again that must not be confused with the ordinary use of that word as pertaining to the individual experience. The object, as *ananda*, is identical with the subject, which is *sat* or pure being. As according to René Guénon, the three are one Being that knows Itself by Itself:

> Thus these three, Sat, Chit, and Ananda ... are but one single and identical entity, and this 'one' is Atma, considered outside and beyond all the particular conditions which determine each of its various states of manifestation.[112]

---

[112] *Man and His Becoming According to the Vedānta*, pp. 98–99. In footnote 7, Guénon notes that in Arabic the three terms have an equivalent in Intelligence (*Al-aqlu*), the Intelligent (*Al-aqil*) and the Intelligible (*Al-maqul*). The first is universal consciousness, the second is its subject and the third its object.

A *yantra* is a visual image. This can be a geometric form such as the well-known Sri Yantra, or a Hermetic or alchemical symbolism, an Egyptian hieroglyph and so forth. It can also be an image of a *deva* or of the Shakti, for example. The mind is concentrated wholly on the image and all thought and other impressions restrained as in *dharana*. The mind is shaped by the object it perceives. After a while, there is no difference between the seer and the thing that is seen. One must also meditate on this fact and understand it. That is the beginning of success with the yantra.

Devotional practices are generally called *bhakti* but one must not think that *bhakti* yoga is separate from *jnana* yoga or that there is no relation between them. The goal remains ever one and the same. The journey of the aspiring yogin is a gradual deepening of meditation so that the various yogic states are acquired. Through the journey, the veils of ignorance are peeled away. From the point of view of the Shakta, the veils of ignorance as well as all states of mind, yogic and non-yogic, belong to Mahadevi Shakti.

Reciting hymns to the Goddess, including her oracles or otherwise composed invocations, forms an essential part of devotion. Mahadevi Shakti has appeared in her Egyptian form as Isis to her devout followers in relatively recent times as well as two thousand years ago or more, as is captured in the Gnostic scripture 'Thunder Perfect Mind', which begins,

> I was sent forth from Mystery,
> And I will come to them that reflect upon me,
> For those that seek me, shall find me.
> Behold me, ye who reflect upon me,
> And listen to me, ye that have ears to hear!
> Ye who have waited for me, take me to yourselves,
> And do not banish me from your sight.
> Do not say hateful things of me, do not hear them spoken.
> Do not be ignorant of me anywhere or at any time.
> Be vigilant! Do not forget me.

Such scriptures can be kept close to one's heart.[113] Some of these, including that quoted above, convey beauty, truth and love to the aspirant as well as perfect yoga instruction. Virtues such as faith, acceptance of the path, obedience to the path and calmness and surrender to God are essential.

---

[113] See 'Thunder Perfect Gnosis' pp. 73–90.

Real *samadhi* is union with God or Shakti, and we must always remember that is no small thing. Men have given their whole lives in service to God and yet have never touched on the knowledge of the real Self (Atma). Others, that obtained full knowledge, did so after spending years of their lives alone in mountain caves. Samadhi is not a sudden 'flash of enlightenment' that comes and soon passes so the person remains as they were before. It means a total and permanent change in the state of the being. An aspirant has to put in the work, but *samadhi* happens by the grace of God, for it belongs to God (or Shakti). Clearly, realisation is not contained solely within the daily practice. So long as we remain attached to worldly things, desiring what the world can offer, and are still concerned by these things, then the degree or gradation of *samadhi* will only be as much as we can bear; any more than that can be injurious to the being.

Both faith (*saradha*) and the practice of recollection (*smrti*) are integral to devotion and are not truly separate. Only a tranquil mind has faith; from faith comes forth tranquility and knowledge. This includes a certain attitude of reverence. By all this we can infer that the Sanskrit word *saradha* means more than the translated word suggests, especially as the conventional meaning of faith is confused with belief in a non-existing thing. Saradha implies a kind of intuitive knowledge; yet the practice is an indispensible part of it; without practice there is no faith. From faith comes increased devotion and a special kind of strength called *virya*.[114] According to Vyasa, the *virya* brings with it the discriminative knowledge that is desired by the seeker. One should note that doubt is an affliction and where there is doubt there is no *virya* and no faith. While these are needed at the beginning of yoga practice, they are also needed for the attainment of the ultimate goal of *kaivalya* liberation. When the goal is liberation then it is only discriminative knowledge that is desired—for nothing else, no other desire for any other object, can bring *kaivalya*.

Recollection is foremost and is a practice (*sadhana*) in itself. One recollects what it was like meditating on an object, and this in turn increases the power and range of the memory. That is why in this day and age written records are kept on the practice, though many fail to understand the need for it. Such is the disorder and confusion of the kind of lives we lead now that nothing can be effectively retained otherwise.

---

[114] Virya has no direct translation in a modern language but is given as 'energy, fortitude and stamina'. It is the special energy needed so that devotion to practice becomes stronger than all obstacles and afflictions arising fron 'ordinary life' and sensorial perception.

Recollection is practiced on God (or Shakti), which is primarily the identification with the name of God, such as AUM. God is to be understood as free of all limitations, even if known through various attributes. To begin with there is a need for verbal assistance, for otherwise the practice of God cannot even be started. AUM is particularly efficacious, whether as the single syllable or as part of a more complex and descriptive mantram. The practice of God, the continuous recollection of God, and the knowledge of God are really all one and the same thing.

The formation of a concept of God as outside the self is an essential beginning part, and this may involve variously qualities such as colour, sound, light and so forth. Once we start to think that God is one with the cogniser, since all these perceptions are made by our instruments of perception, then we move towards the realisation of the pure I-sense, and further, that there is no difference in reality between this God and the I-sense, the knower.

One begins by imagining that God is within a shrine within the heart, the innermost self. This is posited as a sort of 'void' or cavity within the heart. The 'heart' as it is intended in countless sacred texts, and as we mean it here, is not of course something that can be anatomically located. It is more that the sense of the knower, the I-sense, is apparently there in the middle of the chest. It is where one feels that the ego resides, a kind of centre that is not really a place in itself but in so far as the ego awareness is perceived as somewhere in the body, then it seems to be there and not in the head. In fact, when the mental fluctuations are stopped, this feeling of the I-sense in the heart is very strong, and so it is said sometimes that the ego is 'sent down into the heart' and hidden away there, so to speak.

This practice can take one very far indeed. Later, once the I-sense is established firmly through long practice, that awareness can be extended or followed upwards to the head and even beyond the crown, but at that stage it is realised that there is not any difference in reality—the self in the 'heart' and the self in the 'head' are one consciousness and one knower.

Now this practice of placing an image of God in the heart is more suitable for some persons than others—not all practices are there for everyone to do. It is a common mistake made by students who rely more on books than an actual teacher, and even more so if they lack a teacher altogether, to imagine that when a whole range of practices are given in writing, some simple and some very complex, it is meant that everyone should do all of them.

When this practice is done the figure of God should be luminous, as though that luminosity depended from it at source, like the sun. This is naturally regarded with reverence, and a sense of 'holiness'. The person who cannot achieve that might as well not be doing such a practice, although there is something to be said for 'working at it' so long as the feeling is latent.

Next, one imagines that as the figure is within the self then the self is also within that figure, and that it is all and everything. Success comes about when the concentration is fully engrossed in this for a length of time, without any interruption from external means or other thoughts. This induces calmness, otherwise the practice is not being done correctly, and that tranquility in turn leads to increased faith, devotion, reverence, strength, endurance and knowledge. The person contemplates that his own I-sense, his whole self, is within the God as the God is within his heart. In this way, the mind of the practitioner is merged with the mind of God. According to the *Mundaka Upanishad*,

> Brahma or the God within the heart is the target; the sacred syllable AUM is the bow and the ego self is the arrow fired from it. When the mind is made pure and one [i.e. undistracted] then the arrow hits the mark and the self is completely merged in Brahma.

This practice leads to bliss (*ananda*), which is meditation without the need for words or images as a support. One meditates on the blissful feeling alone. When that sense of bliss is transcended then one moves toward the pure I-sense. It is said also that in this practice all obstacles to yoga are removed, for example sickness, afflictions, ignorance and so forth.

Even when meditating on *tattvas*, recollection of knowledge is practiced so it is retained by the mind and fixed thereby. The highest practice is the constant awareness of the difference between the Knower (as *purusha*) and the knowable (*prakriti*, or rather, its productions). This one thought is held in the mind to the exclusion of all else, and this in turn purifies the mind. The pure Consciousness (*purusha*) cannot be attained without recollection *sadhana*. When such awareness is continual, then *samprajñata* 'yoga of knowledge' ensues. The realisation of God is no other than the realisation of *purusha* as the individual Self, for the *boddhi* reflects a ray of that Sun onto the surface of the I-sense, which in fact forms the I-sense with its *tanmatras*, or taken all together, the *ahankara* (ego).

Ishvara, the Lord (or God) is in reality the pure Consciousness and so not a perceptible object. What is perceived as external to the self is the knowable, but the knower is the means of knowing and so not an object to be known except as pure Awareness. It is our own consciousness that perceives God in the self, and God rests only in Itself, which is pure Consciousness. From here comes the true Self-realisation, which comes about through the practice and knowledge of God. One must carefully note that the pure I-sense is a mode of the *boddhi* and is not *purusha* (or Atma). The concentration without an object, called *nirodha*, ensues when there is knowledge of *purusha* and no other knowledge (or object).

What follows uses descriptive *vichara* words to help, though it should be remembered that the pure I-sense and the *boddhi* are not knowable through the senses or reason. The descriptive words are *vikalpa* but helpful. When the mind is engrossed in the pure I-sense it appears like a placid sea, a waveless ocean without limit. From this reflective contemplation arises the knowledge of the knower, the 'I am'. Through this effulgent state the yogin achieves stability. Note that the higher perception is twofold as it can relate to objects or to the pure I-sense.

The knowledge of the *boddhi* comes about when contemplation is practiced on the innermost core of the heart, as previously described. According to Vyasa, the *boddhi* is in some ways comparable to *akasha* ('boundless void') and is resplendent. If this is continued for a long time then the *boddhi* may be perceived as effulgent like the sun, luminous like the moon, or like a shining jewel, for example. We must bear in mind that if we use picture images like this and see them with colour, composition and so forth, we are still at the level of sense and action (the *bhutas* and *vayus*) and not truly knowing the *boddhi*, which is even subtler than the I-sense, for it is the higher principle of the I-sense. Any image or sound must be followed back to its *vayu*, then the *tanmatra* and I-sense, in which case it is no longer an image, a sound and so forth. The effulgence as described is not light as seen with the eyes or as imagined but is 'radiant knowledge', and it is this that enables very subtle things to be perceived. When this blissful state is prolonged it is called *sattvika*.

We can now return to the practice of placing God in the shrine or inner core of the heart, as previously described. This 'cavity' or 'void' is called a lotus and it is not the *anahatha* itself but is posited as either below or within that (as according to different readings). It is also called the abode of Brahma.

We must remember that the pure I-sense is not really an object to be meditated on, as it is the instrument of cognition itself, the knower. That is why merely thinking about the *boddhi* as a luminous jewel or sun, for example, is not the knowledge of the *boddhi*. Nonetheless we can begin by meditating on an effulgence, which is described in the *Svetasvatara Upanishad* as like mist, smoke, sun, air, fire, a fire-fly, lightning, a crystal or moon.

One can then imagine that in the heart there is a limitless, uninterrupted expanse or transparent effulgence, like a sky without colour. Bliss is then gained when the self is imagined as being this expanse, so that the awareness is mingled with it. One becomes the unlimited expanse. The sense of this is radiant effulgence 'free from sorrow' (*vishoka jyotishmati*). It is not the pure I-sense but is a mode of the I-sense, as the pure I-sense is the knower and nothing else but the knower. However, a yogin can concentrate this inner light radiating from their heart upon any object and gain knowledge of it instantly.

What has been described above are ways of getting to the I-sense, but not the I-sense itself. Once proficiency in this engrossment has been gained then the next step is to meditate on the I-sense as pure awareness without an object, as the object is only a means of getting to the I-sense. In this, even the idea of space vanishes away, for even space would imply a subject (knower) and an object (the knowable) that is perceived. There is sentience but without sensorial activity.

The pure I-sense, when arrived at without any other object, is the *sa'asmita samadhi*. The I-sense is the illuminator of all objects, and not an object in itself. It is only by passing through these stages and clearly understanding the differences between them that the more advanced levels of *samprajñata* and *asamprajñata* yoga can be attained. With the latter, even the 'yoga of knowledge' is transcended, for there is no separation between the knower and the knowable.

It also needs to be mentioned here that it is difficult to get into the further states if one is not habitually very tranquil and without desire for sensory objects or the worldly things, which are illusory from the point of view of the supreme Knower, *purusha* or Atma. For this reason meditation on divine or illuminated souls such as *bodhisattvas* does much to help, for those great minds convey a sense of their pure knowledge when contact is made with them. In that way the mind becomes gradually detached from thought and desires.

When *rajas* (action) and *tamas* (dullness or inertia) are removed or put to rest, then *sattva* (enlightening) dominates in the *boddhi*, which is the highest instrument of cognition. This awareness involves total truth, without error—it is more than ordinary knowledge as it does not involve any mental process and is simultaneous. This special knowledge, not gained from words, recollection or inference, attains its fullest development in *samadhi*. That which is written in scriptures, for example, to help others, was derived from this higher knowledge by the sages of old times. This is needed in the practice, but without discrimination no real or direct knowledge can be gained, for it is not gained by reasoning or thinking.

Vigilance

Vigilance is needed at all times and indeed, the further on one gets, the subtler are the obstacles encountered. For this reason the path is described in the *Upanishads* as 'sharp as a razor's edge'. According to the Vedanta there are four obstacles to *samadhi*, and six treasures or virtues that are needed for success. Swami Nikhilananda has elaborated the obstacles in his translation of Shankaracharya's masterpiece, *Atma-Bodha*.[115] He describes how the obstacles become subtler and so even more difficult for the person that has 'detached from the world'; in other words they have had some success at yoga, but are still only 'part timers' when it comes to *samadhi*. So it is of particular interest to us as it really concerns the Savikalpa Samadhi, but seen from the point of view where that is the necessary stage to pass through before the rare attainment of Nirvikalpa Samadhi. The advice that follows then is for those that have gained a measure of success but know there is much further to go before any real mastery is attained.

The four great obstacles are as follows. We give them here starting from the gross, so that the first is that which besets the kind of beginner that will never go far unless they learn to practice self-control. The last is experienced by one that already knows some measure of *samadhi*.

1. Torpidity
2. Distraction
3. Attachment (to objects)
4. Enjoyment of Bliss (*ananda*).

With Torpidity, the aspirant has become to a certain extent detached from the world but they are far from being established in the I-Sense. They then fall into a kind of sleep or inertia, which is dominated by the *tamas* Guna. It is difficult then to make renewed efforts, and often when the aspirant does this, he soon falls into the torpid state again.

---

[115] It has been difficult to find a translation of Shankaracharya's *Atma-Bodha*, 'Way of Self-Knowledge', that can be recommended. The Swami Nikhilananda version is good but littered with modernist ideals such as 'progress' and 'evolution' that have no place in a study of the Vedanta. But for the most part, so long as we keep our guard up, the Swami is good and faithful to the spirit of Shankara and of the Vedanta.

This can go on and on for some years until the aspirant gives it up altogether, having more or less completely succumbed to the *tamasic* state. The torpid state is sometimes described by the Sanskrit term *laya*, but this must not be confused with the method of Kundalini Yoga of the same name. The word means 'dissolution' and so we must understand there is a negative dissolution that only means falling back into an undifferentiated, inert or chaotic state, and there is a positive dissolution, that is the last stage before the final liberation (*moksha*) is attained.

Again, with Distraction, the aspirant has become detached from the world to a certain extent and they may even maintain a regular practice, but they are distracted (*vikshepa*) by ideas and imaginings, or all sorts of things that have no lasting significance. They grasp for one object after another, and when each one fades back into nothingness they find another to replace it. These are sometimes called 'imbecilities of the mind'. These fleeting impressions can arise through undisciplined talk or actions, whether immediately or even as remembered from the near or distant past. Sometimes a particular kind of emotion is evoked in this way, and such can provide a considerable obstacle.

With Attachment (to objects), in similar fashion to that described above, there is an ocean of possibilities in old memories or experiences. Here, because the will has been developed further than the person who habitually falls into Distraction or Torpor, the attachments may suddenly grip the person with violence or passion. It is like a strong gust of wind tossing a boat lying at anchor on the water. The strength of such attachments is not to be underestimated, as well as the harm they can do to the possibilities of ever gaining real *samadhi*.

Finally, there is Enjoyment of Bliss, which is the subtlest of the obstacles to *samadhi*. The bliss is easily mistaken for that of *sa'ananda samadhi* but is in fact of an inferior kind, called *rasavada*, which means 'tasting' or 'enjoying'.[116] Even so, this can be experienced when the suppression of thought has been gained (*sa'ananda*) and, as comparable to aesthetic sense, it becomes a real obstruction from the point of view of Nirvikalpa Samadhi, which is beyond even the first real *samadhi* called *sa'asmita samadhi*.

---

[116] Rasa-vada, 'essence' or 'taste', plus 'wisdom' (though not in the highest sense), is sometimes used to denote alchemy.

This 'glimpse' or 'taste' is a forerunner to the true knowing of Brahma yet it becomes an obstacle, for the aspirant is unwilling to make further efforts. It is precisely this condition in which a person may experience magical visions and ecstasies. These are only secondary and temporary things, and as with the *siddhis* or 'magical powers', their only real use is as a kind of marker to progress. To seek after them is more or less fatal so far as gaining any real knowledge is concerned. As the person may for some time continue to enjoy the bliss of *savikalpa samadhi*, remaining absorbed in the enjoyment of the visions and powers, it can be a really formidable obstruction to the extent it becomes a ring-pass-knot or threshold that cannot be passed.

Sometimes the person is beset by craving from one of his sense organs, which convey sound or hearing, touch, light, taste and smell. There are some that might even be beset by craving from all five, although in that case it is much easier to recognise as the consequences could include general debauchery. When it is one sense in particular, such as light or vision, or taste, then it can be subtle enough to catch out the practitioner of *savikalpa samadhi*. To make things even worse, the person that realises this and commences a heroic battle, and wins it, can immediately be so overwhelmed with happiness that he forgets the goal of yoga completely! According to Swami Nikhilananda,

> Vedantic teachers illustrate this by the story of a man who wanted to lay hold of a treasure buried under a tree and zealously guarded day and night by a powerful dragon. As he came near the tree the dragon challenged him. A vicious and protracted battle ensued. Ultimately the dragon was destroyed. But the man, beside himself with joy at this triumph over his enemy, danced around the tree, forgetting altogether the pot of treasure.

The matter now of immediate concern is how then can we overcome these subtle and formidable obstacles to *samadhi*? We can overcome the torpid state through the study of sacred books, the discussion of sacred things—although one should never discuss God with an atheist, for example, as it will only result in harm to the aspirant, while the atheist remains untouched by any of it. One may sing or chant hymns of praise and indeed, ritual that involves invocation and the recitation of oracles is included here. The sage Ramakrishna himself recommended going on pilgrimages to holy places.

The antidote to the distracted state is patience, perseverance and the rigorous use of discrimination, which loosens the attachments and gradually dissolves away *samskaras*. This includes indifference to phenomena and dispassion. As a final resort, one may wish to recollect how past attachment to worldly objects resulted in evil and suffering.

Once control over the mind is gained through the prolonged continuation of the practice, there is protection from more distraction and attachment to objects. Regarding the enjoyment of bliss, one must not permit the mind to dwell long on temporary happiness, for that is indeed what *rasavada* is. So long as happiness is based on a subject and an object, a knower and a thing that is known, then it is transient. Eventually one must free oneself from all bliss that is merely a reflected or secondary state, and not real *samadhi*. To quote once more from Nikhilananda's translation of *Atma-Bodha*,

> All these obstacles arise owing to the failure of the mind to rest in Brahman. Once the goal is reached there is no falling back. Therefore the aspirant should not relax his efforts until the Ideal is realised. With sincerity and zeal, earnestness and perseverance, patience and love for the Ideal, he ultimately overcomes all obstacles, great and small, through the grace of God and the blessings of his guru. He enjoys the bliss of *nirvikalpa samadhi*.[117]

The Six Treasures or Virtues (Shatsampatti) are as follows:

1. Calmness (*sama*)
2. Self-control (*dama*)
3. Self-settledness (*uparati*)
4. Forbearance (*titiksha*)
5. Concentration (*samadhana*)
6. Faith (*saradha*)

When the mind has been detached from all sense objects, knowing their defects, and rests in Brahma, then Calmness comes about. Hence the word for this, *sama*, is the root of *samadhi* itself.

---

[117] Quotations are from *Self-Knowledge (Atma-Bodha)*, translated from the Sanskrit with Notes, Comments, and Introduction by Swami Nikhilananda [Ramakrishna-Vivekananda Centre, New York].

By 'resting in Brahma' is not meant necessarily the ultimate goal but that the aspirant is a true devotee of the path, and only wants to hear about Brahma from a teacher or from reading the scriptures, hymns and oracles. He wants to discuss and reason only about Brahma, or the goal, and to meditate on their meaning. The student must then cultivate calmness, from which comes peace of mind. The Vedanta has it that such a person is like a fire of blazing charcoal once the wood has been consumed. There is no smoke, no noise. Thus, we need to be wary of having strong convictions, because while we obviously need these to even get started at all, when our conviction is mixed with passions, and seeks outward expression, it works against us and becomes an obstacle.

Self-control refers to the five senses of sound, touch, light or vision, taste and smell. It means restraining the faculties of perception from attachment to their objects, each as according to the nature of the faculty or sense. It also requires discipline over the five faculties of action: speaking, grasping, movement, procreation and evacuation or elimination. The aspirant wishes only to dwell constantly on Brahma, through hearing it, discussing it, and so forth, in whatever way that is done, as well as meditation.

Self-settledness is a function that is developed through practice of the first two virtues mentioned, calmness and self-control, so that we do not fall back into the delusion of the respective objects of attachment. When taken far, this includes the way of the *sannyasin*, which is total world renunciation and a monastic life—something that is obviously difficult if not impossible for most of us today.

Forbearance means enduring the afflictions that come about through contact with sense-objects—for it is not possible to exist without there being contact with sense-objects in one form or another. One does not concern oneself with the need to relieve physical pain or suffering, and one does not worry about it, or suffer anxiety. One is not moved by the heat or cold, pleasure or pain, love or hate, and all such opposites.

The complete concentration upon Brahma, *samadhana*, only comes about when all the above virtues have become the customary mode of the being. Unless a person is literally a one-in-a-million, and even that is more than really exists in the world, they will not get this without practice of yoga, observing all the virtues, study of the scriptures and the help of their teacher.

Faith means far more than belief in the conventional sense of the word, which is passive. By faith, the aspirant is enabled to accept the truth of the Vedanta or other scriptures as taught by a qualified teacher—the term 'qualified' here does not of course refer to profane, outward or conventional qualifications such as a university degree. Faith must be understood as a positive attitude of mind, whereas scepticism for example, which is seen as indispensible by the modern mentality, is in fact negative and derives from egotistic attachment. With faith, there is an intuitive certainty that there is a supreme or ultimate reality or Self (Atma) that is reachable. He who has faith is prepared to make any sacrifice, to go to any lengths so as to attain sure and permanent knowledge of the truth.

Without this very powerful, dauntless attitude, there can be no full realisation of the goal of yoga. According to the wisdom of the *Katha Upanishad*, Nachiketa, 'the man who did not yet know', was armed with Faith or Saradha. He was even prepared to go to the abode of the King of Death to seek the knowledge of the hereafter.

The Way to Samadhi

The *Yoga-Sutras* of Patañjali, taken along with the ancient commentary of Vyasa and more recent commentaries by qualified yogins, is a considerable body of works on a highly technical subject. The yoga teaching was collected and written in Sanskrit by the Patañjali school ('point of view' or *darshana*). It was not translated into Bengali until the last century and it was only in very recent times put into English for the first time. It has, like so much else, suffered abuse from being subjected to over simplification and adaptation to suit the modern mentality. Rendering the teaching in a way that is possible to understand and make practically realisable for modern aspirants requires very careful consideration. It is also essential that anyone doing this has direct knowledge of the realities involved, or it is a case of the 'blind leading the blind'. In *The Way of Knowledge* we gave an overview of the first four levels of Savikalpa Samadhi by way of an introduction to the practice of yoga and discrimination. We can now look at this in much greater detail, so that practitioners will be more fully informed as to what is really involved. It will be helpful to first repeat the overview here:

The first degree or the beginning of Savikalpa Samadhi is called *savitarka samadhi*. The name implies that an object is meditated upon. It is where prolonged *dharana* concentration has produced *dhyana* meditation and there is the first intimation of union between subject and object. The mind is focused on the gross aspect or form of a physical object, for example a *yantra* but it can be anything. This can include a name or symbol or sound. By *savitarka*, the nature of that thing is revealed or known fully.

The second degree of the Savikalpa Samadhi is called *savichara samadhi*. The name implies 'following' or 'furthering', and has a common root with the word for 'devotion'. The mind passes beyond the outer form of objects, and their subtle aspects or qualities such as colour, sound, beauty, love and so forth are understood. When the *tanmatras* are contemplated, the meditation has passed from the gross contemplation to the most subtle.

The third degree of the Savikalpa Samadhi is called *sa'ananda samadhi*, which implies 'bliss' or 'beatitude'. Here, the mind passes beyond the objective world and of reason. There is no reflection, or reflected knowledge, only bliss and tranquility. The pure (*sattvic*) mind is aware only of its own bliss. Here the mind's inner powers of perception are known.

The fourth degree of the Savikalpa Samadhi is called *sa'asmita samadhi*. The name implies the non-existence of the ego (*ahankara*). Even the bliss of the previous stage is surpassed and there is only pure awareness. The pure (*sattvic*) sense of being is that which remains. This fourth degree is analogous, by upward transposition, to the word that Moses heard on the holy mountain, 'I Am That I Am', or 'Being is Being'. It implies the state of Pure Being, which is essentially Ishvara as one step removed from pure Atma. This state surpasses all desire and therefore all fear, and is sometimes called, rather imprecisely, cosmic consciousness. What is important is that the divinity is known within the celestial sphere.

Any summary or overview of the yoga states necessarily blurs some of the important distinctions. For example, the last paragraph on the *sa'asmita samadhi* as likened to the word heard by Moses on the holy mountain is by analogous upward transposition. It implies a state that is in reality further advanced than *sa'asmita*. We can now go into more detail on the practices of the four degrees of *savikalpa samadhi*, as listed above. All of the first four stages of yoga involve the meditation on an object: *savitarka*, *savichara*, *sa'ananda* and *sa'asmita*. The *asmita* is the I-sense, culminating in the pure I-sense or *asmita-matra*. This last is free even from the sense of bliss, which preceded it, for each degree is free of the previous. However, it is not merely 'without bliss', for the pure I-sense is the consciousness of the knower, which transcends the previous state. All nonetheless involve concentration on an object; so even with *sa'asmita* the sense of the ego remains to a certain extent. When the flow of knowledge thus gained cuts off all afflictions at the root, it is called *samprajña yoga*.

Concentrating on a gross object (*savitarka*) is in reality a mixture of the name, the object itself and the knowledge about the object. When this degree is mastered, then *savichara* follows more or less automatically. Full insight is gained into the subtle principles. This involves analytic thought, supported by the knowledge gained in meditation. One must understand then that it is not only a matter of doing the meditation but also one must 'follow' the knowledge by thinking on it later. This begins with the practice of the diary record but does not end there. The word *vichara* itself is indicative of analyses; more specifically it is using the help of words, verbal constructs. One has to pass through this *chara* 'following' state to reach the unmodified *prakriti*, the substantial ground. With analysis, insight is gained into what is harmful or non-harmful, for example, and how to avoid harmful things.

The *sa'ananda* 'bliss' is free from the gross (*bhutas*) and the subtle qualities, involving pure meditation arising from tranquility. In this state the sense organs are at rest (from activity) or peace and so the goal of conservation of energy is automatically gained in the practice itself. One meditates on the bliss alone, which means passing from the subtle elements to the *tanmatras*. There is no need for thinking at this level, or when passing from the gross or subtle elements to this *sa'ananda*. No reason is applied upon gaining the knowledge of the *tanmatras*—otherwise it is not *sa'ananda* but *savichara*, which only begins to touch upon the *tanmatras*.

1. Elemental principles or *tattva-bhutas*: *sa'vitarka*
2. Subtle qualities: *sa'vichara*
3. Subtle roots of the elements or *tanmatras*: *sa'ananda*
4. I-sense: *sa'asmita*

The first two are knowable objects. The third is the knowledge that is bliss arising from tranquility. The fourth is the knower and, as the pure I-sense, it is 'beyond bliss'. It is no longer the 'sense of bliss' but the knower, which is the Self though it is not yet the Atma Self as it is still a reflection made by the ray of the *boddhi*.

Purusha, on the other hand, is not the object of concentration—it is the pure Consciousness (as Atma Itself). It is *purusha* that helps to manifest the I-sense though *purusha* is not the manifestor of the I-sense as such, for that is the *boddhi*. Sa'asmita is not then the knowledge of *purusha* Itself but is the imitation of the mutative ego (*ahankara*). Most precisely, it is called *mahat-tattva*, the 'great principle', which is *boddhi* shaped like *purusha*. It is 'knowing myself' in a distinct and direct way, which comes about through the identity between the pure Consciousness and the *boddhi*. The *boddhi-tattva*, the principle of the *boddhi*, is the first production from *prakriti*. To put this another way, the *boddhi* is the first phenomenon to be manifested from the undifferentiated 'substance'. Knowledge always implies a knower and a thing known. In the Arrested state, the knower-knowable ceases and the *purusha* 'abides in itself'.

It is said by Patañjali that a very subtle connection exists between *boddhi* and *purusha*, and that this can be regarded as an affliction (*klésha*) of the *sa'asmita* state. The *boddhi* is mistaken and thought to be the *purusha* (by Buddhists and others). As an error or *avidya*, it is a subtle one and comes at a relatively advanced level, and yet the full liberation is not then possible and the yogin must suffer rebirth. In *viveka-khyati*, the final realisation, this confusion disappears along with the *boddhi*. For example, we are only aware of the rays of the sun from a point of view of being outside of the sun. From within the sun, there are no rays.

Sa'asmita is the full realisation of the principle of the I-sense, which is the knower, receiver or cogniser (though not Atma Itself). Samprajñata *samadhi* is therefore a partially Arrested state as it requires there still be an object of concentration, even if that concentration is one-pointed. It may then seem as if there are multiple objects in the flow of knowledge but the one-pointed awareness is entirely from the 'I' or knower point of view. Going beyond the *samprajñata* state requires the supreme detachment, which is called *para-vairagya*. It is devoid of objects. In the freedom from objects, the mind is non-existent, or at least it is apparently so. With the *kaivalya* liberation, even the latent fluctuations of mind are shut out, along with the process of knowing. There is an important distinction to be made where the meditation without an object, *nirvija*, does not necessarily lead to *kaivalya*, but the *asamprajñata* state does. In *kaivalya* all latent impressions and fluctuations are stopped permanently, hence the state is truly 'liberation' and total freedom.

We can now go further into consideration of the four degrees of *savikalpa samadhi*, as previously described. The engrossment of *savitarka* is called the *savitarka samapatti*. 'Tarka' means 'with words' (to help). The confusion of the name, the object itself and the knowledge of the object is a *vikalpa* or false cognition. However, it must be emphasised that yogins do not want to know about ordinary objects. The purpose is rather to gain knowledge of the *tattvas* or principles. In this is the beginning of detachment from all objects. When knowledge is gained without verbal inference, it is called *nirvitarka samadhi*. This is direct perception (*pramaña*).

The *nirvitarka samapatti* is when the mind, purified of inference, testimony and so forth, is absorbed solely on the object and no other. This *samadhi* admits to the object as a singular (or unitive) real thing and at the same time as a sort of 'assemblage' of multiple elements that compose a wholeness.[118] The assemblage has practical use but it is no more than mere conventional knowledge. The assemblage then disappears as soon as this is realised, for the realisation removes the causes that go to make it up. In *nirvitarka samapatti* one disregards even the name of the object. This is regarded as a form of mental purification, for it loosens the points of assembly. Words such as 'real' and 'infinite', for example, are applied to Brahma yet they are *vikalpas*, based on no truly perceptible thing; they do not assist us to realise Brahma. Nirvitarka, on the other hand, is truly perceptible fact. We should bear in mind, however, that in spite of all this the sages of old communicated the highest knowledge, which they had themselves fully realised, with the help of words. We should also not forget that theoretical knowledge is indispensible.

The state of retention of impressions received in concentration is *savitarka samapatti*, when it is helped by words. The retention of impressions without words is *nirvitarka samapatti*. One should note that it is possible to utter words, conceiving only the sound or shape of the words, and it can still be *nirvitarka* or *nirvichara*—and this is now more fully explained: The engrossment in the subtle nature of the object—often reduced to a single element or *tattva*—is *nirvichara samapatti*. The *savichara* involves such conditions as time, space and causation. When these are removed it is *nirvichara samapatti*. It is all-embracing and super-reflective, as according to Vyasa. The knowledge derived from *savichara* nonetheless acts as a support, while it is reflected on. When the knowledge is free of all reflective consciousness and only the object remains, then it is *nirvichara samapatti*. This knowledge is not limited to time and space; it reveals all possible properties under all conditions whatsoever. It is the *tanmatra*.

To be really clear, we can now look at what happens with the differing engrossments of the four degrees of the *savikalpa samadhi*, where there is meditation on an object. We will use once again the concentration object of the sun as an example:

Savitarka: The gross form of the sun includes shape, distance, composition and so forth. This requires verbal concepts and the engrossment is called *savitarka samapatti*.

---

[118] Cf. 'The Eagle', *Way of Knowledge* pp. 133–135.

Nirvitarka: All else but the luminosity of the sun is shut out. When even the self is forgotten, this produces *nirvitarka* knowledge about the object (that is, without the help of words or verbal concepts). All objects are seen as one element or a combination of the five *bhuta tattvas* (elementary principles). In this case, light or luminosity is the *tejas* or fire element. The words that assisted us previously are now seen as illusion. In this state of *samapatti* engrossment, which is the superior knowledge of the gross object, by reflex, and with continued practice, the desire for objects such as wealth, family and property is weakened as these are also known as illusory.

Savichara: From the luminosity of the sun we pass to the *tanmatra* of light or fire, which is the higher principle of the element. When freed from inference and testimony, space-time conditions, and when light is known as devoid of any colour or other perceptible properties, then pleasure and pain also cease because these are derived from the gross object. All stupefaction is eliminated. Savichara is also meditated on other objects such as the *ahankara* (ego), which is subtler than the *tanmatras*, the pure I-sense and even the unmanifested or undifferentiated *prakriti*, which consists of the three Gunas in a state of perfect equilibrium.

Nirvichara: The memory is now free of all verbal concepts and only the subtle nature is the object of concentration. This is called the super-reflective *nirvichara samapatti*. However, note that the unmanifested *prakriti* cannot be directly apprehended as an object for *nirvichara*. A yogin can have *savichara* knowledge by merging his mind into *prakriti* and when he re-emerges he uses the help of words and knows *prakriti* that way. This is done by 'holding on' so that while most of the mind was submerged in *prakriti*, a small portion maintained conscious awareness so that on emerging the yogin can say, 'I know *prakriti*!' This last is very subtle and will most likely only be achieved by the experienced practitioner who has direct knowledge of the higher states—the use of the term yogin implies a certain mastery.

Concentration

Concentration gives knowledge of the five *tanmatras* and five *bhutas*. The *tanmatras* are subtle elementary determinations that are the higher or subtler formal principles of the *bhutas* or corporeal and sensible elements. The *tanmatras* are literally 'assignments' or 'measures' and may be likened to the rays of a five-pointed star, where the centre of that star is *jivatma*, the 'creature self'.[119] The *jivatma* is a reflection, through the ray of the *boddhi* or higher spiritual intuition or intellect, of Atma Itself. The *tanmatras* are not outwardly perceptible, as they do not belong to the corporeal domain, as do the *bhutas*. The *jivatma* and its five *tanmatras*, taken together, make up that which is called the *ahankara*, first in the individual order, the individual I-sense. It is at the level of the *jivatma* and its *tanmatras* that the light of Atma shines as a reflection in a clear mirror, for this light is derived from the ray of the *boddhi*, which acts as intermediary between the formless and formal levels. The five *tanmatras* or radials are then as secondary light rays striking out at different angles, in a manner of speaking.

One might then ask why it is that the *ahankara* is here said to be composed of a 'reflection in a clear mirror' when it is also loosely translated as 'ego', a word that has acquired negative connotations? The answer is that the I-sense gets its knowledge of exterior things, perceived as separate from itself, through the *manas* or inward sense, and it is from here that the five sensible elements become intelligible. As we shall see, by the weaving or knitting together of further modifications or determinations, the *ahankara* is prone to the delusion of its own separate existence in a world of objects, and these objects are in fact nothing but objects created by the human mentality and supported by the somewhat magnetic or attractive elements perceivable to the corporeal senses.

In a similar way to how the *boddhi* functions as intermediary between the formless or spiritual level and the *jivatma* with its *tanmatras*, the *manas* or inward sense acts as an intermediary between the integral individuality and the modified sense of the self superimposed by the mentality or cognitive faculty.

---

[119] The 'star' analogy is not in any way part of the Shankhya teaching, from which this science is derived, but it is useful in the context of all we have written previously on this and related subjects.

As the inward sense is the root and the means of the five sensible elements, it is for this reason sometimes called the 'sixth sense', as it is the root of the other five senses—though we should be very careful not to confuse this with the popular use of the term that has given it quite other meanings, devoid of true context.

It is the *tanmatras* and *bhutas* that we are particularly concerned with here, for as we said at the beginning, concentration gives knowledge of them. It is needful to know then that the *tanmatras* are the root of the sensible qualities of sound or hearing, touch, light or vision, taste and smell. One must remember that these are not perceptible or manifested in the sensible order except through the *bhutas*. By analogy the relation of the *tanmatras* to the *bhutas* is as the essential to the substantial.

The yogin that meditates on the *tanmatras* is not affected by the external world. The *tanmatras* are devoid of pleasure, pain or stupefaction. It is at this level, as we said previously, that the light of Atma shines as a reflection in a clear mirror. In the regions of the human mentality and the subtle or psychic realms below that in the natural order, Atma does not shine as a reflection in a clear mirror, for that mirror has already been clouded with the modifications of the sensorial world. These modifications, as we shall see, give rise to what are called the fluctuations of the mind. The fluctuations of the mind must be stilled for otherwise the one-pointed mind that is the primary goal of yoga is not in any way possible.

Now, it is said that 'the symbol is followed back to its source', but what is the exact science of this? This cannot rest on some vague supposition. Take for example the sun as an object. At the gross level (*savitarka*) cognition includes such things as its shape, which is round. It is some distance away. These are mostly spatial cognitions as a physical object occupies space. The sun also has movement, or at least appears to from the terrestrial point of view. We perceive that from our own faculty of 'action'.

By 'following' (*savichara*) we can move on to the subtler qualities of the sun. It has luminosity and radiates light in all directions. It not only has colour but is also the source of all colour. From light comes vision, one of the five senses. Now which of the corresponding five elements is the sun, at least predominantly (as nothing in nature is a single element)? Heat and light are both the product of fire. Therefore the sun is predominantly of the nature of *igni*, fire, or otherwise the *tejas tattva* element.

To follow further, to the subtler realms of the inward sense (*manas*), which is the source of the senses and gross elements, we eliminate sense and other mental impressions and meditate on the *tanmatra* of light. Meditating on the *tanmatras* means that the yogin is no longer subject to any external impressions. Once the meditation has entered the realm of the *tanmatras*, we are only one step away from the centre of the individuality and the I-sense. We may recollect that the *jivatma* is likened to the centre of a five-rayed star, and the five rays are the *tanmatras*, which cannot be heard, touched, seen, tasted or smelled, because they are the principial source for what later can be sensed by the five senses. We are using 'sooner' or 'later' here as a *vikalpa* figure of speech, because what is being described is not sequential but simultaneous. When the centre of the I-sense has truly been entered then Atma is perceived (though indirectly) as a reflection of the ray from the *boddhi*, unclouded and clear.

The student may well then ask at this juncture, 'But is not this, what is being described, only the centre of the ego-self?' The answer is that yes indeed it is! But few persons will ever reach it. And that is because the mind is composed of modifications, which in turn give rise to the fluctuations, the *samskaras* and *kléshas*. Most will spend their whole lives imprisoned in their own mentality, which is both the prison and the jailor who makes sure they are kept locked up at all times. There is no escape from it but by concentration. Dreaming is not an escape because while the senses and faculty of action are withdrawn, the mentality is still present.

Only concentration, the practice, and discrimination over a lengthy period of time can defeat the prison guard and break out of the compound forever. In the meantime, there will be temporary excursions out of the prison but once there is knowledge of what is beyond then the return to the body and mind can never be the same as it once was. This forms a part of what initiation really is. So long as we believe in the products of mind, thinking this or that to be real, or thinking it to be our Self, then we are in the state that is called ignorance or *avidya*, which means 'not seeing' or 'not knowing'.

In the *Yoga-Sutras* that were developed from the Shankhya *darshana* or school of thought, some of the terms used are different from those used by Shankara and others. The supreme knowledge is here defined as the realisation of the principle of *purusha* or pure Self. In this sense, *purusha* is more or less interchangeable with Atma.

The knowledge of the distinction between the *boddhi* and *purusha* is called *viveka-khyati*. That is to say, in order to truly know the difference between *boddhi*, the 'ray of the sun', and the *purusha*, the sun itself, which is self-luminous, one must know this from the point of view of *purusha*, which properly belongs to the formless realm. This knowledge prevents relapse into the empirical life, and is also called Dharmamegha, which means to be constantly with the divine presence.[120] In passing, it is worth noting that the empirical knowledge or 'experience' is made much use of in neo-spiritualist commentaries and even teachings. Experience, by definition, belongs to the realm of the modifications of the mind through the sensible perceptions and so 'spiritual experience' is really an oxymoron.

There are five adjectives used in the Patañjali *Yoga-Sutras* to describe the pure Consciousness, or *chiti-shakti*, and these are Pure, Infinite, Immutable, Untransmissible and the Illuminator (of things presented by the *boddhi*). It is by this illumination of things that the *boddhi* becomes known, and this leads to the awareness of the objects that are related to the *boddhi*. The pure Consciousness is the illuminator but it is neither involved nor active, nor is it mutable or subject to change. For this reason of its detachment, it is called 'untransmissible'.

We know of the three Gunas that *sattvas* is calmness and tranquility and has an upward tendency towards wisdom, while *rajas* is active and prone to agitation and seeks development on its own plane; *tamas* is inertia, tending downwards, or towards ignorance. While *sattvas* can be influenced by *rajas* and *tamas*, the pure Consciousness is not as it is fully self-luminous and infinite. It is worth noting here a further distinction in terms used. The technical use of the word 'infinite' in no way implies an infinite number or aggregate of finite units. Its meaning does not include any finite conception. There is nothing within the manifest universe, either physical or subtle that can truly be called infinite.

Sattva is the predominant Guna in what is called *viveka-boddhi*, the final realisation, because it is not influenced by *rajas* or *tamas*. The *sattva* is the revealer of the *boddhi*, and so it is called the *sattvika* manifestation, which is the discriminative knowledge or realisation.

---

[120] Dharmamegha has no direct translation equivalent but can literally mean 'cloud of virtue'. See *Way of Knowledge*, 'Gradations of Samadhi'.

When this difference between the *purusha* and *boddhi* becomes permanent, when there is no more relapse into the empirical state, then *viveka-khyati* comes about, otherwise called the 'arrested' state. Viveka-khyati plus total renunciation of the world is the onset of final liberation or *kaivalya*.

When the subject is relieved even of the last trace of the I-sense, then it is said that the Seer (*purusha*) abides in his own nature. As the *boddhi* is now regarded as separate from *purusha*, from the self-luminous *purusha* (or Atma) point of view it thereafter becomes an object of knowledge.

To become absorbed in pure being, to return to the Self as resting or abiding in Its own Self, the mind must be freed from the influence of the Gunas. From the individual or the corporeal point of view, it then seems as if the mind has returned to its own matrix (*avyakta*) and so effectively no longer exists. From the spiritual point of view however, the mind only appears to have vanished. In reality it continues in a state of the perfect equilibrium of the Gunas. All that has gone, which appears from the ordinary point of view as a 'sacrifice', is the misery and suffering that arises from all co-relations of the Self and the objects.

It is important to understand then that freedom from *rajas* and *tamas* in the *sattvika* state is not freedom from those Gunas as such but they no longer get in the way of the discriminative knowledge. To recapitulate on the higher reaches of the path of yoga: Dharmamegha is where the mind abides in its own nature as pure *sattva*, free from *rajas* and *tamas*. Kaivalya is the final liberation where the mind merges into its constituent cause.

Such are the further reaches of the path of yoga, but to attain any yogic state it is necessary to control the modifications of the mind, called *vrittis*. Of these, Patañjali gives five types only, as all other modifications can fall into one or more of them. The modifications can be harmful (*kléshas*), as based on ignorance, or harmless (*akléshas*), as used in discrimination for the yoga of knowledge (*jnana*). The harmless modifications are naturally opposed to the Gunas, or their influence as an obstruction to yoga. The latent impressions formed by the modifications are what give rise to fluctuations of the mind. The fluctuations go on continually if unchecked by discipline; it is as though they were turning on an unceasing wheel.

When impressions (as experience) are retained by the mind through the power of memory or recollection, then *samskaras* come about, which are the latent impressions, and it is these that give rise to the fluctuations of the mind, the endless turning of the wheel of delusions, one after another. It has been said of the *vrittis* that they may be harmless, as leading to the goal, or harmful, as leading away from it and to ignorance. A table of negative and positive *vrittis* could never be made, or at least that is impossible without making a complete distortion of the science. The same *vrittis* can be harmful or harmless at different times, and depending on their use and what stage of development one has reached.

The same can be said of the *siddhis* or 'magical powers', of which there are two kinds, harmful and harmless, and yet they are the same powers, but to discuss these would take us away from our subject. To give an example of harmful and harmless *vrittis*: there are certain ideas or ideals that can be very helpful, even indispensible on the path, for they contribute to the acquisition of the final knowledge. They are harmless in that context, but from the supreme point of view these are unreal (*vikalpa*), of the nature of illusion, and so it might be injurious for a person at a much further stage of spiritual development to practice them. In all this, it is the inversion of such ideas or ideals that is at all times harmful.[121]

The *vritti* of the recollection (through the power of memory) of thoughts relating to the Self (as Atma) can lead to knowledge eventually, and so is harmless. The recollection of thoughts that are opposed to such realisation, however, is harmful. Ordinary sleep (*nidrā*) is harmful as one may be prone to falling into the *tamasic* lower states, but when the discriminative knowledge is retained in the mind by the same recollection, then it is no longer harmful but is needed for health, and so it is beneficial for the spiritual practice. Dreamless or deep sleep as defined by Patañjali, *nidrā*, is not the same as the *prajna* that is one of the three states of being designated by the mantric Aum. Nidrā is inclusive of any state of vacuity without cognition. For example, there is a phenomenon encountered by some practitioners that meditate with *smriti* and fall asleep. When they wake up, they have no knowledge whatsoever of where they have been, only knowing that they must have fallen asleep. The condition is not in any way useful for yoga, and must be stopped through the use of the discrimination of cognitive self-realisation, which is what is being described here.

---

[121] It is precisely this inversion of principles that characterises the modern mentality.

The five harmful and harmless modifications (*vrittis*) of the mind are defined as follows:

Pramaña	correct cognition
Viparyaya	false cognition
Vikalpa	cognition of a thing not existing
Nidrā	dreamless sleep
Smrti	recollection

The *vrittis* are cognition of conscious mental states. Stopping them leads ultimately to the cessation of all mentation whatsoever. Thus discrimination is a constant vigil, sometimes called 'self enquiry'. The *vrittis* are seen here to apply to the waking state but discrimination may equally be carried through to the dreaming state. The arrested (or liberated) state is attained by the yogin by the cessation of all cognitive fluctuations. The *sattva* element of the mind is thus freed from variations (called *prakhya*). It is through *sattva*, unaffected by *rajas* and *tamas*, that the higher states are known.

What then is the mind? The mentality, *chitta*, is the power to cognise, to will and retain by blending all the knowledge relating to the five senses. This includes the experience of the movement of objects, which owes to the faculty of action (*rajas*), or their inertia (*tamas*), by the five *vayus*, which are the vital (*prana*) forces of the body. This comprises such feelings as pleasure and pain, all of which are inherent in the inner faculties. Feelings such as happiness or sorrow cannot be controlled but are eliminated by shutting out the valid cognition (*pramaña*) that gives rise to them. All modifications (*pratyayas*) have as their constituents the three Gunas. Chitta has three functions:

Cognition *knowing*
Conation *will, volition*
Retention *latent impressions*

All fluctuations are *chitta*, the mind, generally speaking. The mind is known by its fluctuations and when the fluctuations cease then the mind as such is not there either. For example, fluctuations arise from retention by memory of past cognitions, and likewise of feelings, experiences, of things willed, actions performed and so forth. The *chitta* has two properties:

Pratyaya modification
Samskara impressions

Pratyaya, the modification of the mind, is called *chitta-vritti*. As fluctuations are cognised, thought of or known, they are thus transformations of the *boddhi*, which is the transformation of *sattva*. The *boddhi* is knowledge itself and is the principle from which mind depends. It is not to be thought of as in any way dependant on the mind therefore, which would be an inversion of the natural order. It can be thought of as an intermediary between the higher or spiritual (formless) states of being and the human state, which is defined by its mind or mentality, as associated with a body and so is in turn identified with the world (as exterior). A body is not only the gross or physical body; there is a subtle body, for example. The *boddhi* and *chitta* (mind) are terms sometimes interchanged in various texts but the modifications of the *boddhi* are not the *boddhi* when this is taken in the sense of the higher or spiritual intellect or intuition.[122] The term is thus used in different ways as according to the point of view; so in one sense it refers to the higher intellect but used in another way it might only be another word for mind. Sometimes it is even used to refer to an elemental principle (*tattva*). So as to eliminate confusion, in our writings we always use *boddhi* in the higher sense, not in the sense of its modifications through the mental faculties.[123]

The words *chitta* and *manas*, the mind and the inward sense, are also used sometimes to mean the same thing but to be exact they are not the same. Manas is the inner power by which the internal and external senses are set in motion. Mental perception is due to *manas* in the same way that visual knowledge, for example, is due to the eyes. It is for this reason that *manas* is called a 'sixth sense', as previously mentioned, but to be precise it is only by *manas* that the five senses are known.

The mind is the instrument of will or conation. As such it is the inner centre of knowledge and action, while *chitta-vritti* is nothing other than knowledge itself. Chitta-vritti is specifically the knowledge of all retentions of the mind, all thoughts and actions whatsoever.

---

[122] For reason of the interchangability of *boddhi* (as subject to modifications) and *chitta*, the *chitta-vritti* is sometimes called *boddhi-vritti*.
[123] The *atma* is sometimes used in texts to mean only an individual or the 'creature self (*jivatma*), and so we might hear of '*atmas*', plural; but we always mean the Self as opposed to the mind or individual self (*ahankara*) when we use the word Atma.

What then is perception? Firstly, there is direct perception: 'this is a cat'. Secondly there is reflective perception: 'I am seeing a cat'. Thus there are three things involved: there is 'a cat', there is 'seeing' and there is 'I'. The knowledge of the cat is therefore a modification of the I-sense. Of the meditation practice, it is sometimes said that 'a symbol is followed back to its source'. This takes place in stages. Firstly, one must identify which of the five senses is involved (*bhutas*). The senses have their formless root in the five *tanmatras*. The source of the *tanmatras* is the pure I-sense, and furthermore, the I-sense is a reflection of the *boddhi*. Ultimately, the source of the *boddhi* is known in *purusha*, the immutable principle.

When the mind contacts an external object, via the senses, it is modified. Pramaña, the first of the five *vrittis* or modifications, is the instrument of knowing something correctly.[124] Usually there follows self-identification with the modification; that is, the (real) Self is mistaken for the mental modification—*the mind is shaped by its modifications.*

Pramaña ('perception') is also constituted of two other secondary things: Inference and Testimony. Inference is made up of the general characteristics of a knowable object. The sage Vyasa, in the ancient commentary on Patañjali, gives the example of motion: the moon and stars have motion—they change position, as does a person. A mountain does not change location and so does not have motion. To know one of two related things is to know the rest, by Inference. This forms a part of perception.

Authoritative testimony is to hear the words of a reliable person. This is called *agama-pramaña*—the testimony is here conveyed or is otherwise transmitted to the hearer. In this case the person sending the thought has experienced and thus knows what he is talking about. Otherwise it is not a valid testimony. Agama-pramaña is a separate source of *pramaña*, the valid or correct cognition or knowledge. If one then went on to make a study, one would be proving by Inference. Some possess the power of thought transference, as well as knowing what is in another's mind. The direct transfer of cognition, by telepathy, is a different cognition than direct perception or Inference. Such a reliable person is called an *āpta*, which means he conveys or transmits sure knowledge through verbal testimony. However, words alone are not *agama*, as there must be a transferred or transmitted cognition.

---

[124] See the five harmful and harmless *vrittis*, p. 144.

Viparyaya is the false kind of knowledge or cognition, literally a 'superimposition', based on an unreal notion of a thing: it is to know a thing as different from what it really is. It is delusion. Such delusion is only dissolved by concentration, by which the mental power (*prama*) is able to show a real thing. There are five parts to the *vritti* of *viparyaya*: nescience, from which arises the other *kléshas*, egoism, attachment (to objects), aversion (or hatred) and fear of death.

Vikalpa is based on words or language suggestive of a non-existing thing. It is nonetheless useful and necessary, as is verbal and written language. For example, 'the nature of *purusha* is not created' is expressive of no positive quality, only the absence of creation. Vikalpa has no real existence beyond words. It is useful knowledge arising out of the meaning of a word but without a corresponding reality. However, real or essential knowledge destroys all the unreal *vikalpas* such as 'infinite' or 'immeasurable', or 'void', for further examples. To put this another way: however useful these verbal notions may be, realised truth called *rta* in Sanskrit cannot be known until the imaginary cognition is eliminated from the mind.[125]

Nidrā or 'dreamless sleep' is the modification arising from inertia, vacuity or negation and is to be carefully distinguished from *prajna*, one of the three states of being symbolised by Aum. When awake, the faculties of thought, senses and action are present. When dreaming, only thought is present. In dreamless sleep all three are withdrawn; it is the condition called obscurity (*tamasic*). This is overcome through self-cognition; constant recollection; single-pointed concentration on the real Self (Atma).[126] The states of waking, sleeping and dreamless sleep are then here understood to be mental modifications that owe to retention. It is by practice and detachment (that leads ultimately to renunciation) that the continuous fluctuations may be stopped—all other practices are included in them.

Developing the habit of discrimination turns the flowing river of mind away from evil and opens the floodgates of knowledge—the mind is turned in the right direction. Thus *moksha* deliverance requires both practice and detachment. Practice is also the effort needed to attain tranquility (*sthiti*), through the cessation of all the fluctuations of the mind.

---

[125] Rta or *rita* is also 'to set in order', from whence 'ritual'. True cognition or knowledge is the only way that anything can really be properly organised; truth must be the basis, and that is the value of effective ritual.

[126] In the case of insomnia there is no stoppage of the fluctuations and so this is not yoga. One-pointedness is thus the only real cure for insomnia.

Finally, *smrti* is the modification based on reproduction of a previous impression, without admixture from other sources. Two things are here important: knowledge of the object and the power of original cognition, which is that of *boddhi*. Furthermore, there are two types of recollection: firstly of a real thing and secondly of an imagined thing. A recollection can be startling or surprising, because in the object and the cognition is the knower, which produces a new or further cognition. That new knowledge is *pramaña*. Smrti is also part of the practice, the recollection of the Self (Atma) or the recollection of previous meditation states that further the goal. Other kinds of recollections may be harmful, for example false or erroneous ideas, past actions that brought suffering, a conversation that took place earlier, and so forth. Those are eliminated by discrimination, removing the cause.

One cannot control happiness or sorrow but one can eliminate the valid cognition or *pramaña* that gives rise to these. For example: everything and everyone in this world is born and they die. Everything else also passes away continuously by the power of the great Maya. Why would anyone want to bring yet more souls into this miserable world? And yet they do, every hour of every day. All this gives rise to sorrow, which is suffering. It is miserable and it is no good for yoga. The fact that creatures and all things are born and die is a valid cognition or *pramaña*. But all perceptions, even when they are valid are nonetheless perceptions and the perceptible is illusion from the point of view of Atma. So the remedy for such sorrow is to recollect that Atma is without birth and without death, and is forever free from all pain and suffering.

That is the way of discrimination. We can't do it all at once, but 'a little goes a long way', and it brings *virya*, which is the spiritual strength needed to overcome all obstacles. Over time, the Shakti destroys the afflictions and poisons in the steadfast devotee. Her knowledge and power, of which she is the embodiment, conveys the *virya*.[127]

Without discrimination, faithfully and habitually written in the record afterwards, the practice is not a practice and does not lead to further and real knowledge.

---

[127] Virya—see p. 120 and footnote.

Attachment and Fascination

When there is irresistible attachment to the objects of desire, which often owes to thwarted past actions of one kind or another, then the objects become magnetised, in a manner of speaking, through the constant attention being placed there. As was said earlier,

> Pursuing the objects of desire ... creates habits of the mind, through the mental impressions. In Sanskrit these are called *samskaras*. These pile up like hills and mounds, so we are not able to see beyond them.[128]

A 'vampiric force' is a lurid term but one that is accurately descriptive of the *samskaras*. The mental faculty or cognition of recollection called *smrti* is clearly involved. Through such 'magnetisation', the objects then appear to be powerful or charged with force, although in reality the power is only that which has been invested in them by our attention on what is really only an imaginary thing—and that is still the case even if the recollection is based on what is termed a 'valid cognition' at the beginning. That can be easily proved because as soon as we take our attention away from it and put it somewhere else, the object no longer exists. It will nonetheless *subsist* until such a time as it has become completely eliminated, which only comes about through one-pointed concentration of mind in meditation practice.

There are two kinds of concentration. The first is yogic, where the mind is trained to meditate on an object that is helpful to the practice. Most often, such an object is God, Ishvara or Shakti in one of her countless forms. The second is anti-yogic, and is something that everyone is able to do and does all the time although without knowledge (*avidya*). That is the kind of concentration where one habitually returns to the harmful thought impression or recollection and broods on it; to all intents and purposes it places power in the imaginary thing. In the case of the practitioner, it drains away all the *virya*, the special strength, endurance and power that is needed for persisting with the practice so it becomes effective. We will find for example that even if we turn our mind to other things, the object of desire—or thwarted desire or action it makes no difference—will come to the surface and claim our attention before we realise it has even happened.

---

[128] 'Concentration', p. 138.

It is as though the thought or object has overpowered our mind and will. It is seductive so that no matter what thought is in perception, that thought will cunningly turn into the one thought that is the obsessional object. It is in short the power of obsession and that is why 'vampiric' is an apt term. It only takes an instant for the obsessional thought to return. Yet it only takes an instant of yoga discrimination to eliminate it at source.

It will be helpful if we summarise and recapitulate the practice of discrimination and the different kinds of cognition as according to the *Yoga-Sutras*. Discrimination is achieved through mental process. Firstly, we must identify which of the five kinds of cognition is chiefly involved:

Pramaña is direct or true perception.

Viparyaya is false cognition; literally 'superimposition' or 'leading away'.

Vikalpa is the figure of speech, which only has meaning in the words alone. It is nonetheles useful.

Smrti is the recollection of any former impression.

Nidrā is nescience or sleep, which is no different from ignorance.

The five cognitions of the mind are potentially harmful or helpful to the practice, because *the mind is shaped or moulded by what it perceives*. The mind takes on the shape of the objects, and so the self is identified with those objects, leading to a false idea of the self. The false idea of self is what is vaguely called the 'ego' in modern languages, for in reality the ego or *ahankara*, to use the exact Sanskrit term, is composed of the pure I-sense, *jivatma* 'centre' and its five *tanmatras* or subtle non-perceptible *tattvas* (principles). We have likened this in other writings to a five-rayed Egyptian star with a circle and point in the centre, which is a more or less exact correspondence. It is not the human 'ego' as that is understood in ordinary parlance; it is the centre of the individuality. As such it is not to be confused with Atma Itself, the immutable, infinite principle or True Self. Once the objects that shape the mind are cleared away completely then the I-sense is able to reflect a 'ray of the sun', as it were, that ray being a metaphor for the highest non-individual suprahuman intuition (*boddhi*) and the sun being an analogy for the Atma Itself.

According to the systematised knowledge represented by the structure of grades or degrees, every Zelator ought to be tested by such glamours as we have described above. It is worthwhile that the practitioner should recollect that even those glamours or fascinations that lead the mind away to empty stupefaction are given by the power of Shakti, through her mysterious *maya*. This is the 'every spell and scourge of God' mentioned in the Bornless invocation, that must be realised as obedient to the Shakti power, for all is a manifestation of that same power. We can practice discrimination and concentration, which is the only remedy, yet at the same time so long as we think that we are in control of everything and that we cause things to happen or not happen, we remain in ignorance. All power is with Shakti and must be given to her.

The error of all 'psychological thinking' can then clearly be understood in one sense at least as a misappropriation of power. It relies on the person being able to 'fix things up' by making various adjustments without any resort to a higher principle beyond human will and imagining. The systematic adjustments are based on purely sensorial, recollective or even environmental factors and apparent causes. The remedies are thus only another form of hypnosis or fascination. Yet all this is confused with something 'spiritual' in the teachings of neo-spiritualism and psychotherapy. In fact, it could not be further away from anything truly spiritual or metaphysical.

While there is a particular correspondence between such fascinations and enchantments and the Zelator grade, the power of such attachments does not stop there. To a certain extent this shows how tabulated correspondence systems are as much a hindrance and a nuisance as they are a helpful aid, and when we use them we need to exercise caution. For example, there are vices and virtues that apply to various grades or stations on the Tree of Life symbol, yet one does not need to be an Adeptus Minor to suffer the affliction of pride, which is of course a very ordinary thing. If the Adeptus Minor has really touched upon the I-sense, through prolonged meditation and discrimination, then it is true that an ordinary vice like pride or egoism can be become super-amplified to the even worse affliction of 'spiritual pride'. Spiritual pride is an oxymoron as pride can never be spiritual; it is a type of *vikalpa* 'figure of speech'. But it is easily possible for the person that has known a degree—even a 'taste'—of the individual centre to imagine they have reached much further, in which case they become like a caricature of the 'small god', or 'false prophet'. As a matter of fact, even persons that have attained nothing but self-imagined 'psychic powers' have set up their own schools, in which case it is truly like the blind leading the blind.

Even one who has realised Nirvikalpa Samadhi might yet be seized by a powerful *samskara* that has emerged through previous actions (*karmas*). And in that case, the power is even greater—the further along the path the mightier is the pull if the object is in any way succumbed to, that is, if the practitioner allows it to move their mind in any given direction. Only the Dharmamegha yogin is really free from such things. It can then be seen why persistence and endurance on the path are essential. As soon as the first step is taken then a further step must follow, and another and another, until the individual has reached the limit of their possibilities. For some, though it is very rare in the present times, even that limit can be transcended through the means of various intermediaries, so that there is knowledge of higher states than the human, and even the illimitable possibilities of the final and total immersion in Brahma or ultimate Reality.

Patañjali Eight Limbs of Yoga

The Eight Limbs of Yoga is widely known and used in various ways and by diverse schools, some traditional and some even anti-traditional or anti-spiritual. The eight precepts consisting of abstentions, observances and yoga practice are concerned with the practices and requirements for any person that aspires to the yoga of knowledge. The Eight Limbs of Yoga forms a small portion of the whole body of works that make up the *Yoga-Sutras*. It is frequently made subject to erroneous interpretations and is used in ways that dilute and denature the intended meaning and use. We will therefore provide here a non-sectarian commentary based on the ancient texts and doctrine, without any 'social' or humanist distortions.

The *yamas*, though they are called 'abstentions', are practices in effect and when properly understood they are simply an expression of the truth of any individual being. The *niyamas*, called 'observances', are similarly what is 'seen', as an outward attitude to the beginner, while knowledge of these reveals them as the simplest, most natural state of the being.

The Eight Limbs of Yoga

1. Yamas: harmlessness; truthfulness; non-stealing; continence; non-covetousness
2. Niyamas: cleanliness; contentment; fiery aspiration; self-study; self-surrender (to the path, which is God)
3. Asana (seated posture)
4. Pranayama (control of breath)
5. Pratyahara (withdrawal of senses)
6. Dharana (concentration, fixation)
7. Dhyana (true meditation with sustained concentration)
8. Samadhi (union with God—the goal, which is yoga)

The first two *yamas* and *niyamas* are commonly referred to, even by so-called experts, as moral requirements, and sometimes even as social ethics. However, although that is certainly how they appear to the uninitiated, they are really nothing of the kind. These are practical requirements so that the goal of yoga is achievable and as such they have no relation with society or any morality; all morality is arbitrary by definition. The timeless wisdom does not change with the expedient requirements of any social order.

The ancient commentaries of sages on the *Yoga-Sutras* are emphatic that 'harmlessness' is not to be interpreted as Jainists and others do. Jainists must walk very carefully lest they step on an ant and if they find a flea in their bed they might have to move to another bed. The sages insist that one must not harbour thoughts that involve harm to another being. Obviously that also includes deeds but extreme interpretations are heterodox and do not accord with the primordial and universal tradition.

Truthfulness can be taken as far as the level of understanding goes. With greater knowledge, greater exactitude is required. One must not speak falsehood merely because it will please someone.

Non-stealing includes not stealing the thoughts of other persons, and this is subtler than it appears because there can be thoughts of a 'collectivity', such as popular opinion, what one might read in a newspaper or some form of social media—if one would read such things, which would then contradict 'truthfulness'. Stealing also includes thoughts of envy, resentment of others. One should not claim gifts or favours from others and even when they are freely offered one should not always accept something; for example if it is given by a person with an unclean or evil mind.

Continence is sometimes construed as sexual abstinence, which is sufficient for many persons. A more complete understanding involves the conservation of all energy for the Great Work. This includes speech, such as idle chatter, and thought.

Non-covetousness is self-explanatory once it is realised what misery and suffering is caused by attachment to objects of desire. To desire or yearn for objects that belong to someone else is also a subtle form of stealing.

Of the *niyamas*, cleanliness includes purity of mind, so that all thoughts that are harmful to the path are eliminated. Most especially, even if evil thoughts enter the mind, they must not be retained so they become afflictions.

Contentment is acceptance of the path, and the level of attainment. From discontentment is bred the untruth of imagining that one is much further along than one really is. That is an impediment to yoga. With contentment comes tranquility, which is necessary if the yoga practice is to advance beyond the veriest beginning.

The fiery aspiration brings forth *virya*, a special kind of faith, strength and endurance that is built up through continuance of right practice. Nothing can be achieved without fiery aspiration.

Self-study means constant vigilance and discrimination—which is an exact science. It also means developing a reflective attitude of mind. It must not be construed 'psychologically', which involves development of a mentality that is totally anti-yogic as it encourages *tamas* and tends towards the *asuras* or demonic nature.

Self-surrender to God (and so the path itself) cannot be done without faith (*saradha*) and as a consequence the *virya* that comes about through the practice of yoga and discrimination. The profane or uninitiated person does not comprehend this at all and imagines it to be a sort of passivity that he can only see as 'negative'. Self-negation on the other hand does not require mortification, as that is in fact only an inverse form of conceit or flattery. The self, through the senses and mental impressions, is a superimposition upon the Real or True Self. Any sacrifice is only what appears from the point of view of ignorance. From the point of view of the Self, freedom is gained from the misery and suffering of countless afflictions.

The last six limbs of yoga are the practice itself, commencing with seated *asana* or posture, which does not involve, as some like to think, difficult or even impossible or unnatural contortions of the body. Likewise with the control of the breath, which when properly understood is the direction of *prana* or subtle vitality.

The withdrawal of the senses here refers to the physical senses of hearing, feeling, seeing, tasting and smelling, for at the beginning it is valid to concentrate the mind on the subtle (*tattva*) elements. When seated for meditation one closes the eyes so the sight is transferred within.

Concentration means to hold one object in the mind and no other. When this is sustained, then *dhyana* or true meditation is possible, and knowledge can be gained of any object.

Samadhi or union with God, sometimes called 'transcendence', is the goal of yoga. The word 'yoga' is inclusive of both the means and the goal.

AUM: Reality and Unreality

The *Mandukya Upanishad* forms part of the *Atharva-Veda*. It is one of the shortest of the *Upanishads*, consisting of only twelve verses; yet it sets out to explain the whole of reality.[129] *Mandukya* means 'teacher' or 'teaching', though the origin of the noun is lost to antiquity.[130] Gaudapada's *Kārikā*, the very ancient commentary, is in four parts.[131] It is impossible to summarise the treatise as it is of vast scope and we shall not attempt to do that here. What we will do is set forth a few pertinent lines of thought that might provide the basis for further study from the source texts. The commentary emphasises two paths, the lesser mysteries and the greater, and sets out to prove that ultimately the knowledge of non-dual reality is the only real bliss, all else partaking of the nature of the unreal. The studying of scriptures, for example, as partaking of the lesser path, does not eliminate ignorance directly but shows indirectly the reality of the non-dual Brahma. It is only through direct realisation that ignorance is totally destroyed forever. Once the *jivatma* (individuality) identifies and realises itself as Atma, which is no different than Brahma, the phenomenal universe is destroyed, like a mirage in the desert or the rope seen as a snake in half-light. The direct knowledge of Brahma is *vidya*, knowledge ('seeing'), while the knowledge of duality is called *avidya*, ignorance ('not seeing').

---

[129] Source texts used are *The Upanishads* (volume two of four) translated by Swami Nikhilananda and *Eight Upanishads* (volume two of two) translated by Swami Gambhirananda [Advaita Ashrama]. Some use is also made of the abbreviated *The Upanishads* translated by Eknath Easwaran, to help make the source text more accessible to the reader not well-versed in brahmanic scriptures [Penguin Arkana].

[130] A further root meaning is 'frog', which could imply 'leaping', since the text concerns the highest knowledge of absolute Advaita Vedanta. *Mandukya* might also have originated from a family name, as Vedic tradition was passed on from father to son in the time-honoured manner.

[131] Gaudapada was the teacher to Shankara's guru, Govindapada. Gaudapada is very little known to the Western world but is renowned as the first Vedantic sage after the Upanishadic period.

 The first chapter is called *Agama-Prakarana*.[132] This chapter takes the form of a cosmology, determining the nature of the sacred syllable AUM so the student can come to understand the essence of Atma. The second chapter is called *Vaitathya-Prakarana* and seeks to show, through the science of perception, how the unreality of duality may be understood. The third chapter deals with the non-duality of Atma Itself, lest there be any confusion regarding this. The fourth chapter concerns causality, as regarded from various points of view. We will begin here by summarising AUM and the four corresponding states of waking, dreaming, dreamless sleep and that which surpasses them all (*turiya*). To this end we include a carefully modified translation of the *Mandukya Upanishad* verses that are the subject of the key commentaries of Guadapada and Shankaracharya.

> AUM, the word, is all this. A clear explanation is as follows: All that is past, present and future is, indeed, AUM. And whatever else there is, beyond the three-fold division of time—that also is truly AUM.
> Brahma is all, and the Self is Brahma. This Self has four states of consciousness.
> The first is called Vaishvanara, in which one lives with all the senses turned outwards, aware only of the external world.
> Taijasa is the name of the second, the dreaming state in which, with the senses turned inward, one enacts the impressions of past deeds and present desires.

The letter A in Sanskrit makes the sound that pervades all speech in the same way that *vaishvanara*, the waking state, pervades the whole universe. The letter U, *taijasa*, symbolises the dreaming state and is the intermediary between A and M. It includes the knowledge of the subtle states. The letter M, *prajna*, symbolising dreamless sleep, is expressive of absorption and dissolution. Vaishvanara (A) and *taijasa* (U) express the coming into and out of dissolution and the origination from undifferentiated *prakriti*. A and U merge into M, *prajna*, forming OM. Vaishvanara and *taijasa* are conditioned by cause and effect; they thus partake in the non-apprehension and misapprehension of reality.

---

[132] A *prakarana* is a short work confined to a particular topic, whereas a *shastra* is a broader discourse, inclusive of a variety of topics and using subtle logic in its thesis.

For the above reason in Vedantic texts both waking and dreaming are considered as closely related, for what is perceived in the normal mode of consciousness or waking state partakes as much of the nature of dream as does sleeping, through its incorrect cognitions.

> The third state is called *prajna*, of deep sleep, in which one neither dreams nor desires. There is no mind in *prajna*, there is no separateness; but the sleeper is not conscious of this. Let him become conscious in *prajna* and it will open the door to the state of abiding joy.
> Prajna, all-powerful and all-knowing, dwells in the hearts of all as the ruler. Prajna is the source and end of all.
> Those who know this find their true Self and are able to measure [know] the minds and hearts of men by seeing with the inward eye of the heart.

Prajna is the Knower *par excellence*, that is to say, without any conditions or particularities. The state of dreamless sleep (M) is conditioned by cause and there is usually no recollection of it, so it is frequently paired with nescience or ignorance. However, when compared with meditation, where the being passes to higher states, it is no different from the brahmanic state, which is one-pointed. It is possible for one who is qualified to pass through the Brahma Sun-Door or symbol into the 'state of abiding joy', though it is impossible for an ignorant person to achieve the same simply by making use of the same symbol. Rarer indeed is the one that can leap straight to the *turiya* condition (described below) without continuous devoted practice (including devotion to their guru) and observances over a lengthy period of time. Those who 'know the minds and hearts of men' are gurus that have direct knowledge of Nirvikalpa Samadhi. The verse concerns the *siddhis* that come about spontaneously as a consequence of that 'abiding joy'.

> The fourth is the superconscious state called *turiya*, neither inward nor outward, beyond the senses and the mind, in which there is none other than Atma. It is the supreme goal of life. It is infinite peace and bliss, non-dual. Realise Atma!

There is a fourth state called *turiya* where no conditions exist. This is the soundless or 'point' aspect of AUM. In the realised state of *turiya* there is a total cessation of all phenomena. This concerns the higher states of Samadhi as alluded to above, of which it would be too much of a digression to enter into more fully here. Of *turiya*, it is thus said sometimes that the universe is 'destroyed', though it is more accurate to say the universe is transformed.

Lord Shiva is often described as the Destroyer in relation to the Trimurti Gods but likewise, it is more accurate to think of him as the Transformer, which is to say, transformation as passing beyond form altogether, not changing from one form to another.

> The mantram AUM stands for the supreme state of *turiya*, without parts, beyond birth and death, symbol of everlasting joy. Those who know AUM as the Self become the Self. Verily, they are merged in Atma.

Turiya, as in the case of Atma Itself, cannot be identified or described by anything in manifestation. It does not lie outside the three states but is their changeless and unrelated substratum, so to speak. The soundless AUM is experienced in the state of *turiya* that transcends the individual human state. AUM is the true symbol that should be meditated in the heart for it expresses Brahma in all the four states. 'He who knows this, merges himself in Atma.'

Om Tat Sat

The second chapter of Gaudapada's *Kārikā* commentary concerns the nature of illusions. The *Vaitathya-Prakarana* uses reason to prove the unreality of dualism for those not accepting the Vedic authority of the *shruti* texts. In this regard, using a strictly scriptural approach rests on dogmatic thinking. Shankaracharya teaches that the unreality experienced as duality can be clearly established with reason. This is where Buddhists and Jainists fail in their nihilistic theories. For example, some schools of Buddhist thought would have it that all that is *maya*, or illusion to them, has absolutely no ground in reality at all and is of the nature of a void or emptiness. If that were true then nothing could exist at all. According to the Tantras, 'What is here is there also, and what is not here is not there either'. Both 'void' and 'emptiness' are not real as they only negate any positive expression. There is no void in nature and space is not truly empty, for it must be a container for something. Even the unmanifest contains the latent possibilities of all that can be manifested.

Such false notions then come about through *vikalpa*, which is something true only of a figure of speech such as 'void'. Without discrimination, this can become a *viparyaya* or illusion based on ignorance. This is tantamount to the pursuit of worthless objects of the mind. However, Shankara did not set out to condemn the Buddhists but to prove to them, through the common ground of ordinary reason, that there is no conflict between Advaita and the Vedic texts, and that there need be no conflict between Buddhism and the scriptures.

If one would deny or reject Atma, for example, then this must presuppose the existence of the denier and the thing denied! The duality is resolved simply through recollecting the nature of the Real as non-dual, without subject or object.

The mind creates and experiences a stress or a movement (*spanda*) that causes apparent duality. The mind as subject has cognition (*pratyaya*) of objects (*artha*), and names those objects by word (*s'abda*) or language.[133] The dreaming and waking states differ in how they are experienced. The two states are unreal from the metaphysical point of view. However, the phenomena experienced in the waking and dreaming states are appropriate to their own plane. There are degrees of reality, so to speak, but relative to Atma or the supreme principle, objects perceived in both the waking and the dreaming state are as nothing; they are essentially unreal.

The experience of the dream state takes place internally and the experience of the waking state is observed externally. The dream state is of the subtle realm and is the intermediary (U) between the waking (A) and dreamless (M) states of being. The falsity of objects residing within the dream state is due to the perceived smallness of the space in comparison to what is observed in the waking state. On waking, after having been asleep, the objects perceived in the dream state disappear. The example that is given is this: an elephant in the waking state cannot fit inside a person but appears to do so during the cognising of the dream state. The key difference here is the limitation of space owing to the peculiar conditions of the mind.

It follows, time and space being inseparable, that the time identified with a dream is limited in comparison to that which has been experienced. While dreaming a person travels to a faraway land or village and upon waking they realise they have not moved from the place where they have slept. The dream state is an illusion as the objects perceived during the dreaming state disappear upon waking. Objects removed still leave impressions upon the mind, however. Note that the mind is shaped by its impressions, real or not. Hence the need for discrimination and control of thought in yoga practice. According to the Gaudapada *Kārikā*, II: 5–6,

> Thoughtful persons speak of the sameness of the waking and dream states on account of the similarity of the objects [perceived in both states] on the grounds already mentioned.

---

[133] Cf. *Garland of Letters*, p. 13, Woodroffe.

If a thing is non-existent both in the beginning and in the end, it is necessarily non-existent in the present. The objects that we see are really like illusions; still they are regarded [by the unknowing] as real.

Ideas in the dream state are revealed by the inner light of Atma where objects in the waking state are shown forth by sunlight, fire, and so forth. Internal (indistinct) and external (vivid) objects are mere imagination as they are perceived owing to the peculiar conditions of the mind. The power of imagining properly belongs to Ishvara, Lord of the Universe, for the object of creation is already present in the Lord's mind—nothing can be created that is 'new'. From the uninitiated viewpoint, however, the power is (falsely) attributed to *jivatma*. Thus, the artist will talk about 'my work', or 'my creativity', all of which arises from the ignorance of unknowing and belief in separation. From the Advaitan perspective, all of that creation, even on the cosmic level, is in the realm of *maya* and so unreal.

The individual ordinarily considers the objects of perception as reality. Even worshippers of God attribute forms to Ishvara. The forms superimposed on Atma create an illusion that is mistaken for reality. External factors and objects are distinguished by two related points in time. These are imagined with the awareness of the *jivatma* self experiencing ideas by cause and effect that are retained as memories. Trees move by the action of the air and once the air current ceases the tree is back where it began. The apparent measure of time would be perceived between when the wind began and ended. The phases of the Moon are another example. The face of the Moon never changes, only how we experience it in the waking state as it reflects the Sun. This is imagination superimposed upon the non-dual Self.

The *Yoga-Sutras* (Patañjali), when understood, do not in any way disagree with Advaita or with the Vedantic scriptures. However, the point of view is to assist the practitioner who must attain spiritual realisation gradually, over time, which is achieved through devotion and yoga meditation. This involves a science of the mind. The perceived impressions create modifications of the mind known as *vrittis*. At the commencement of yoga, the *savitarka* meditation is to worship the object that is being concentrated on to the exclusion of all else. He who experiences the *savichara* meditation, which means literally 'following', becomes a devotee; the subtle qualities of the object are then touched upon.

This opens the door in turn to higher states of consciousness, though still within the realm of the individual I-sense. The devotee becomes absorbed into the object of worship. At the further reach of what is possible, the yogin with high intellect and that has no desire for worldly or sensorial things can work towards liberation (*moksha*). Yet, from the point of view of absolute Advaita, no one works towards liberation. In the reality of the non-dual, all categories of experience cease to exist save in the sense they are an imagined superimposition upon Atma. The Self exists truly as non-imagined entity and a substratum to all illusions. Time, space and motion are absent in reality, having no relation with it at all; the non-dual (*turiya*) is the substratum of illusion.

The mind takes the shape of the object that is worshipped in ritual. The worshipper or devotee does not partake in idolatry when Atma is known as the substratum of all forms. The mind perceives all objects through the various faculties of perception, the *indriyas* and *tanmatras*. The thought impressions create *upadhis*, likened to 'waves', as a form of vibration. The mental impressions are retained through the mind's faculties such as memory, and for this reason they can be either helpful or harmful at different stages of the individual development.

The Sanskrit word *sadhana* means 'realisation'. The root *sadh* means to accomplish an aim, and so *sadhana* is usually taken to indicate a practice where such realisation is the goal. In ritual and other practices, the Self is realised gradually with the support of symbols or objects of worship. The worship of a symbol absorbs the devotee and the devotee comes to realise the symbol as Brahma. With discrimination, such single-minded devotion can direct the practitioner toward truth. These objects, even though they are ignorance (*avidya*) from the metaphysical point of view, could not exist without the Self (Atma). After experiencing non-duality, if only for a moment, one should then fix the memory to recollect and to continuously think upon non-dual reality. Thus recollection forms an important part of any practice.

When ritual is done over a lengthy period of time and it acts as a support to yoga concentration and meditation (*dhyana*), then both the practice (*sadhana*) and the practitioner (*sadhaka*) become an expression of *dharma* or True Will. The fuller realisation is when Ishvara is known as the first veil upon Atma, and that Atma and Brahma are one.

Om Shanti! Shanti! Shanti!

PART THREE: OTHER WORKS AND REVIEWS

Uniformity against Unity

It will help the reader that is unaccustomed to the metaphysical analogies of Guénon to provide an overview of the symbolism of the metaphysical 'point' and the extension of this into space as a cross, whether two-dimensional or three-dimensional.[134] A cross of vertical and horizontal bars can symbolise Will and Love or Spirit ('essence') and Being ('substance'), for example.

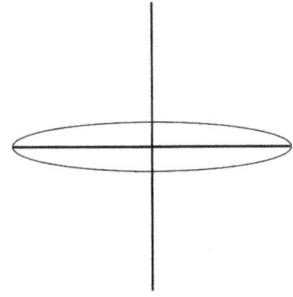

It must first be understood that the vertical axis does not occupy space and time at all. It extends from the principial 'point', which is outside of manifestation. It is through the self-polarisation of the principle, for instance as *purusha* and *prakriti*, 'essence' and 'substance', that manifestation is able to take place. To represent the formation of cyclical manifestation the horizontal axis becomes extended into a circle. In fact, it is not a closed circle and more closely resembles a spiral. An entire state of being is symbolised by one circumference, yet it is really spiralic; no states of being are truly discontinuous. The spiral can extend upwards and downwards and so it is really more like a double helix. It is only necessary to add that an indefinite series of further reflected or duplicated points can be 'located' along any of the radii that can extend from the vertical axis to the circles or spirals—of which there are also an indefinite (though not infinite) number.

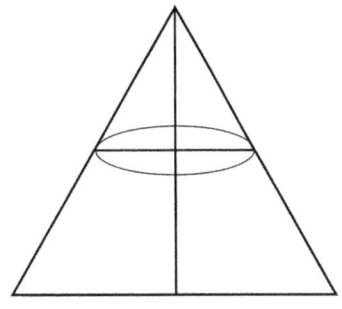

If we place a triangle about the cross we can place Quality or 'essence' at the apex with the principial source of manifestation.[135] Quantity must always involve number, and all numbers are necessarily discontinuous; Quantity is therefore placed at the base of the triangle. The base must then represent total or absolute Quantity; yet this can never be reached in manifestation, which nonetheless tends towards it.

---

[134] This subject is examined in considerable depth across several works of Guénon, including *The Symbolism of the Cross*, *The Multiple States of Being* and *Traditional Forms and Cosmic Cycles*.
[135] Cf. *The Reign of Quantity and the Signs of the Times*, René Guénon.

In the present times, as we near the end of the Manvantara, our world is increasingly dominated by the suppression of quality in favour of quantity. Eventually, it reaches a point of no return. As the world cannot proceed further towards quantity, which is effectively *below* manifestation, the entire world is withdrawn back into the principle. This is called in Sanskrit the *mahapralaya* or the 'great dissolution' at the end of time.

Quality is the content of essence, which by transposition belongs to the principle Itself. Principial unity is pure being, the non-manifest principle of all manifestation. It contains within Itself all possibilities whatsoever and is not limited in any way. It is infinite and therefore not contained by anything. As It is non-manifest It is not in the world, although as universal spirit It permeates all things without being those things. To use the geometric analogy, principial unity at the summit of the vertical axis or axial pole of manifestation contains synthetically within Itself all qualities and determinations that are possible in the domain of manifestation. Through the course of manifestation there is a movement away from unity, from the essential pole. This can be viewed as succession, as in time cycles, or as simultaneous as in the hierarchical elements of a being. At the lowest end of the axis is the substantial pole, pure quantity with indefinite 'atomic' multiplicity implied therein; the only distinction between its elements is numerical.[136]

As we have shown above, the domain in question can be represented by a triangle where the apex is the essential pole, pure quality, and the base is the substantial pole, pure quantity. The quantitative multiplicity of indefinite 'points' increases towards the base.[137] The domain of manifestation is indefinite, thus the base is indefinitely removed from the apex. In fact the base, being pure quantity, can never be reached for pure quantity is actually below manifestation. However that may be, manifestation in the course of its development tends more and more towards it. The apex becomes increasingly remote and disappears from view—and this corresponds to the existing conditions of our world as we find it. In pure quantity, 'units' are only distinguished one from another numerically—and this makes it clear that pure quantity is beneath manifested existence. There is always quality in manifestation, even at the lowest point of a cycle, otherwise it would cease to exist.

---

[136] For the fallacy of 'atomism', see Guénon, *Reign of Quantity* [ibid].
[137] Using the geometric analogy of *Symbolism of the Cross* [ibid], any line has an indefinite number of 'points'—as many as can occupy the same space.

Leibnitz refers to the 'Principle of Indiscernibles' and by this he means that there can be no two beings that are alike in every respect. This is because of the limitlessness of universal possibility, where there cannot be any repetition whatsoever. If two beings are said to be identical then they are not two beings, but one and the same being. In order for there to be discernible difference between beings, there must be a qualitative difference. Thus the determination of beings can never be purely quantitative. This overrides mechanistic conceptions like those of Descartes. Also, it makes atomism a false theory. If atomism is about reducing things to a conceptual 'one' without any quality being involved, it cannot be true. Leibnitz goes on to say that if beings did not differ qualitatively 'they would not even be beings', but something like divisions exactly resembling each other of a homogenous space and time. Such divisions have no real existence, but only what the scholastics called *entia rationis*. Note however that Leibnitz does not have adequate ideas of space and time. He defines space as the 'order of coexistence' and time as the 'order of succession', but considers them from only a logical point of view, thereby reducing them to homogenous containers without quality and so without any effective existence. In fact, space and time have an ontological nature. They exist as conditions determining the special modality distinguished as corporeal existence.

Uniformity, to be in any way possible, presupposes beings deprived of all quality, reducing them to units that can be counted. Obviously this is not true in reality but the efforts of man to impose it robs beings of all qualities and turns them into something very much like machines, machines being the typical product of the modern world demonstrating the predominance of quantity over quality. Uniformity is the exact opposite of unity; it suppresses quality. Modern thinking mistakes uniformity for unity. The fact that this is everywhere apparent is revealed by the separativity and alienation that comes about as a consequence. Uniformity is brought about by forcing everything whatsoever to fit discontinuous quantity that is number, or numerical logic. It results in homogeneity that is only separated by number. Quantity is always separate and cannot unite; likewise everything that proceeds from matter produces nothing but antagonism in many divers forms between fragmentary units that are at a point directly opposite to true unity, pressing toward that point with all the weight of a quantity no longer balanced by its qualities.

From a social point of view, the democratic and egalitarian also robs beings of all discernible difference or quality by insisting that they are all the same and that everyone can do anything. Democracy reduces all to numbers and 'equality' makes everyone the same. Uniformity instead of unity is thus a topsy-turvy ideal.[138] Education suppresses quality, though it cannot do this absolutely, so results will never be identical. However, it moves in a downward direction and it could not be any other way since it is quantity, and quantity is the bottom, actually below manifested existence.

It is at this end of the domain of manifestation where we now are. Modern man has used the prevailing conditions to impose uniformity as a false unity on the world and all beings in it. Uniformity relies wholly on number to realise itself in forms such as machines both mechanical and digital, and in an indefinite amount of statistics and data collection and production. In the current time, all is produced by and reduced to more or less faceless data streams becoming a prison both literal and virtual. The protection of data only exists, for example, because it is the data of the person that counts and not their qualities. As it is purely quantitative, the Act itself along with much other related legislation has to be continually updated. What counts, they say, is number, yet it is number, which is pure quantity, that is at the bottom end of the axis, the furthest away from principial unity. Indeed, the essential pole of existence is entirely lost from view.

There are some who would cry out in objection, 'But individuality is encouraged in our society. I have all my qualities!' But what is it that is really being encouraged, however? Uniformity automatically presupposes individuals as being without quality or essence, which by transposition is the spiritual, principial unity. The modern world emphasises the separateness of a person as uniformity is contrary to unity, which requires quality or essence. Instead of allowing the faculties to exist in conformity with their principle, thereby to know spiritual reality, they are rigorously suppressed.

---

[138] Some of our readers suffer the affliction of being politically minded. For their benefit we should point out that we are not interested in politics in any way whatsoever and that we are not proposing some alternative kind of political system. All political systems are anti-initiatic by definition. It should be obvious from everything we have written that we have no interest in changing the social order, which is an exoteric concern. Any person that retains any kind of political affiliation is impervious, ipso facto, to any spiritual influence.

The faculties are redirected to sub-infra levels of reality by anti-traditional uniformity enforced in all areas of 'normal' life and by the productions of the modern world, and thus even by choice of the person. There is apparently something for everyone, but these 'somethings' are designed in a uniform manner in conformity with pure materiality, which involves gross distortion and inversion of the truth. We have arrived at a time when there is suppression of even the ordinary senses. The audio faculty is suppressed, for example, through being subjected to higher and higher levels of environmental and other noise. The visual faculty is suppressed through digital and virtual images, which are a substitute. Computers, phones and television bombard the senses with information that limits the whole range possible to a mere fraction. Separation from others, sometimes even enforced by law, is the ultimate or 'end result'.

Conventional science knows nothing existing beyond the physical and mental state, and its knowledge of this is extremely limited as it is based on theory, supposition and experimentation. Our language lacks precise terms for the higher states so we will need to resort to the Hindu doctrines before we can explain why it is such a tragedy that the 'essence' of the individual should be suppressed and even removed from the being entirely—for some branches of science seem compelled towards this end. Essence is the principle that forms the individuality; it is not itself part of the individuality or corporeal domain. Similarly, what is called in Sanskrit the *boddhi* or higher intellectual faculty is at the formless level and has no part in the ego or *ahankara*.

The true 'Name' or signature of an individuality is called Nama, and from Nama comes Rupa, the form of the individuality.[139] The True Self and therefore True Will of an individual, group or collective, can only be known via the *boddhi*. The Nama is quite close to what is sometimes called the Holy Guardian Angel; it has the possibility, through transposition, of entering the supra-sensible and non-individual states while yet retaining its 'true name'. When even the ordinary senses are suppressed, the subtle or psychic senses undergo distortion. The ways to the higher states are eventually sealed off completely. Thus it can be seen how the suppression of quality and imposition of quantity in all things is truly an anti-spiritual force.

---

[139] See 'Name and Form: Nama and Rupa', *Way of Knowledge*.

The Serpent Power

Sir John Woodroffe's seminal work *The Serpent Power* is a highly technical and thoroughgoing study of Kundalini Yoga that has been a considerable influence on modern thinking regarding what was once a subject wrapped in almost total obscurity. Over the last fifty years or more distorted notions of Tantra have arisen through both theory and practice being removed from all doctrinal contexts. Woodroffe himself is not entirely without blame in this respect; in order to drive home his particular fondness for the 'physical' yoga and *siddhis* or 'magical powers', he renders the differences between methods of yoga somewhat ambiguously, as we shall see. The present article is in no way an analysis of the entire book, which would take another whole book to accomplish. We here focus on the section, 'Theoretical Bases of Yoga', which is central to understanding the more detailed applications of the knowledge.

We learn that the doctrine of the chakras is to be found in other *shastras*, not only the Tantras. Only the accomplished yogin can really take Kundalini to the *sahasrara* chakra. There are nonetheless preliminary practices, without which the *sadhaka* (practitioner) is not considered fit to worship a Deva. Such daily practices involve 'worship' alone, which means use of imaginative or mental images; properly speaking it is worship (*upasana*) rather than yoga (union) in the real sense. The lotuses or chakras have a central significance, because by the use of their symbolism the Shakti is worshipped in various parts of the body, or apparently so. Apart from anything else this purifies and prepares the *sadhaka* from the ground upward as it were, commencing with the elemental *bhutas*. There are other forms of yoga that are not concerned with that at all, it should be noted.

One interesting point raised by Woodroffe is that critics of Tantrik practice, both from within Hinduism and outsiders, quite often seem ignorant of the fact that references to it appear in some of the earliest *Upanishads* and *Puranas*. It is not in any way separate from Vedic knowledge and neither is it truly heterodox, though we have often been led to believe that is so.

The Indian schools have it that the 'heart' is considered to be the seat of waking consciousness. It should be noted that the heart has a 'cavity', which is the seat of the soul, so it is more than another word for 'mind', which is in fact the domain of the Moon in traditional knowledge whereas the heart's intelligence is symbolised by the Sun.

The three states of consciousness are waking, dreaming and dreamless sleep. Waking consciousness is, from the metaphysical point of view, the most deluded, for the mind is ensnared in its many objects, which it takes to be real. In dreaming sleep the external senses are withdrawn, although the representative faculty continues to be active or awake. Thus it is possible to experience the phenomenon of dreaming, which is a continuation of consciousness in the subtle as opposed to the gross state. In dreamless sleep all the faculties are withdrawn and for this reason nothing is remembered of it. The three states are symbolised by the three letters of AUM. The secret of AUM is that it includes a fourth state beyond these, called *turiya*, in which Atma and Brahma are one, and which is called Knowledge.

By analogy, yoga meditation practices follow the withdrawal of faculties that takes place in the three states. First, there is withdrawal of the physical senses and of the identification with sense objects. On the subtle level there can be a qualitative appraisal of objects, for we are still involved with the plane of form. In Western occultism a great deal of emphasis is placed on the subtle plane, which is there given a general umbrella term, the 'astral'. However, the subtle senses too must be withdrawn in real yoga, otherwise this only reaches as far as 'worship', which is the preliminary practice. No object, whether gross or subtle, is Atma or the Real, and so the discrimination of what is real and not real forms a vital part of yoga and not only *jnana* yoga as exemplified for example in the teachings of Shankaracharya. It is the *boddhi*, the higher intellectual faculty that is completely outside and beyond the individual human state with all its perceptions of false knowledge, that is alone able to truly tell the difference between what is real and what is not real. At the beginning there is 'practice'.

The author provides a useful list of some of the many source texts that refer to the practice of yoga, in particular the lotuses or chakras. Before so doing he mentions the *brahmarandra*, which allows the continuation of the 'vital nerve' called *shushumna* so as to form the *sahasrara* chakra that is above the crown of the head. This forms the entry and exit point for the *prana* (vital breath) that is the path to Knowledge.

The *Hamsa Upanishad* insists that the knowledge contained therein should be communicated only to the student of peaceful mind and who is self-controlled and devoted to his guru. The *Upanishad* mentions by name the six chakras in the context of raising the *vayu* (air-spirit 'going forth') from the *muladhara*, and which really constitutes Kundalini Yoga.

The word *ham-sa* denotes the breath and is also associated with Brahma and the swan, as one of the symbols of Brahma or wisdom in general. The Hamsa is here considered to be the *jiva* or individual self, situated in an eight-petalled lotus immediately below the *anahatha* or heart chakra. It is here that the Goddess is worshipped (Ishta Devata), since the *jiva* is otherwise involved with all kinds of actions, objects and predispositions that arise from ignorance. At the centre of the lotus or labyrinth, so to speak, is 'dispassion'.

The *Brahma Upanishad* mentions the naval, heart, throat, and head, as places where the four quarters of Brahma shine—or the four centres from which Brahma may be (partially) attained. The two chakras below these are not mentioned here but are called 'tamasic', that is leading to the lower states through inertia, avarice, passions and so forth.

The *Dhyanabindu Upanishad* refers to hearing the *anahatha* sounds, which are internal and not external. The *Upanishad* makes mention of meditation on Vishnu in the naval, Brahma (seated on a lotus) in the heart and Rudra (a form of Kali) in the forehead. However, in verse 13 meditation is directed on a hundred lotuses with one hundred petals each, and after that on Sun, Moon and Fire—which have a relation with the Caduceus of Hermes, where the two serpents are Sun and Moon and the central axis is Fire. It is Atma here that rouses the lotus and that takes the honey from it, so to speak, passing then to the three principles mentioned.

It may be seen from this how greatly modern forms of yoga have simplified the knowledge, so that there are persons who will think there must be seven chakras, not six and not ten, and will even argue that they must be seen in a particular colour that is the 'correct' colour, as according to their sophistry.

The *Amritanada Upanishad* refers to the five elements and above them *ardhamatra* (*ajna*). The elements (*tattvas*) are those in the chakras, for example the *anahatha* is the entrance for *vayu* (air). The Gate of Liberation is then somewhat beyond this. It is said that the subtle breath (*prana*) and the inward sense (*manas*) go along the way that the yogin sees (*pasyati*), which means that the 'breath' passes upwards from *muladhara* according to the mind and will (intention) of the yogin. It should be borne in mind also that the Sanskrit word *prana* means a lot of things, and that 'breath' is an analogy not to be taken literally. It can be almost anything, including food or sustenance or the person themselves.

For this reason it is stated elsewhere that 'prana eats prana', and the same is said of the *devas*. So one might think of 'food of the gods', for example, whether sacraments to be imbibed or sacrifices. Also, that the rising upward of *prana* is one of the first principles of all sacrifice when that word is correctly understood. So it is that we might hear an ignorant person say they are 'giving up' something, meaning they are going to do without it because it might be good for them in some way. That has nothing at all to do with a sacrifice in the real sense.

The *Kshurika Upanishad* speaks of the 72,000 *nadis* and of *ida*, *pingala* and *shushumna*. All of these, apart from the *shushumna*, are served by the yoga of meditation. Here again, the practitioner is instructed to get himself into the white (pure) *nadi* and to drive *prana-vayu* through the centre of the heart lotus. Various physical techniques of Hatha Yoga are mentioned in the commentary, as well as 'heating' the Kundalini by internal fire.

There are many more books, not least of which are the ones composed by the great sage Shankara himself, which include the much celebrated *Ananda Lahiri*.[140]

There is a curious interlude worthy of note. Woodroffe mentions that the Tantras have been the subject of modern criticism, which is not at all surprising to learn. However, he goes on to produce a lengthy summary of a letter passed on to him from the disciple of an unnamed guru, a Hindu that had an English education.[141] This was elicited by the gift of the traditional Sanskrit texts that form the basis of *The Serpent Power*.[142] The guru begins by stating that yoga as a means of liberation (*moksha*) is attained through *jnana* (knowledge) and *karma* ('action' or quite often ritual practices). He does not mention *bhakti* yoga (devotional) but this will be explained later. He warns, quite correctly, that there is more than one kind of 'bliss' (*ananda*), and that physical bliss, whether of the gross or the subtle order, cannot in any way lead to liberation, which can only be attained through direct and permanent abiding with Brahma, the supreme.

---

[140] See Woodroffe, *Hymns to the Goddess*, pp. 180–189.
[141] *Serpent Power* pp. 273–276 [Dover edition 1974].
[142] 'Traditional', that is to say, the Sanskrit texts were originally the property of an ancestral Hindu family, as was customary.

The distinction made between types of 'bliss' (*ananda*) is quite essential, and is one that has been blurred by modern writers for a century and that has not in any way abated.[143] A person might even think they get 'bliss' through drink or drugs, but clearly that does not lead to *moksha* liberation! And yet, some neo-spiritualist groups and individuals have even gone so far as to suggest that it might, gaining the devotion (and fees) of many a drug addict.

The guru then denounces the Buddhists as atheists, not without some justification, and that they 'locked up these two doors which gave entry to liberation' (that is, *jnana* and *karma* or knowledge and practice). He then goes on to denounce the Westernised attempts at making a religion out of Hinduism. In particular, the Arya-Samaja, of whom he says claimed to be 'knowers of Brahma', was a kind of 'church' religion that was an attempt to subvert Hinduism from within by the British Colonialists, aided and abetted by the Theosophists. It did not last for very long in fact. He also mentions the cult known as the Brahmos, which Sri Ramakrishna seems also to have experienced some difficulty with for their strange ideas.[144]

A very interesting view is put forward, presumably not of his own invention as it is based on scriptural knowledge: Vishnu, the Lord of the Manvantara, manifested these false doctrines, including the Buddha himself, so as to wipe out the knowledge of the Vedas in the Dark Age of Kali Yuga. However, the plan was subtle. By producing *shastras* that were suited to the dark minds of people in the Kali Yuga, it became possible that they might still rise from it 'to higher things'. He then singles out the *Satchakra Sadhana* as particularly materialistic.

---

[143] Thus we have, in a book on the cult of Mithras that was published quite recently, supposedly written by a Sufi ('master') that also happens to be a member of various neo-spiritualist groups, a description of yoga that means no more than getting into a sort of trance, or of being 'spaced out'.

[144] The reader is referred to the works of René Guénon where all this is verified, in particular *An Introduction to the Study of the Hindu Doctrines* and *Theosophy: History of a Pseudo-Religion*. In another book, *Studies in Hinduism*, the whole of chapter three is devoted to the subject of Kundalini Yoga, where special reference is given to the book *The Serpent Power*. It must also be mentioned that with regard to the present study, and any Hindu texts in a modern language, one must read and understand Guénon's book *Man and His Becoming according to the Vedānta*, without which, one is not in any way properly equipped.

He qualifies this by saying that the bliss attained through the leading of the Kundalini to the *sahasrara* is not to be denied, as it is affirmed by those who have experienced it—but that this bliss (*ananda*) is momentary and merely a superior kind of physical bliss, which, as with all things of the body, disappears (and so is not the Real strictly speaking). He uses a method of discrimination similar to that of Shankaracharya and says that it is not Brahma and so cannot possibly be liberation.

Most interestingly, in respect of liberation, he mentions that one must leave the *sahasrara* through the piercing of the *brahmarandra* and so departing from the corporeal state. Such Tantriks as he has previously described seek to remain in the body, 'and thus to obtain liberation cheaply'. It seems that later, in his comment, Woodroffe chooses to interpret this as though it means the person has to die before they can get liberation. In fact, 'leaving the corporeal state' happens in advanced levels of *samadhi* and even to a certain extent in Kundalini Yoga, but there is usually a return to the physical state, of course. Woodroffe admits that in translating the letter from Bengali and then paraphrasing it, he has 'pointed' the translation so as to accentuate the acerbic nature of it. So he has quite deliberately misrepresented the gift he received from a genuine guru and we cannot trust the rest of his summary.[145]

Whether the guru really denounces *all* forms of Tantras we cannot know for sure, though that is how Woodroffe has made it appear. The guru says that the Tantras are a Dharma, which means they are suitable for some persons, and that also makes the Tantras a part of Vedic knowledge. He is alleged to have said that the lotuses or chakras are not real because they cannot be seen—the kind of argument that would only be raised by a profane person—but this part of the letter was very amusing, because he also says that some tantrik gurus are like sellers of lotuses at a garden party! All in a variety of different colours, and so forth. It does not take that much of a stretch of the imagination to think that even a century ago in India there might have been some gurus like that.

---

[145] Why would he do this? It transpires that Woodroffe has certain objections to matters of fundamental principle that are integral to the doctrine, including what *yoga* even is. He uses such false (or fabricated) arguments as a lever to push forward his own views on such matters, as we shall see.

The worship of *devas* and *devis* in lotuses is a form of external worship, but none of the old books suggest that the chakras are physically present in the body, or could be seen under a microscope, for example. They are interior, that is to say relatively existent on the subtle plane not the gross, and in that way the external worship is converted into internal worship. Woodroffe is able to clarify for us the apparent omission of *bhakti* yoga when only *jnana* and *karma* are mentioned. Bhakti may partake of the nature of either the first or second. In a footnote:

> Thus, the offering of flowers and the like to the Divinity partakes of the nature of Karma; whilst Bhakti in its transcendental aspect, in which by love of the Lord the devotee is merged in Him, is a form of Samadhi.

Laya Yoga—which is broadly the subject of *Serpent Power*—combines both *jnana* and *karma* yoga, and it is *jnana* by which liberation is alone gained:

> In the Ajna is Manas and Om, and on this the Sadhaka meditates. The Sadhaka's Atma must be transformed into a meditation on this lotus. His Atma is the Dhyana of Om, which is the inner Atma of those whose Buddhi is pure.

That is to say, the practitioner must identify himself with the Atma in the meditation on the lotus. The meditation on the Sanskrit AUM (or Om), once the deceptions of the mind have been cleared away so as to allow the pure ray from the *boddhi*, which alone can reveal Atma, means that the real Atma becomes the 'inner Atma'. This is more or less the inner guru in more than one tradition although most also insist that a human guru is needed if knowledge is to become effective realisation. One might make comparison with both the Mahadevi Shakti as inner teacher, or the Guardian Angel of the Western tradition—though with all due caution in regard to the latter as it has been rather obfuscated by occultists that have made of it something 'mystical' as an excuse to cover their own lack of any real knowledge.

> He realises that he and the Brahman are one, and that Brahman is alone real (Sat) and all else unreal (Asat). He thus becomes an Advaitavadi or one who realises the identity of the individual and universal Self.

And as for worship, and lest we think the practitioner achieves all this on his own efforts (let alone without a guru),

The Devi [Shakti Devi], by dissolving Kundalini in the Para-bindu, effects the liberation of some Sadhakas through their meditation upon the identity of Shiva and Atma in the Bindu. She does so in the case of others by a similar process and by meditation on Shakti. In other cases this is done by concentration of thought on the Parama-purusha [supreme essence of the Mahadevi Shakti or her true nature] and in other cases by the meditation of the Sadhaka on the union of Shiva and Shakti. In fact, the worshipper of any particular Devata should realise that he is one with the object of worship.

There are thus many ways but all ways lead to the same goal, and as for worship as a support to knowledge, one might say there are as many ways as there are individual practitioners. From the renowned *Ananda Lahiri* of Sri Shankaracharya:

Kuharini, Thou sprinklest all things with the stream of nectar which flows from the tips of Thy two feet; and as Thou returnest to Thine own place, Thou vivifiest and makest visible all things that were aforetime invisible; and on reaching Thy abode Thou resumest Thy snake-like coil and sleepest.

Thus, 'after union with Shiva, Kundalini makes her return journey'. It is only after repeated unions, and at the will of the yogin (which by that time is no less than the will of God), that the final journey is made, from which there is no return to the physical body—or any body or individuality at all, since the yogin becomes a *mukta*, finally liberated.

The Yogi thus does claim to secure the bliss of Liberation by making entry thereto through the doors of Karma and Jnana Yoga.

General Principles

We now move on to the general principles that underlie the practice as described. We must answer the question, 'How does the raising of Kundalini Shakti and her union with Shiva effect the state of ecstatic union (*samadhi*) and spiritual experience?' Some of the terms used by Woodroffe are not in any way suitable and 'ecstasy' is in no way descriptive of *samadhi*. In fact, in so far as yoga or 'union' is concerned, ecstasy is almost the exact reverse, as its literal meaning is 'to go out from oneself'. However, there is the pure meditative approach and there is the Kundalini Yoga that is the subject of the present work, and these are distinctly different in *means*, at least, if not the goal, which must always remain one and the same.

Unfortunately, the difference is obfuscated in *The Serpent Power*, presumably by the fact that Woodroffe's understanding of yoga is not based on principial knowledge but on the applications and means or methods of knowledge, which can only ever be secondary. We will attempt with what follows to rectify this difficulty as best we can, for it can otherwise lead to real misunderstanding.

The first method is that in which *samadhi* is attained by what Woodroffe terms as 'intellective process' of meditation (*kriya jnana*), with the aid of preliminary techniques such as *mantra* or Hatha Yoga, by which is meant control of breath and assuming the *mudra* (seated posture in this case). This involves stilling of the mind and complete detachment from the world, from worldly preoccupations and pursuits. According to the author, in this first kind of yoga, pure meditation, the supreme state may be realised (i.e. *moksha*) but without the union that is experienced as taking place in the body through Kundalini. And that is because the union apparently taking place in the body is in fact an appearance only, due to ignorance. It transpires later that either the author did not understand this or that he deliberately sought to subvert it. Union 'taking place within the body' is meaningless and cannot in any case be yoga union, as that involves the higher intellect no matter what means are employed towards that goal.

He goes on to say that the second method does not preclude the 'intellective process' [by which is really meant mentation, not intellect in the true sense] but the Shakti of the body as Kundalini is united with her Lord or Shiva (as consciousness) so as to procure the same end result as that of *jnana* yoga. Though it is the yogin that arouses Kundalini, it is the Shakti alone that gives knowledge (*jnana*), for *she is that knowledge*. This is easily understood if it is known that the intellectual intuition, which has nothing to do with the 'intellective process' mentioned earlier, is the *boddhi* and in certain respects this is none other than the Shakti Herself. However, we must call into question whether the author understood what yoga is, given that he has muddled the means with the end or the goal itself, and has first explained 'intellectual mentation' as a preliminary training of mind but then later confuses this with the goal of yoga itself, of which intellective process forms only a part of the means and has nothing to do with that goal. He also makes no reference to the vital part that discrimination plays in all forms of yoga practice. We must bear in mind that 'yoga' is not only the means but is expressive of the goal itself.

According to the author, advocates of *jnana* yoga and Kundalini Yoga often regard their way as the highest but in fact none of these ways are truly separate, and this is echoed in the traditional saying that Raja Yoga, which includes all of these methods, is the highest.

Now it is needful to explain that what kind of yoga practice is more suitable is down to individual possibilities and the range of powers that the person possesses at the outset. The *dhyana yogin* (master of meditation) does not neglect the body or indeed practice any form of mortification, as is sometimes supposed, as that is 'more apt to produce disordered imagination' than true realisation. On the other hand, he is not in any way as concerned with the body as the practitioner of Hatha Yoga is. A *dhyana yogin* may even be weak or sick of the body, and so short-lived. The author here makes a difference between the Jivanmukti who obtains liberation in the flesh, which he says is not the complete liberation as the person is still subject to sickness and death, and the one that obtains it when he dies, where it can be complete and perfect. He insists that in the case of Laya Yoga or Kundalini, where the central power in the body is raised, the same illumination can be gained. However, he has blurred somewhat the fact that raising the Kundalini alone does not gain liberation or even real initiation in itself, as was mentioned by the nameless guru he quoted from previously. Perhaps he would have benefited from paying more careful attention. There is also some ambiguity with his insistence on 'bodily power' as that could only be a preparation, suited to some persons but not others, and not by any means resulting in illumination of the kind referred to. By the end of this, he reverses the doctrine, asserting that 'union of the body' is superior, which is an impossibility.

The *Shakta Tantra* claims to give both enjoyment (any form of sensorial or intellectual enjoyment or indeed suffering) in this world and the next, and liberation (*moksha*) from all worlds. This is quite correct but the author does not comprehend the contextual meaning:

> If the ultimate Reality is one which exists in two aspects of quiescent enjoyment of the Self in Liberation from all form and of active enjoyment in objects—that is, as pure 'Spirit' and 'Spirit in matter'—then a complete union with Reality demands such unity in both of its aspects. It must be known both 'here' and 'there'.

The 'here' and the 'there' has been taken out of its context and a different meaning applied. Reality in the supreme sense cannot be said to have 'two aspects', which is dualism. When reality has aspects it is a only a relative degree of reality that we are considering. This last sentence has been taken out of the *Vishvasara Tantra*:

> What is here is there, what is not here is nowhere.

This is in some ways similar to the Hermetic 'as above and so below' maxim, for it concerns the relationship of the macrocosm and the microcosm, and is quite essential in understanding how all this yoga of lotuses and so forth can be in any way effective. Woodroffe has changed the meaning and rendered it in dualistic terms. There is also no 'spirit in matter' and 'matter' is in any case a word that does not exist in Sanskrit. We can guess that what is meant here is the enjoyment in sense objects that pertain to the physical or gross level as well as the enjoyment of perfect knowledge of the supreme principle or spirit. That would then seem to be a flat contradiction of Hindu doctrines; one cannot have one's cake and eat it too. However, it is the word *quiescent* that makes it clear there is no disagreement after all; it is only that the author seems to be driving a particular kind of wedge through the teaching, and in this he confuses what he terms as the 'fundamental bodily power' with spiritual realisation.

It transpires later in the text that, if Woodroffe practiced anything at all, then he must have been one of those tantriks described earlier by the nameless guru, and that are addicted both to the body and the *siddhis* or magical powers. The bias would then explain how he was led to confusing the means of yoga with the goal, which is always the same. If he was not a practitioner then it is a salutary lesson in how erudition does not in any way equal knowledge in any real or true sense. Now, *quiescence* is non-action, something that is vital to the Eastern paths (including Taoism) but that is almost completely incomprehensible to the Western mentality—and that by now is unfortunately a mentality (and type of education) that has distorted all traditions in the world. Clearly the kind of 'enjoyment' spoken of here is not one that is accessible to 'anyone', and neither is it a common state of affairs. So Woodroffe has opened the way, perhaps inadvertently, to what will amount in some persons to anti-metaphysical interpretation of the Tantras. He goes on to compound this:

It is held to be false teaching that happiness hereafter can only be had by neglect to seek it now, or in deliberately sought for suffering and mortification.

There is firstly confusion between religious 'salvation' of a 'happy hereafter' and *moksha* Liberation of the Advaitans. Any deliberate suffering or mortification has no true place in the Tantras or in any traditional doctrine, but Westerners have often used their own bias towards action (*karma*) as a weapon to undermine and subvert Hinduism. One might then also wonder exactly what the source of such 'false teaching' alluded to actually is? Unfortunately the claim rests on the kind of vague generalisation that is so much loved by neo-spiritualists in search of evidence to support their self-invented theories. The real teaching on this is in fact very clear. According to the *Bhagavad Gita* 17: 5, with the commentary by Shankara,

> Those persons who, given to ostentation and pride, and possessed of passion, attachment and strength, undertake severe austerities not sanctioned in the scriptures.[146]

In the context, it has previously been written that while one in thousands may be devoted to the gods, which owes to the state of *sattvas* (wisdom, clarity and peace of mind), most creatures and men are of the nature of *rajas* and *tamas*, which is *karma* (action) and ignorance. The next verse relates that those who torture all the organs in the body in fact torture that divine Person (in this case Krishna Himself), in so far as the body is its product and Atma Itself the Witness. And those who do this are 'possessed of demoniacal conviction'. These do not discriminate, as according to Shankara, and such only comes about through disobedience to all scriptural injunctions. And further more, as Shankara explains, these men, as having a demoniacal nature, must even be rigorously avoided: 'This is an instruction.'

Furthermore, the notion of postponing either salvation (the lesser mystery) or liberation (the greater mystery) to the 'hereafter' is something peculiar to certain kinds of religious thought and has nothing to do with Hinduism. It is as though one has to create an argument that is entirely imagined to support the distortion of the teaching so as to make it fit with the modernist fixation with body, mind and the desire for action—all of which are ultimately ways of ignorance, which the Hindu doctrines and Tantras insist on.

---

[146] *Bhagavad Gita with the commentary of Shankaracharya*, translated by Swami Gambhirananda [Advaita Ashrama, Second Edition April 2018].

> It is the one Shiva who is the supreme blissful experience, and who appears in the form of a man with a life of mingled pleasure and pain. Both happiness here and the bliss of liberation here and hereafter may be attained if the identity of these Shivas be realised in every human act.

The Tantrik *sadhaka*, when fulfilling any of the natural functions of the body, does so, saying and believing 'I am Shiva'. Thus he recognises that his life and the play of all its activities are not separate things to be egotistically pursued, rather they are all conceived as part of the divine action in nature (Shakti) manifesting and operating in the form of man. What then follows is descriptive of devotional practices. For example, in the Shakta ritual, when drinking wine one should imagine that it is the Shakti that is drinking it and not oneself. This forms part of the ongoing and continual observance. It is not merely a matter of saying that 'everything is divine' and so nothing matters!

> To fully realise Her, as such, is to perfect this particular manifestation of Hers which is himself.

This requires careful qualification: Shiva 'appears as a man' with all the common afflictions of men, but this is an illusion that owes to ignorance of the true state of affairs. To 'perfect this particular manifestation of Hers' means perfecting the individual self, which is misleading in so far as the individual (*ahankara*) only exists relatively to the state of ignorance; it cannot really be perfected as such. It is always, by its very nature, subject to contingencies. It is not the Real.

> Who is more divine, he who neglects and spurns the body or mind that he may attain some fancied spiritual superiority, or he who rightly cherishes both as forms of the one Spirit which they clothe? ... The *Kularnava Tantra* says: 'By what men fall, by that they rise'.

The last paragraph, 'Who is more divine...' is quite a subtle distortion of the teaching and requires special treatment: 'By what men fall, by that they rise' is meaningless when removed from its metaphysical context, as the author has done. One must discern spirit in all being and activities, it is true. It is also possible to sink and never rise again! Once again we have the false argument raised, as if all traditional teaching apart from the Tantras were against the body and mind. As for 'spiritual superiority', that could only be the boast of a profane person so it is, or should be, completely irrelevant in the present context. Neither the renunciationist nor the slave of the senses is divine so long as they are in the human state.

Woodroffe goes on to say that such things as may cause a man to fall *may* be impediments, but if rightly conceived they may equally become 'instruments of attainment'. One might then wonder how this can be? All such things belong to the realm of action, and so have a purely relative existence. It is nonetheless true that those 'things that men may cast aside' may have been cast aside in ignorance, without true discrimination or any knowledge at all, in which case it makes no difference either way. Ignorance remains ignorant and only knowledge destroys ignorance. The Tantras do not in any way refute or contradict the unity of the Hindu doctrines, but it might seem so as according to some of what is put in the author's conclusions.

In the next twenty or so pages that follow he really does seem to be making a 'scientistic' case for Tantra, going so far as to use vague, populist terms like 'cosmic energy'. This involves a completely futile discussion with a learned friend of Woodroffe's, a discussion based on physics, which cannot, by definition, in any way explain metaphysical doctrine. After this, Woodroffe then concludes with the complete reversal of the doctrine as previously mentioned, where he wants to assert 'physical enjoyment' or bliss as a higher or more complete yoga union, which once again confuses the means with the goal, which must always remain the same. What is so very surprising is that his conclusions are a more or less total contradiction of all he has gathered together and presented from various schools of thought in the previous forty or so pages. We can examine the idea of what constitutes rising and falling from a metaphysical point of view, so as to dispel all possible confusion:[147]

Metaphysical knowledge is the principle from which all other knowledge derives, the latter being contingent knowledge, which includes philosophy in the etymological sense. There are thus two points of view, one ascending and one descending. The descending point of view, by which 'men fall', implies the development of knowledge that starts from the principle but necessarily becomes increasingly remote from the principle. The other point of view, 'by that they rise', is one by which men may proceed from the inferior to the superior, or from the exterior to the interior if we want to put it that way. This involves the gradual acquisition of knowledge.

---

[147] See Guénon, *Spiritual Authority and Temporal Power* p. 73, which we have here paraphrased in part.

It then becomes clear that the author seems to lack any truly metaphysical comprehension of the texts, and takes a literal and 'scientific' view, which then explains why he thinks physicality to be superior to all else. We cannot suppose there was any insincerity in this, but he has gone to elaborate lengths to 'make his case', rather in the way of a legal attorney—a case that happens to be a departure from the principial unity that underpins all of the Hindu doctrines.

We are in no way proposing abstention from anything, or of the 'giving up of things' that we have already explained as a false notion of sacrifice. It is the over-simplification of doctrines, or as it is in this case the deliberate and in some ways quite subtle distortion of them, that we must be opposed to, for it leads to confusion, some of which is to push a point of view that might even be called 'political', and with some justification. It is what the guru of the letter given to Woodroffe began with, when he talked of those who will 'throw dust in the face' of others so as to plant their false notions. It is easily possible that in the case of Woodroffe, such subversion crept in unawares, as there is quite a bit of difference between his conclusions at the end of the piece and the more detailed observations that preceded them.

Thus the exposition, otherwise quite brilliant and very learned, is marred by what can only be an anti-traditional bias typical of the modern mentality. And this is very unfortunate, as it will only have reinforced the prejudice that readers of the book will retain; very often without even knowing it is there. With all that said, *The Serpent Power* is a remarkable treatise, well worth anyone's time and trouble, but one must always keep both eyes wide open when reading any traditional or ancient subject in a modern language as the subversion can easily pass notice yet all the while obtaining its damaging effect, which is sometimes to completely reverse the meaning of symbolism.

The System of Antichrist
Truth and Falsehood in Postmodernism and the New Age

Book by Charles Upton [Sophia Perennis 2001]

Here is a case of postmodern writing against postmodernism. A good portion of this substantial tome is dedicated to denouncing the influential gurus of the New Age. The author, in spite of the 'spiritual master' status afforded him by his publishers, seems never to have dropped the populist style of writing. He has an insatiable appetite for the exposé, and has even gone so far as to deconstruct New Age celebrities such as Depak Chopra ('Entrepreneural Hinduism'). He is also prepared to take on the very horrible distortions of doctrine proposed in *The Celestine Prophecy* and *A Course in Miracles*. That certainly might provide a service for those who have been duped by these fake New Age inventions, of which *A Course in Miracles* is clever in presenting an appearance of real traditional doctrine while subversively altering such diverse sources of it as Hinduism and Gnosticism to fit the prejudice of the authors, or rather 'channellers'. Upton usefully shows how the motive for the work was hatred of Christianity in the first place.

The author devotes considerable space to what amounts to a relentless victimisation of writer Carlos Castaneda—to whom he says he was introduced at a hippy beach party in California in the late 60s. Commenting on *Tales of Power*, where Castaneda enters the otherworld or *nagual*, the author says that Castaneda,

> Comes closer than anywhere else in his books to the classic mystical experience, as in the *tonal* he drinks his fill of mental and imaginative experience.

This is rather strange if we consider that mystical experience must usually have a religious framework. In fact, the teachings of don Juan, whoever that might have been, have nothing to do with mysticism. The shortcomings of mysticism are well explained in *The Fire from Within*, Carlos Castaneda. This relates to the 'mold of man', an analogy used by don Juan that causes grievous offence to Upton, for it is descriptive of the 'personal God' or God-reflection. According to don Juan, it is nothing more than a kind of 'stamp', a seal or impression by which man is defined and limited. This happens to be in accordance with much of the Hermetic and Gnostic texts, as well as to Qabalistic doctrine. Don Juan explains it here with vigorous symbolism that is in perfect agreement with traditional metaphysics:

> He said that I had to go beyond the mold, that the mold was merely a stage, a stopover that brought temporary peace and serenity to those who journey into the unknown, but that it was sterile, static. It was at the same time a flat reflected image in a mirror and the mirror itself. And the image was a man's image ... He [don Juan] assured me that even if I was able to *see*, I was bound to make the same misjudgment that mystics have made. Anyone who *sees* the mold of man automatically assumes that it is God.

In fact this angered Castaneda almost as much as it has angered Charles Upton; perhaps not surprisingly, both men had a Catholic upbringing, although it could have been any form of dogmatic religious fundamentalism, which is always a distortion of the one true and universal religious doctrine, which is that of love. Even Shankarāchārya himself has alluded to this 'mould of man', as noted by René Guénon in *The Symbolism of the Cross*, p. 129.

> Even before any outward expression takes place, this insufficiency [of the individual human understanding] already reveals itself in formal thought ... any idea that is thought of with intensity ends by adopting to some extent a human form, namely that of the thinker; to use a striking simile of Shankarāchārya, it might be said that 'thought flows into man as molten metal is poured into the founder's mould'. The very intensity of the thought makes it occupy the whole of the man, more or less as water fills a vessel to the brim; it then assumes the shape of that which contains it and limits it, in other words it becomes anthropomorphic.

Later, Castaneda has a further vision of the 'mold of man', which brings him to his knees, in spite of what he has just learned. Don Juan chastises him:

> He called me pious and careless and said I would make a great priest; now I could even pass for a spiritual leader who had a chance *seeing* of God. He urged me, in a jocular way, to start preaching and describe what I had *seen* to everyone.

To help Castaneda understand this better, don Juan remarks on the fact that the 'personal God' is always anthropomorphised in male form.

> 'Very cozy, eh', don Juan added, smiling. 'God is a male. What a relief!'

After the brief excusing of Castaneda, with the 'classic mystical experience', Upton passes from faint praise to unrestrained loathing:

> And yet—what invincible narcissism. His identity is blown sky-high, yet all the scattered fragments are still fragments of Carlos. Nowhere in those unimaginable worlds does he *meet anyone else*—only Carlos, Carlos, Carlos.

While taking apart the postmodern faux spirituality, Upton's writing style is very much in the postmodern vein. He fills pages with personal confessions and anecdotes; it can come as quite a jar to find so much of 'I' and 'me' in a book that claims to be 'traditionalist'. For example,

> How easy it is to satirize Carlos Castaneda, to unpack all my rhetorical irony against a worthy and vulnerable target on the darker side of things. But remember, I was there too. I dabbled in the black arts—believing all the time, of course, that there was nothing black about them, that I could love and serve God while playing the 'lyric sorcerer' ... a very apt term of Castaneda's, given that poets, especially failed poets, love to think of themselves as magicians. I spent three days and two nights in the cabin of a local witch, a woman to whom men were attracted when they had decided to commit suicide ... I sat there eating her drugs as a way of doing penance...

Haven't we all been there, or somewhere like it? Even if it might not have occurred to us that the dubious pleasure was a way of doing penance. One feels like saying, 'What? Only three days and two nights!' Upton will not be restrained by attacking the ideas alone; he must also attack the man, often from an entirely imagined perspective. Every so often, as if stricken by conscience, he puts in an aside to his imagined victim, where he piously preaches to him, pointing out the error of his ways. He then goes back to the assault with the red-hot irons of Holy Wrath—for page after page.

It is merely derogatory to denounce someone's ideas by throwing an unqualified term at them, such as 'black arts', as if that were enough. However, it would take more than a few lines of abuse to explain exactly what is meant by the 'black arts' and why the term is being applied in this instance. The author puts such considerations to one side so he can concentrate on writing about himself and his opinions, which he wishes to freely exercise without the need for tiresome explanations. As for 'rhetorical irony', it seems to be somewhat lacking in this book, or if it is there, it might be that it is hard to see when wrapped in layers of hatred and contempt.

It is certainly true that we have to pick our way very carefully through the 'teachings of don Juan' to find corroboration with authentic tradition. Does that mean, though, that it has no value whatsoever? Some of the knowledge of the 'emanations of the Eagle' contained in Castaneda's *The Fire from Within* is in perfect accord with what René Guénon has set forth in at least three books, and is in accordance with the Hindu doctrine.

And likewise, the Dreaming Attention explained in the same book agrees very well with what Guénon said with utmost clarity in 'The Dream State or Condition of Taijasa', *Man and his Becoming According to the Vedānta,* and in 'Analogous Considerations drawn from the Study of the Dream State' in *The Multiple States of the Being.* Given the emotionalism the author displays when attacking what he sees as worthy of His Righteous Vengeance, he might have learned something from this line from don Juan (*The Fire from Within*),

> Beware of those who weep with realisation for they have realised nothing.

One emotional outburst is as good as another. Although well schooled in the religious and theological dogma of the 'personal God', to which he always seems to resort when feeling threatened by things he dislikes, when the author slips into the vernacular as in the above quoted passage on Castaneda he becomes even more careless. What exactly is a 'failed poet', one wonders, even while the author clearly self-identifies with the description? Similarly, when he says that some regard Sri Ramakrishna as a 'lesser saint', what can that mean? Surely a person is either a saint or they are not a saint? If a hierarchy of saints should exist, he has certainly not elucidated on this.

The world of don Juan's sorcerers, real or imagined, places an emphasis on the earth as central to existence, the source of all. That much is consistent with Native American Indian teaching, for what is called the 'earth' in that language also includes the 'sky'. Presumably, because there is no Demiurge in this, no tyrannical or benevolent All-father, the author finds it extremely offensive and goes on the attack. Such a malignant interpretation of the sky and earth tradition as is given here owes either to incomprehension of symbolism or a wilful distortion of meaning. In the Qabalah, for example, Malkuth, the 'earth' or Kingdom, is said to be Kether, the 'crown', but after another fashion. The earth and heaven are not separate in reality but owe to a unitive principle, without which neither could exist. It is not the earth that is an illusion as such; it is the narrow view by which we habitually perceive it.

Clearly, in the teaching of don Juan it is simply not necessary to make too much of a distinction between the 'above and below' of it all. The separation exists solely in the dualistic mentality of Charles Upton. Dualism automatically comes about when the belief in the 'personal God' becomes separated from its true principle, a principle that is purely metaphysical.

When exotericism (that is, religion) becomes separated from the esotericism that gave it life and substance, all that is left is a husk, an empty shell, a mere semblance of what it once was. In an attempt to equilibrate this emptiness, men must then go on the warpath, seeking evil everywhere but in the one place it resides, which is in their own hearts.

Aleister Crowley, quite rightly perhaps, only gets a passing mention. But when that reference is known to be factually inaccurate (Crowley did not found the OTO), one inevitably loses confidence in the other 'facts' that are recounted. For example, we can easily believe—we may even *want* to believe—that former US president Jimmy Carter admitted to seeing a UFO, or that George Bush attended a conference organised by the 'Moonies'. However, no references are given, no sources—there is nothing to reassure us that this is not merely something the author overheard in a bar in Los Angeles while getting stoned with his witch friend. Let's hope he gave her more than a pious lecture in return for so generously putting up with him for three days.

More seriously, the treatment of Gnosticism in this book is no more than a polemic one could find in any exoteric religious study in all the centuries since the persecution of Gnostics as 'heretics', a view that Upton obviously endorses. That again is rather strange, because some Gnostic texts most certainly predate Christianity in any form that we would recognise it now. One could equally say that the Roman mandatory form of Christianity was a heretical form of Gnosticism. He begins this assault (p. 82) by declaring that Gnosticism is 'an extremely heterogeneous group of religious sects'. Gnosticism is no more a religion than Hinduism, as religion is exoteric by definition. He then goes on to bluff us by saying that Gnostics have been attacked in general terms, and indeed slandered—then goes on to do that very thing!

It is hard not to think that the misrepresentation of Gnosticism that follows is born from a simple inability to understand metaphysical symbolism, for he gives a sweeping generalisation of Gnosticism, and without any source references to support his negative opinions. He claims that the Gnostic doctrines posit the fall of man to have taken place 'within the Godhead' (without qualifying that term), as opposed to 'a manifestation of Godhead in space, time, and human consciousness'. In fact any such manifestation within the human consciousness defines and thus limits God as the Demiurge, so that 'He' must then be seen either as an evil tyrannical despot or a good, kind uncle.

Gnostic texts make it clear in any case that the evil Demiurge was born of the lower, inferior waters—that is, time and space precisely, and as such is not of the Godhead or 'within the Godhead' (Ref. 'The Sethian Gnosis', GRS Mead, Hermetic sourceworks.) The Demiurge is in the way of a 'reflection of a reflection', which is only a relative degree of reality strictly limited to the corporeal point of view.

Gnosticism teaches (broadly speaking) that faith is the necessary exotericism and knowledge the esoteric goal. For example, *Pistis Sophia*, 'wisdom in faith'. This author, however, wants to assert an entirely erroneous opposition in Gnosticism between faith (*pistis*) and knowledge (*gnosis*). He thus makes what Guénon would have termed a 'formal rejection of traditional doctrine', for the teaching, as with that on the Demiurge, is completely in accordance with the Vedanta, and with Guénon's expositions on the Vedanta. He goes on to compound error with falsehood, so as to conclude that Gnosticism itself is false, and not the falsity of his own incomprehension of sacred texts. The volleys of exhortations to the Demiurge, 'His Blessing', and so forth, are what seem to pass with some people as 'metaphysics', which this is certainly not.

The conclusion of the book, which is what it is purportedly all about, 'System of Antichrist', comes as a crashing disappointment. Having no insights or particular point of view, the author falls back on a reductionist way out of the dilemma, positing that the Antichrist is no different than a personal force, the human ego, or otherwise a collective form of the ego (which really amounts to much the same thing). He seems, by the end of the book, to have run out of energy, so that he fails to deliver that which he promised at the outset. In so doing, perhaps he forgot why he used the term coined by Guénon, 'System of Antichrist', in the first place. That term, we would remind him, is far more descriptive of the completely inhuman and mechanical entity we are now up against.

That brings us, at last, to the American-centrism of some authors, including this one. One could easily gain the impression that Europe is only a place that exists in books! In fact, even anything south of the Mexican border takes on a kind of 'twilight' connotation here. It seems surprising in a way that the publishers let the author get away with using slang terms that are almost completely unknown outside the USA.

In our view, the book would be so much better, and might even be readable, without the personal anecdotes and interventions, which place it in the category of 'personal journey books' rather than that of the metaphysicians. That would also easily reduce the book's content to one third of the present size. That does seem rather unlikely, though, given the journalistic style that gulps down vast tracts of 'information', 'news' and hearsay and hurls it out the other end in packages after the fashion of a combine harvester. But it may be that the bedazzling of useless information and 'personal story' are exactly what readers like to read about these days.

All that being said, this book has moments of clarity, for example in the section on *A Course in Miracles* we have already mentioned, and where Charles Upton has been very careful to pinpoint the errors that litter such pretentious New Age propaganda.

The Kingdom of Agarttha

Book by Saint-Yves d'Alveydre [Inner Traditions]

The full name and title of the author is Marquis Alexandre Saint-Yves d'Alveydre (1842–1909). We are fortunate to have this book, which very nearly became a 'lost book' as all the first edition copies but one, which belonged to Papus, were destroyed. The remarkable account of the secret subterranean Kingdom of Agarttha, with roots passing upward to link centres around the world, was also the subject of a later book by Ossendowski, *Beasts, Men and Gods*, which in places bears such a strong resemblance to the first that he was accused of plagiarism. The city was not always submerged but became so from the beginning of the Age of Kali Yuga. At the end of time—a date is given by Ossendowski that is very near the present time—the Argartthians will return to the surface. It sounds fantastic but much of this involves universal symbolism in common with various ancient traditions. Nonetheless, given the predisposition of Saint-Yves, perhaps typical of his time, the book might also be seen as a sort of testimonial to the madness and confusion of occultism since the revolutionary period in France.

René Guénon was able to see much of significance regarding the primordial tradition in the two tales, the first by Saint-Yves and the second by Ossendowski; he was not interested as to whether the accounts were obtained by vision, dream or, as the authors claimed, secret knowledge gained while travelling through Asia. Agarttha was what inspired one of Guénon's most controversial books, *The King of the World*. He was perfectly clear that he had no interest at all in 'evidence' or research to verify whether or not such a place 'actually' exists under the earth. By Chapter Seven of *The King of the World* it becomes obvious why the symbolism should arouse such interest. To quote him,

> Traditions telling of a 'subterranean world' are found among many peoples, and we do not intend to collect them all here, especially since some do not seem to have any direct relevance to our topic. It is worth noting in a general way, however, that the 'cult of the caverns' is always more or less linked to the idea of an interior place, or a central place, and that in this connection the symbol of the cave and that of the heart closely converge. On the other hand, in Central Asia and in America and possibly elsewhere, there actually are caverns and underground sites where certain initiatic centres have been able to persist for centuries.

But aside from these particular facts, from all that has been reported on the subject it is not difficult to say that it is precisely considerations of a symbolic nature that have determined the choice of these subterranean locations for the establishment of initiatic centres, much more than any simple reasons of prudence. Perhaps Saint-Yves may have been able to explain this symbolism, but he failed to do so, and this is what lends the appearance of fantasy to certain portions of his work.[148]

The Introduction to *The Kingdom of Agarttha* is sadly marred by scholarly myopia. Joscelyn Godwin's grasp of metaphysics is non-existent so he is only able to understand anything in terms of psychic phenomena. He thus uses this in his attempt to explain how Saint-Yves must have worked. While it is not improbable that Saint-Yves used occult methods, none of that explains how the symbolism accords so well with the kind of knowledge of ancient traditions that is very little known to anyone outside of closed initiatic circles. That always infuriates academics and so Godwin wastes no time in trying to make a case for Guénon's credulity, as he puts it. He is not reading Guénon; he has thrown the book away and is self-writing a script to support his opinions. We see what is coming when he first introduces the young Guénon as 'embarking on an esoteric career', an idea utterly foreign to Guénon's way of thinking. The plot thickens as we are told, perhaps to disarm us, that René Guénon was in 'confident possession of the highest metaphysical doctrines, which would provide the foundation for the Traditionalist or Perennialist school of spiritual philosophers'. Guénon made it clear there is a difference to be discerned between 'Traditional' and 'Traditionalist', and that he wanted nothing to do with any Traditionalists. As for a school of spiritual philosophers, Guénon insisted in almost every book he wrote that metaphysics is in no way comparable to any philosophy; he never used such terms to describe his interests. Is this plain ignorance on behalf of Godwin, or is it wilful misrepresentation? The latter seems likely, for on page 12, he first quotes Guénon from *The King of the World*:

> Independently of the evidence offered by Ossendowski, we know from other sources that stories of this kind are widely current in Mongolia and throughout Central Asia, and we can add that there is something similar in the traditions of most people.

Godwin uses this completely straightforward statement for the stone on which to grind his axe:

---

[148] *The King of the World*, 'Luz: Abode of Immortality', p. 42.

> Unfortunately Guénon does not appear to support his claim to privileged access by telling us what these sources are, nor what degree of similitude is meant by 'stories of this kind'.

Guénon did not say anything about having 'privileged access'; all he said was that he knew the stories were existent in Asia from other sources than Ossendowski. As for the similitude of 'stories of this kind', Godwin feigns complete ignorance of the countless tales of gods or men descending into the underworld across many traditions. Guénon covered the whole subject in depth in *Symbols of Sacred Science*. However, anyone could compile a list of places where subterranean caves or labyrinths exist, and which at one time were used as initiatic centres. For merely one example, a labyrinth of chalk caves exists in Chislehurst, southern England. These still contain Druidic altars and certain edifices carved into the rock. The caves are said to extend for hundreds of miles; most of the labyrinth remains unexplored to this day. The greater part of the remains of the ancient Egyptian civilisation, for a further example, is underground. Vast caverns and labyrinths were cut out of the side of mountains.

In a footnote on page 43, Guénon relates how the Native American Indians tell of a tree by the means of which some men that lived below the surface of the earth were able to gain entrance to the surface, while others of the same race continue to dwell in the subterranean world. It seems this might have been the inspiration for Bulwer-Lytton's *Vril: the Power of the Coming Race*.[149] It is plainly absurd if taken literally, but such stories are more than symbolic in the ordinary sense of that; initiatic 'secrets' are only secret because profane minds are unable to construe the real meaning, and that meaning can only be conveyed through symbolism.

As we said, nothing infuriates profane scholars so much as the mere mention of any 'privileged access', by which is meant initiated knowledge. This is made clear by the use of the expression 'privileged access' in the first place, which betrays total incomprehension of what initiation is and how it works. In fact, all Guénon said was that he knew it from 'other sources' than the book by Ossendowski. For obvious reasons, he would not disclose his sources and so betray his friends and colleagues.

---

[149] It might sound astonishing to some, but former subterraneans still walk the surface of the earth. While these are not recognised by terrestrials, they usually recognise each other. They frequently become involved in initiatic organisations, if they can find one that is genuine at this late stage of the Kali Yuga.

However, Guénon is unique in being the only writer in a modern language to disclose some matters that are of interest only to initiates. In fact, when such things are made known to academics, they cannot possibly make any use of them, nor do they even recognise what is put before them as having any value. As for the 'degree of similitude' with other stories, we have already given a few examples here and Guénon said more than enough in his book to convey what is needed to those with sufficient wit and wisdom to comprehend it.

To round off the attack, Godwin mentions 'certain believers in Guénon's infallibility', which is news to us as we were not aware of his position at the Vatican! Apparently 'they'—by which he seems to be referring to a certain Jean Robin—see Guénon as 'an emissary from the King of the World'. Finally, throwing all caution to the wind, Godwin takes a completely normal statement from a colleague of Guénon's, to the effect that Guénon's Hindu contacts would not want the matter of Agarttha to be divulged, and manages to twist it round into an assertion that Guénon definitely believed, as Saint-Yves appeared to, that the 'kingdom of Agarttha does exist', that is to say, as an actual location beneath the earth. He thus brings in false evidence to support his slur that Guénon is 'credulous'. Once again we are shown that postmodern scholarship and gutter press journalism are not very distant relatives. The facts and information pulled in to supply context to this extraordinary book is nonetheless worthwhile and needed. It is sadly the case that the academics, who are well qualified to collect facts and search the libraries of the world—to which they certainly do have 'privileged access'—seem never to exercise restraint when it comes to the free expression of their profane opinions on matters they do not understand at all.

It would be helpful, given a book that almost defies criticism by its very nature, to quote something from *The Kingdom of Agarttha*. The following, from the first chapter, should convey to anyone that has made a serious study of the works of Guénon why it is that the symbolism used so engrossed the attention of the latter, inspiring one of his most accessible yet arcane books, *The King of the World*.

> During the great prayer days, during the celebration of the cosmic Mysteries, although the sacred hierograms are recited in a tone little more than a whisper inside the immense underground dome, a strange acoustic phenomenon takes place on the surface of the earth and in the skies.

The travellers and caravans that wander far during the light of day or on clear nights come to a halt, both man and beast, anxiously listening.

It seems to them that the Earth itself has opened its lips to sing.

An immense harmony with no visible cause is in fact floating through space.

It unfolds in growing spirals and tenderly shakes the Atmosphere with its waves, then rises to be engulfed in the Heavens, as if seeking there for the Ineffable.

All that can be seen in the distance during the night is the trembling of the Moon and the Stars watching over the slumber of the mountains and valleys, while in the day all that is visible is the resplendence of the Sun over the most enchanting sites to be found on this Earth.

Whether Arabs or Parsis, Buddhists or Brahminists, Karaite Jews or Subbas, Afghans, Tartars or Chinese, all travellers respectfully gather their thoughts, listen in silence, and softly utter their orisons in the Great Universal Soul.

Such is the shape taken by the hierarchy of Paradesa from its base to its apex, a veritable pyramid of light enclosing the bond of an impenetrable secret.

The Simple Life of René Guénon

Book by Paul Chacornac [Sophia Perennis]

René Guénon (1886–1951) remains an obscure and enigmatic figure to this day, and is still very little known or read by English speaking people. Yet he always was and still is influential in places where one would least expect to find it. Guénon was a very private individual. He originally wanted his books to be published anonymously, but gave in eventually to the requirements of modern publishing, which make that almost impossible. René Guénon is his family name, although in some very early articles and reviews he wrote under pseudonyms such as 'Palingenius' and 'The Sphinx'. Guénon always insisted that personal details and 'life stories' are completely irrelevant to the subject of his interest. So why did Paul Chacornac, his publisher, write a biography in the first place? It is best if we hear it in his words:

René Guénon repeatedly said that personalities count for nothing in the traditional domain, the only domain of any importance in his view. We cannot, however, alter the fact that the modern world is more interested in personalities than in their work; and if their life stories are not told, legends often arise that go far wide of the mark, and perhaps even contradict the facts. We believe therefore that we serve the truth, albeit in a modest way, by establishing or re-establishing, the facts concerning René Guénon's life— and we intend to confine ourselves to the facts. In other words, to speak in fashionable jargon, no 'psychoanalysis of René Guénon' will be found here.

That last point should assuage any doubts as to whether this biography of René Guénon is worth studying, though of course such a 'psychoanalysis' would not be expected in any serious work, especially one that is sensitive to its subject concerning the most important spiritual teacher and prophet of modern times.

After Guénon's death on 7th January 1951, a surprising number of articles and biographies were published in France, but only two biographies have been translated into English. It seems obvious to choose the one written by his publisher, who was a close friend of the man for many years.

In spite of the title of this book, the facts concerning Guénon's life are really quite extraordinary, and there is no space here to summarise even what is most cogent. His knowledge of Hinduism and other traditions was not in any way book-learned, though he seems to have read almost everything that can be read. When Hindu masters of the Advaita Vedanta tradition made a rare visit to Europe early in the twentieth century, they somehow found their way to René Guénon—or he found his way to them, we cannot know for sure. Guénon 'knew people'—many people, and had access to information that does not appear anywhere but in his works. According to an article that appeared in the review *Jayakarnataka* (edited in Dhawar, India),

> This author presents the rare case of a writer who expresses himself in a Western language, and whose knowledge of Eastern philosophy has been direct, that is to say derived essentially from masters of the East. It is in fact to the oral teaching of these masters that Guénon owes his knowledge of the doctrines of India, of Islamic esoterism, and of Taoism, as well as of the Sanskrit and Arabic languages; and this sufficiently distinguishes him from European and American orientalists, who have no doubt worked with Asians, but have asked only for help to facilitate the bookish research characteristic of Western erudition.

Guénon's first book was *Introduction to the Study of the Hindu Doctrines* (1921), which, as according to Chacornac, was possibly not the best title for it as at least half of it is an introduction to tradition in general. He aimed to make it known what divides the modern world from a normal world, that is to say, a traditional one. It is perhaps needless to say that the India that Guénon was referring to at that time no longer exists, and that his worst fears concerning Western global domination have by now become fully realised. The second part of the book is doctrinal while the last part examines Western misconceptions about Hinduism.

In the same year the second book, a large tome, on the history and facts concerning the disproportionately influential and damaging Theosophical movement, was published. In *The Spiritist Fallacy*, Guénon goes far beyond a mere debunking of neo-spiritualism and discloses real secrets concerning the subtle or astral plane. Once again, this is best heard in the words of Paul Chacornac:

The Spiritist Fallacy is a copious and extensively documented work, as was Guénon's preceding one [*Theosophy: History of a Pseudo-Religion*]; but whereas *Theosophy* is almost solely an historical and critical work, *The Spiritist Fallacy* comprises doctrinal expositions on both metaphysical and cosmological questions, and gives the reader an insight into the subtle world, which has never before been publicly discussed in a Western language. Among its chapters, 'Explanations of Spiritist Phenomena', 'Immortality and Survival', 'Representations of Survival', 'Communication with the Dead', 'Reincarnation', and 'Satanism', rank among the masterpieces in Guénon's corpus.

And furthermore,

The Spiritist Fallacy echoes to some extent the same concerns voiced in *Theosophy*, for the spiritualists had acquired the habit of attributing to Eastern traditions, particularly Hinduism, both their doctrine of reincarnation and their practice of evoking the dead.

The fundamental doctrinal work of René Guénon was *Man and his Becoming according to the Vedānta* (1925), which appeared in embryonic form as early as 1911. He admitted of the impossibility of producing any comprehensive exposition on 'the purest metaphysics in Hindu doctrine', and so used the nature and constitution of the human being as a launching point. In fact, in it he expounded the fundamental principles of all traditional metaphysics:

Not since the fourteenth century had this doctrine been expounded in the West—and here in lucid language free of symbolism. By degrees he leads up to the doctrine of the Supreme Identity and its logical corollary—the possibility that the being in the human state might in this very life attain liberation, the unconditioned state where all separateness and risk of reversion to manifested existence ceases.

It is not in any way possible to mention all of the works of Guénon, but mention must be made of some of the curious circumstances that surrounded the book *The King of the World*—a work that is packed with otherwise completely unknown esoteric matters. It seems that one or two of the Hindu Advaitan masters that Guénon had remained in contact with objected to the book's publication on grounds that too much had been said, and too precisely. Guénon thought otherwise, and gave his reasons for so doing as the dire circumstances that the world had by then entered into by 1927, which made it clear that things could only get worse. It is fortunate for his readers that he made that decision, although his Bengali contact or contacts declined to communicate further.

It will be surprising to some to learn that one of his friends performed a psychometry reading on a paper knife at Guénon's house in Paris—at the request of the latter, who knew of his ESP experiments. The result was an extraordinarily accurate vision concerning the palatial residence of the Advaitan master in question, and of the break in relations that ensued.

Guénon was a member of many organisations over the course of his lifetime. Early on in his life, while still in his twenties and before he had completely renounced neo-spiritualism, he was a member of an occult organisation called the Universal Gnostic Church, and received a mysterious appointment, under strange circumstances, to lead a reformed Order of the Temple of seven degrees. Of the mysterious appointment, Guénon had this to say, in *The Spiritist Fallacy*, part 1, chapter 7:

> A communication, expressing events in fact unknown to all those present, can nevertheless come from the 'subconscious' of one of them; for one is normally very far from knowing all the possibilities of the human being in such a situation. Each of us can be connected through this obscure side of ourselves to beings and things of which we have never had any knowledge in the ordinary sense of the word; and innumerable ramifications can ensue, to which it is impossible to ascribe definite boundaries.

The degrees of the reformed *Ordo Templi* included such titles as Egyptian Rosicrucian, Knight of the Guard of the Inner Temple and Hermetic Adept. This detail is not mentioned to show inconsistency in Guénon's work, because he was always consistent even if he modified his views on some things over the course of time, as we all must do, but it is to indicate that his activities, involvements and teaching were frequently paradoxical in nature. It is this, added to the fact that his subject of interest and writing was almost exclusively metaphysics, or at least derived from a metaphysical point of view when it leaned towards social criticism, that has made the works of Guénon a revelation to a few while remaining completely inaccessible to a majority of others—though for those who have the intellectual capacity, it is always through their innate disinclination to see beyond their own prejudices.

Furthermore, it seems almost incredible that some have used the above facts concerning Guénon's early life as an excuse to write him off as no more than an occultist. There are only two possible explanations for this: either they did not read any of his books but have only read what other people think of them, or they actually read a book but understood absolutely nothing of what they read.

Selected Works of Oliver St. John

Hermetic Astrology (2015)
Magical Theurgy (2015)
The Enterer of the Threshold (2016)
Liber 373 Astrum Draconis (2017)
Hermetic Qabalah Foundation—Complete Course (2018)
Babalon Unveiled! Thelemic Monographs (2019)
Ritual Magick—Initiation of the Star and Snake (2019)
Nu Hermetica—Initiation and Metaphysical Reality (2021)
The Way of Knowledge in the Reign of Antichrist (2022)
Thirty-two paths of Wisdom (2023)
The Law of Thelema—Hidden Alchemy (2024)
Metamorphosis—Hermetic Science and Yoga Power (2024)
Advaita Vedanta—Question of the Real (2025)
Egyptian Tarot and Tarot Cards (2025)

Contact the O∴ A∴

Universal Gnostic Collegium: Contact details and information is posted on our website at www.ordoastri.org

www.ingramcontent.com/pod-product-compliance
Lightning Source LLC
Chambersburg PA
CBHW050145170426
43197CB00011B/1973